Frank Barrett

A Set of Rogues

Their wicked Conspiracy, and a true Account of their Travels and Adventures

Frank Barrett

A Set of Rogues

Their wicked Conspiracy, and a true Account of their Travels and Adventures

ISBN/EAN: 9783337178369

Printed in Europe, USA, Canada, Australia, Japan

Cover: Foto ©ninafisch / pixelio.de

More available books at **www.hansebooks.com**

A SET OF ROGUES

TO WIT

CHRISTOPHER SUTTON
JOHN DAWSON
The Señor Don SANCHEZ
DEL CASTILLO de CASTELAÑA
and MOLL DAWSON

THEIR WICKED CONSPIRACY

AND A TRUE ACCOUNT OF THEIR TRAVELS AND ADVENTURES

TOGETHER WITH MANY OTHER SURPRISING THINGS, NOW DISCLOSED FOR THE FIRST TIME, AS THE FAITHFUL CONFESSION OF CHRISTOPHER SUTTON

BY

FRANK BARRETT

Author of "The Admirable Lady Biddy Fane,"
"The Great Hesper," etc.

New York
MACMILLAN AND CO.
AND LONDON
1895

All rights reserved

CONTENTS.

CHAPTER I.

Of my companions and our adversities, and in particular from our getting into the stocks at Tottenham Cross to our being robbed at Edmonton.................................... 1

CHAPTER II.

Of our first acquaintance with the Señor Don Sanchez del Castillo de Castelaña, and his brave entertaining of us............ 10

CHAPTER III.

Of that design which Don Sanchez opened to us at the Bell...... 18

CHAPTER IV.

Of the several parts that we are appointed to play............ 27

CHAPTER V.

Don Sanchez puts us in the way of robbing with an easy conscience 34

CHAPTER VI.

Moll is cast to play the part of a fine lady; doubtful promise for this undertaking..................................... 46

CHAPTER VII.

Of our journey through France to a very horrid pass in the Pyraneans 52

CHAPTER VIII.

How we were entertained in the mountains, and stand in a fair way to have our throats cut........................... 61

CHAPTER IX.

Of the manner in which we escaped pretty fairly out of the hands of Señor Don Lopez and his brigands................... 70

CHAPTER X.

Of our merry journeying to Alicante...................... 79

CHAPTER XI.

Of our first coming to Elche and the strangeness of that city 88

CHAPTER XII.

How Don Sanchez very honestly offers to free us of our bargain if we will; but we will not........................... 96

CHAPTER XIII.

A brief summary of those twelve months we spent at Elche...... 104

CHAPTER XIV.

Of our coming to London (with incidents by the way), and of the great address whereby Moll confounds Simon, the steward... 114

CHAPTER XV.

Lay our hands on six hundred pounds and quarter ourselves in Hurst Court, but stand in a fair way to be undone by Dawson, his folly 127

CHAPTER XVI.

Prosper as well as any thieves may; but Dawson greatly tormented 135

CHAPTER XVII.

How Dawson for Moll's good parts company with us, and goes away a lonely man 144

CHAPTER XVIII.

Of our getting a painter into the Court, with whom our Moll falls straightway in love 152

CHAPTER XIX.

Of the business appointed to the painter, and how he set about the same 161

CHAPTER XX.

Of Moll's ill humour and what befel thereby 170

CHAPTER XXI.

Of the strange things told us by the wise woman 180

CHAPTER XXII.

How Moll and Mr. Godwin come together and declare their hearts' passion, and how I carry these tidings to Dawson .. 185

CONTENTS.

CHAPTER XXIII.

PAGE

Don Sanchez proposes a very artful way to make Mr. Godwin a party to our knavery, etc............................ 197

CHAPTER XXIV.

I overcome Moll's honest compunctions, lay hold of three thousand pounds more, and do otherwise play the part of rascal to perfection.. 203

CHAPTER XXV.

A table of various accidents................................. 212

CHAPTER XXVI.

How Moll Dawson was married to Mr. Richard Godwin; brief account of attendant circumstances...................... 220

CHAPTER XXVII.

Of the great change in Moll, and the likely explanation thereof.. 233

CHAPTER XXVIII.

Moll plays us a mad prank for the last time in her life......... 237

CHAPTER XXIX.

Of the subtile means whereby Simon leads Mr. Godwin to doubt his wife... 247

CHAPTER XXX.

How we are discovered and utterly undone................... 254

CHAPTER XXXI.

Moll's conscience is quickened by grief and humiliation beyond the ordinary 259

CHAPTER XXXII.

How we fought a most bloody battle with Simon, the constable, and others 265

CHAPTER XXXIII.

We take Moll to Greenwich; but no great happiness for her there 271

CHAPTER XXXIV.

All agree to go out to Spain again in search of our old jollity 281

CHAPTER XXXV.

How we lost our poor Moll, and our long search for her 288

CHAPTER XXXVI.

We learn what hath become of Moll; and how she nobly atoned for our sins 300

CHAPTER XXXVII.

Don Sanchez again proves himself the most mannerly rascal in the world 308

CHAPTER XXXVIII.

How we hear Moll's sweet voice through the walls of her prison, and speak two words with her, though almost to our undoing . 313

CHAPTER XXXIX.

Of our bargaining with a Moorish seaman; and of an English slave 322

CHAPTER XL.

Of our escape from Barbary, of the pursuit and horrid, fearful slaughter that followed, together with other moving circumstances 330

CHAPTER XLI.

How Dawson counts himself an unlucky man who were best dead; and so he quits us, and I, the reader 340

A SET OF ROGUES.

CHAPTER I.

Of my companions and our adversities, and in particular from our getting into the stocks at Tottenham Cross to our being robbed at Edmonton.

THERE being no plays to be acted at the "Red Bull," because of the Plague, and the players all cast adrift for want of employment, certain of us, to wit, Jack Dawson and his daughter Moll, Ned Herring, and myself, clubbed our monies together to buy a store of dresses, painted cloths, and the like, with a cart and horse to carry them, and thus provided set forth to travel the country and turn an honest penny, in those parts where the terror of pestilence had not yet turned men's stomachs against the pleasures of life. And here, at our setting out, let me show what kind of company we were. First, then, for our master, Jack Dawson, who on no occasion was to be given a second place; he was a hale, jolly fellow, who would eat a pound of beef for his breakfast (when he could get it), and make nothing of half a gallon of ale therewith,— a very masterful man, but kindly withal, and pleasant to look at when not contraried, with never a line of care in his face, though turned of fifty. He played our humorous parts, but he had a sweet voice for singing of ditties, and could fetch a tear as readily as a laugh, and he was also exceeding nimble at a dance, which was the strangest thing in the world, considering his great girth. Wife he had none, but Moll Dawson was his daughter, who was a most sprightly, merry little wench, but no miracle for beauty, being neither child nor woman at this time; surprisingly thin, as if her frame had grown out of proportion with her flesh, so that her body looked all arms and legs, and her head all mouth and eyes, with a great towzled mass of chestnut hair, which (off the stage) was as often as not half tumbled over her shoulder. But a quicker little baggage at mimicry (she would play any part, from an urchin of ten to a crone of fourscore), or a livelier at dancing of Brantles or the single Coranto never was, I do think, and as merry as a grig. Of Ned Herring I need only here say that he was the most tearing villain imaginable on the stage, and off it the most civil-spoken, honest-seeming young gentleman. Nor need I trouble to give a very lengthy description of myself; what my character was will appear hereafter, and as for my looks, the less I say about them, the better. Being something of a scholar and a poet, I had nearly died of starvation, when Jack Dawson gave me a footing on the stage, where I would play the part of a hero in one act, a lacquey in the second, and a merry Andrew in the third, scraping a tune on my fiddle to fill up the intermedios.

We had designed to return to London as soon as the Plague abated, unless we were favoured with extraordinary good fortune, and so, when we heard that the sickness was certainly past, and the citizens recovering of their panic, we (being by this time heartily sick of our venture, which at the best gave us but beggarly recompense) set about to retrace our steps with cheerful expectations of better times.

WE SET FIRE TO A BARN. 3

But coming to Oxford, we there learned that a prodigious fire had burnt all London down, from the Tower to Ludgate, so that if we were there, we should find no house to play in. This lay us flat in our hopes, and set us again to our vagabond enterprise; and so for six months more we scoured the country in a most miserable plight, the roads being exceedingly foul, and folks more humoured of nights to drowse in their chimnies than to sit in a draughty barn and witness our performances; and then, about the middle of February we, in a kind of desperation, got back again to London, only to find that we must go forth again, the town still lying in ruins, and no one disposed to any kind of amusement, except in high places, where such actors as we were held in contempt. So we, with our hearts in our boots, as one may say, set out again to seek our fortunes on the Cambridge road, and here, with no better luck than elsewhere, for at Tottenham Cross we had the mischance to set fire to the barn wherein we were playing, by a candle falling in some loose straw, whereby we did injury to the extent of some shilling or two, for which the farmer would have us pay a pound, and Jack Dawson stoutly refusing to satisfy his demand he sends for the constable, who locks us all up in the cage that night, to take us before the magistrate in the morning. And we found to our cost that this magistrate had as little justice as mercy in his composition ; for though he lent a patient ear to the farmer's case, he would not listen to Jack Dawson's argument, which was good enough, being to the effect that we had not as much as a pound amongst us, and that he would rather be hanged than pay it if he had; and when Ned Herring (seeing the kind of Puritanical fellow he was) urged that, since the damage was not done by any design of ours, it must be regarded as a visitation of Providence, he says: "Very good. If it be the will of Providence that one should be scourged, I take it as the Divine purpose that I should finish the business by scourging the other"; and therewith he orders the constable to take what money we have from our pockets and clap us in the stocks till sundown for payment of the difference. So in the stocks we three poor men were stuck for six mortal hours, which was a wicked, cruel thing indeed, with the wind blowing a sort of rainy snow about our ears; and there I do think we must have perished of cold and vexation but that our little Moll brought us a sheet for a cover, and tired not in giving us kind words of comfort.

At five o'clock the constable unlocked us from our vile confinement, and I do believe we should have fallen upon him and done him a mischief for his pains there and then, but that we were all frozen as stiff as stones with sitting in the cold so long, and indeed it was some time ere we could move our limbs at all. However, with much ado, we hobbled on at the tail of our cart, all three very bitter, but especially Ned Herring, who cursed most horridly and as I had never heard him curse off the stage, saying he would rather have stayed in London to carry links for the gentry than join us again in this damnable adventure, etc. And that which incensed him the more was the merriment of our Moll, who, seated on the side of the cart, could do nothing better than make sport of our discontent. But there was no malice in her laughter, which, if it sprang not from sheer love of mischief, arose maybe from overflowing joy at our release.

Coming at dusk to Edmonton, and finding a fine new inn there, called the "Bell," Jack Dawson leads the cart into the yard, we following without a word of demur, and, after putting up our trap, into the warm parlour we go, and call for supper as boldly as you please. Then, when we had eaten and drunk till we could no more, all to bed like princes, which, after a night in the cage and a day in the stocks, did seem like a very paradise. But how we were to pay for this entertainment not one of us knew, nor did we greatly care, being made quite reckless by our necessities. It was the next morning, when we met together at breakfast, that our faces betrayed some compunctions; but these did not prevent us eating prodigiously. "For," whispers Ned Herring, "if we are to be hanged, it may as well be for a sheep as a lamb." However, Jack Dawson, getting on the right side of the landlord, who seemed a very honest, decent man for an innkeeper, agreed with him that we should give a performance that night in a cart-shed very proper to our purpose, giving him half of our taking in payment of our entertainment. This did Jack, thinking from our late ill-luck we should get at the most a dozen people in the sixpenny benches, and a score standing at twopence a head. But it turned out, as the cunning landlord had foreseen, that our hanger was packed close to the very door, in consequence of great numbers coming to the town in the afternoon to see a bull baited, so that when Jack Dawson closed the doors and came behind our scene to dress for his part, he told us he had as good as five pounds in his pocket. With that to cheer us we played our tragedy of "The Broken Heart" very merrily, and after that, changing our dresses in a twinkling, Jack Dawson, disguised as a wild man, and Moll as a wood nymph, came on to the stage to dance a pastoral, whilst I, in the fashion of a satyr, stood on one side plying the fiddle to their footing. Then, all being done, Jack thanks the company for their indulgence, and bids 'em good-night.

And now, before all the company are yet out of the place, and while Jack Dawson is wiping the sweat from his face, comes the landlord, and asks pretty bluntly to be paid his share of our earnings.

"Well," says Jack, in a huff, "I see no reason for any such haste; but if you will give me time to put on my breeches, you shall be paid all the same." And therewith he takes down his trunks from the nail where they hung. And first giving them a doubtful shake, as seeming lighter than he expected, and hearing no chink of money, he thrusts his hand into one pocket, and then into the other, and cries in dismay: "Heaven's mercy upon us; we are robbed! Every penny of our money is gone!"

"Can you think of nothing better than such an idle story as that?" says the landlord. "There hath been none behind this sheet but yourselves all the night."

We could make no reply to this, but stood gaping at each other in a maze for some seconds; then Jack Dawson, recovering his wits, turns him round, and looking about, cries: "Why, where's Ned Herring?"

"If you mean him as was killed in your play," says the landlord, "I'll answer for it he's not far off; for, to my knowledge, he was in the house drinking with a man while you were a-dancing of your antics like a fool. And I only hope you may be as honest a man as he, for he paid for his liquor like a gentleman."

That settled the question, for we knew the constable had left never a penny in his pocket when he clapt us in the stocks.

"Well," says Jack, "he has our money, as you may prove by searching us, and if you have faith in him 'tis all as one, and you may rest easy for your reckoning being paid against his return."

The landlord went off, vowing he would take the law of us if he were not paid by the morning; and we, as soon as we had shuffled on our clothes, away to hunt for Ned, thinking that maybe he had made off with the money to avoid paying half to the landlord, and hoping always that, though he might play the rogue with him, he would deal honestly by us. But we could find no trace of him, though we visited every alehouse in the town, and so back we go, crestfallen, to the Bell, to beg the innkeeper to give us a night's lodging and a crust of bread on the speculation that Ned would come back and settle our accounts; but he would not listen to our prayers, and so, hungry and thirsty, and miserable beyond expression, we were fain to make up with a loft over the stables, where, thanks to a good store of sweet hay, we soon forgot our troubles in sleep, but not before we had concerted to get away in the morning betimes to escape another day in the stocks.

Accordingly, before the break of day, we were afoot, and after noiselessly packing our effects in the cart in the misty grey light, Jack Dawson goes in the stable to harness our nag, while I as silently take down the heavy bar that fastened the yard gate. But while I was yet fumbling at the bolts, and all of a shake for fear of being caught in the act, Jack Dawson comes to me, with Moll holding of his hand, as she would when our troubles were great, and says in a tone of despair:

"Give over, Kit. We are all undone again. For our harness is stole, and there's never another I can take in its place."

While we were at this stumble, out comes our landlord to make sport of us. "Have you found your money yet, friends?" says he, with a sneer.

"No," says Jack, savagely, "and our money is not all that we have lost, for some villain has filched our nag's harness, and I warrant you know who he is."

"Why, to be sure," returns the other, "the same friend may have taken it who has gone astray with your other belongings; but, be that as it may, I'll answer for it when your money is found your harness will be forthcoming, and not before."

"Come, Master," says I, "have you no more heart than to make merry at the mischances of three poor wretches such as we?"

"Aye," says he, "when you can show that you deserve better treatment."

"Done," says Jack. "I'll show you that as quickly as you please." With that he whips off his cap, and flinging it on the ground, cries: "Off with your jacket, man, and let us prove by such means as Heaven has given all which is the honester of us two. And so he squares himself up to fight; but the innkeeper, though as big a man as he, being of a spongy constitution, showed no relish for this mode of argument, and turning his back on us with a shake of the head, said he was very well satisfied of his own honesty, and if we doubted it we could seek what satisfaction the law would give us, adding slyly, as he turned at the door, that he could recommend us a magistrate of his acquaintance, naming him who had set us in the stocks at Tottenham Cross.

The very hint of this put us again in a quake, and now, the snow beginning to fall pretty heavily, we went into the shed to cast about as to what on earth we should do next. There we sat, glum and silent, watching idly the big flakes of snow fluttering down from the leaden sky, for not one of us could imagine a way out of this hobble.

"Holy Mother!" cries Jack at length, springing up in a passion, "we cannot sit here and starve of cold and hunger. Cuddle up to my arm, Moll, and do you bring your fiddle, Kit, and let us try our luck a-begging in alehouses."

And so we trudged out into the driving snow, that blinded us as we walked, bow our heads as we might, and tried one alehouse after the other, but all to no purpose, the parlours being empty because of the early hour, and the snow keeping folks within doors; only, about midday, some carters, who had pulled up at an inn, took pity on us, and gave us a mug of penny ale and half a loaf, and that was all the food we had the whole miserable day. Then at dusk, wet-footed and fagged out in mind and body, we trudged back to the Bell, thinking to get back into the loft and bury ourselves in the sweet hay for warmth and comfort. But coming hither, we found our nag turned out of the stable and the door locked, so that we were thrown quite into despair by the loss of this last poor hope, and poor Moll, turning her face away from us, burst out a-crying — she who all day had set us a brave example by her cheerful merry spirit.

CHAPTER II.

Of our first acquaintance with the Señor Don Sanchez del Castillo de Castelaña, and his brave entertaining of us.

I WAS taking a turn or two outside the shed, — for the sight of Jack Dawson hugging poor Moll to his breast and trying to soothe her bodily misery with gentle words was more than I could bear, — when a drawer coming across from the inn told me that a gentleman in the Cherry room would have us come to him. I gave him a civil answer and carried this message to my friends. Moll, who had staunched her tears and was smiling piteously, though her sobs, like those of a child, still shook her thin frame, and her father both looked at me in blank doubt as fearing some trap for our further discomfiture.

"Nay," says Jack, stoutly. "Fate can serve us no worse within doors than without, so let us in and face this gentleman, whoever he is."

So in we go, and all sodden and bedrabbled as we were, went to follow the drawer upstairs, when the landlady cried out she would not have us go into her Cherry room in that pickle, to soil her best furniture and disgrace her house, and bade the fellow carry us into the kitchen to take off our cloaks and change our boots for slip-shoes, adding that if we had any respect for ourselves, we should trim our hair and wash the grime off our faces. So we enter the kitchen, nothing loath, where a couple of pullets browning on the spit, kettles bubbling on the fire, and a pasty drawing from the oven, filled the air with delicious odours that nearly drove us mad for envy; and to think that these good things were to tempt the appetite of some one who never hungered, while we, famishing for want, had not even a crust to appease our cravings! But it was some comfort to plunge our blue, numbed fingers into a tub of hot water and feel the life blood creeping back into our hearts. The paint we had put on our cheeks the night before was streaked all over our faces by the snow, so that we did look the veriest scarecrows imaginable; but after washing our heads well and stroking our hair into order with a comb Mistress Cook lent us, we looked not so bad. And thus changed, and with dry shoes to our feet, we at length went upstairs, all full of wondering expectation, and were led into the Cherry room, which seemed to us a very palace, being lit with half a dozen candles (and they of wax) and filled with a warm glow by the blazing logs on the hearth reflected in the cherry hangings. And there in the midst was a table laid for supper with a wondrous white cloth, glasses to drink from, and silver forks all set out most bravely.

"His worship will be down ere long," says the drawer, and with that he makes a pretence of building up the fire, being warned thereto very like by the landlady, with an eye to the safety of her silver.

"Can you tell me his worship's name, friend?" I whispered, my mind turning at once to his worship of Tottenham Cross.

"Not I, were you to pay me," says he. "'Tis that outlandish and uncommon. But for sure he is some great foreign grandee."

He could tell us no more, so we stood there all together, wondering, till presently the door opens, and a tall, lean gentleman enters, with a high front, very finely dressed in linen stockings, a long-waisted coat, and embroidered waistcoat, and rich lace at his cuffs and throat. He wore no peruke, but his own hair, cut quite close to his head, with a pointed beard and a pair of long moustachios twisting up almost to his ears; but his appearance was the more striking by reason of his beard and moustachios being quite black, while the hair on his head was white as silver. He had dark brows also, that overhung very rich black eyes; his nose was long and hooked, and his skin, which was of a very dark complexion, was closely lined with wrinkles about the eyes, while a deep furrow lay betwixt his brows. He carried his head very high, and was majestic and gracious in all his movements, not one of which (as it seemed to me) was made but of forethought and purpose. I should say his age was about sixty, though his step and carriage were of a younger man. To my eyes he appeared a very handsome and a pleasing, amiable gentleman. But, Lord, what can you conclude of a man at a single glance, when every line in his face (of which he had a score and more) has each its history of varying passions, known only to himself, and secret phases of his life !

He saluted us with a most noble bow, and dismissed the drawer with a word in an undertone. Then turning again to us, he said : " I had the pleasure of seeing you act last night, and dance," he adds with a slight inclination of his head to Moll. " Naturally, I wish to be better acquainted with you. Will it please you to dine with me ? "

I could not have been more dumbfounded had an angel

asked me to step into heaven; but Dawson was quick enough to say something.

"That will we," cries he, "and God bless your worship for taking pity on us, for I doubt not you have heard of our troubles."

The other bowed his head and set a chair at the end of the table for Moll, which she took with a pretty curtsey, but saying never a word, for glee did seem to choke us all. And being seated, she cast her eyes on the bread hungrily, as if she would fain begin at once, but she had the good manners to restrain herself. Then his worship (as we called him), having shown us the chairs on either side, seated himself last of all, at the head of the table, facing our Moll, whom whenever he might without discourtesy, he regarded with most scrutinising glances from first to last. Then the door flinging open, two drawers brought in those same fat pullets we had seen browning before the fire, and also the pasty, with abundance of other good cheer, at which Moll, with a little cry of delight, whispers to me:

"'Tis like a dream. Do speak to me, Kit, or I must think 'twill all fade away presently and leave us in the snow."

Then I, finding my tongue, begged his worship would pardon us if our manners were more uncouth than the society to which he was accustomed.

"Nay," says Dawson. "Your worship will like us none the worse, I warrant, for seeing what we are and aping none."

Finding himself thus beworshipped on both hands, our good friend says:

"You may call me Señor. I am a Spaniard. Don Sanchez del Castillo de Castelaña." And then to turn the subject, he adds: "I have seen you play twice."

"Aye, Señor, and I should have known you again if by nothing but this piece of generosity," replies Dawson, with his cheek full of pasty, "for I remember both times you set down a piece and would take no change."

Don Sanchez hunched his shoulders cavalierly, as if such trifles were nought to him; but indeed throughout his manner was most high and noble.

And now, being fairly settled down to our repast, we said no more of any moment that I can recall to mind till we had done (which was not until nought remained of the pullets and the pasty but a few bones and the bare dish), and we were drawn round the fire at Don Sanchez's invitation. Then the drawers, having cleared the tables, brought up a huge bowl of hot spiced wine, a dish of tobacco, and some pipes. The Don then offered us to smoke some cigarros, but we, not understanding them, took instead our homely pipes, and each with a beaker of hot wine to his hand sat roasting before the fire, scarce saying a word, the Don being silent because his humour was of the reflective grave kind (with all his courtesies he never smiled, as if such demonstrations were unbecoming to his dignity), and we from repletion and a feeling of wondrous contentment and repose. And another thing served to keep us still, which was that our Moll, sitting beside her father, almost at once fell asleep, her head lying against his shoulder as he sat with his arm about her waist. As at the table, Don Sanchez had seated himself where he could best observe her, and now he scarcely once took his eyes off her, which were half closed as if in speculation. At length, taking the cigarro from his lips, he says softly to Jack Dawson, so as not to arouse Moll:

"Your daughter."

Jack nods for an answer, and looking down on her face with pride and tenderness, he put back with the stem of his pipe a little curl that had strayed over her eyes. She was not amiss for looks thus, with her long eyelashes lying like a fringe upon her cheeks, her lips open, showing her good white teeth, and the glow of the firelight upon her face; but her attitude and the innocent, happy expression of her features made up a picture which seemed to me mighty pretty.

"Where is her mother?" asks Don Sanchez, presently; and Dawson, without taking his eyes from Moll's face, lifts his pipe upwards, while his big thick lips fell a-trembling. Maybe, he was thinking of his poor Betty as he looked at the child's face.

"Has she no other relatives?" asks the Don, in the same quiet tone; and Jack shakes his head, still looking down, and answers lowly:

"Only me."

Then after another pause the Don asks:

"What will become of her?"

And that thought also must have been in Jack Dawson's mind; for without seeming surprised by the question, which appeared a strange one, he answers reverently, but with a shake in his hoarse voice, "Almighty God knows."

This stilled us all for the moment, and then Don Sanchez, seeing that these reflections threw a gloom upon us, turned to me, sitting next him, and asked if I would give him some account of my history, whereupon I briefly told him how three years ago Jack Dawson had lifted me out of the mire, and how since then we had lived in brotherhood. "And," says I in conclusion, "we will continue with the favour of Providence to live so, sharing good and ill fortune alike to the end, so much we do love one another."

To this Jack Dawson nods assent.

"And your other fellow,—what of him?" asked Don Sanchez.

I replied that Ned Herring was but a fair-weather friend, who had joined fortunes with us to get out of London and escape the Plague, and how having robbed us, we were like never to see his face again.

"And well for him if we do not," cries Dawson, rousing up; "for by the Lord, if I clap eyes on him, though it be a score of years hence, he shan't escape the most horrid beating ever man outlived!"

The Don nodded his satisfaction at this, and then Moll, awaking with the sudden outburst of her father's voice, gives first a gape, then a shiver, and looking about her with an air of wonder, smiles as her eye fell on the Don. Whereon, still as solemn as any judge, he pulls the bell, and the maid, coming to the room with a rushlight, he bids her take the poor weary child to bed, and the best there is in the house, which I think did delight Dawson not less than his Moll to hear.

Then Moll gives her father a kiss, and me another according to her wont, and drops a civil curtsey to Don Sanchez.

"Give me thy hand, child," says he; and having it, he lifts it to his lips and kisses it as if she had been the finest lady in the land.

She being gone, the Don calls for a second bowl of spiced wine, and we, mightily pleased at the prospect of another half-hour of comfort, stretch our legs out afresh before the fire. Then Don Sanchez, lighting another cigarro, and setting his chair towards us, says as he takes his knee up betwixt his long, thin fingers:

"Now let us come to the heart of this business and understand one another clearly."

c

CHAPTER III.

Of that design which Don Sanchez opened to us at the Bell.

WE pulled our pipes from our mouths, Dawson and I, and stretched our ears very eager to know what this business was the Don had to propound, and he, after drawing two or three mouthfuls of smoke, which he expelled through his nostrils in a most surprising unnatural manner, says in excellent good English, but speaking mighty slow and giving every letter its worth:

"What do you go to do to-morrow?"

"The Lord only knows," answers Jack, and Don Sanchez, lifting his eyebrows as if he considers this no answer at all, he continues: "We cannot go hence without our stage things; and if we could, I see not how we are to act our play, now that our villain is gone, with a plague to him! I doubt but we must sell all that we have for the few shillings they will fetch to get us out of this hobble."

"With our landlord's permission," remarks Don Sanchez, dryly.

"Permission!" cries Dawson, in a passion. "I ask no man's permission to do what I please with my own."

"Suppose he claims these things in payment of the money you owe him. What then?" asks the Don.

"We never thought of that, Kit," says Dawson, turning to me in a pucker. "But 'tis likely enough he has, for I observed he was mighty careless whether we found our thief or not. That's it, sure enough. We have nought to hope. All's lost!"

With that he drops his elbows on his knees, and stares into the fire with a most desponding countenance, being in that stage of liquor when a man must either laugh or weep.

"Come, Jack," says I. "You are not used to yield like this. Let us make the best of a bad lot, and face the worst like men. Though we trudge hence with nothing but the rags on our backs, we shall be no worse off to-morrow than we were this morning."

"Why, that's true enough!" cries he, plucking up his courage. "Let the thieving rascal take our poor nag and our things for his payment, and much good may they do him. We will wipe this out of our memory the moment we leave his cursed inn behind us."

It seemed to me that this would not greatly advance us, and maybe Don Sanchez thought the same, for he presently asks:

"And what then?"

"Why, Señor," replies Dawson, "we will face each new buffet as it comes, and make a good fight of it till we're beat. A man may die but once."

"You think only of yourselves," says the Don, very quietly.

"And pray, saving your Señor's presence, who else should we think of?"

"The child above," answers the Don, a little more sternly than he had yet spoken. "Is a young creature like that to bear the buffets you are so bold to meet? Can you offer her no shelter from the wind and rain but such as chance offers? make no provision for the time when she is left alone, to protect her against the evils that lie in the path of friendless maids?"

"God forgive me," says Jack, humbly. And then we could say nothing, for thinking what might befall Moll if we should be parted, but sat there under the keen eye of Don Sanchez, looking helplessly into the fire. And there was no sound until Jack's pipe, slipping from his hand, fell and broke in pieces upon the hearth. Then rousing himself up and turning to Don Sanchez, he says:

"The Lord help her, Señor, if we find no good friend to lend us a few shillings for our present wants."

"Good friends are few," says the Don, "and they who lend need some better security for repayment than chance. For my own part, I would as soon fling straws to a drowning man as attempt to save you and that child from ruin by setting you on your feet to-day only to fall again to-morrow."

"If that be so, Señor," says I, "you had some larger view in mind than that of offering temporary relief to our misery when you gave us a supper and Moll a bed for the night."

Don Sanchez assented with a grave inclination of his head, and going to the door opened it sharply, listened awhile, and then closing it softly, returned and stood before us with folded arms. Then, in a low voice, not to be heard beyond the room, he questioned us very particularly as to our relations with other men, the length of time we had been wandering about the country, and especially about the tractability of Moll. And, being satisfied with our replies, — above all, with Jack's saying that Moll would jump out of window at his bidding, without a thought to the consequences, — he says:

"There's a comedy we might play to some advantage if

you were minded to take the parts I give you and act them as I direct."

"With all my heart," cries Dawson. "I'll play any part you choose; and as to the directing, you're welcome to that, for I've had my fill of it. If you can make terms with our landlord, those things in the yard shall be yours, and for our payment I'm willing to trust to your honour's generosity."

"As regards payment," says the Don, "I can speak precisely. We shall gain fifty thousand pounds by our performance."

"Fifty thousand pounds," says Jack, as if in doubt whether he had heard aright. Don Sanchez bent his head, without stirring a line in his face.

Dawson took up his beaker slowly, and looked in it, to make sure that he was none the worse for drink, then, after emptying it, to steady his wits, he says again:

"Fifty thousand pounds."

"Fifty thousand pounds, if not more; and that there be no jealousies one of the other, it shall be divided fairly amongst us, — as much for your friend as for you, for the child as for me."

"Pray God, this part be no more than I can compass," says Jack, devoutly.

"You may learn it in a few hours — at least, your first act."

"And mine?" says I, entering for the first time into the dialogue.

The Don hunched his shoulders, lifting his eyebrows, and sending two streams of smoke from his nose.

"I scarce know what part to give you, yet," says he. "To be honest, you are not wanted at all in the play."

"Nay, but you must write him a part," says Dawson,

stoutly; "if it be but to bring in a letter — that I am determined on. Kit stood by us in ill fortune, and he shall share better, or I'll have none of it, nor Moll neither. I'll answer for her."

"There must be no discontent among us," says the Don, meaning thereby, as I think, that he had included me in his stratagem for fear I might mar it from envy. "The girl's part is that which gives me most concern — and had I not faith in my own judgment — "

"Set your mind at ease on that score," cried Jack. "I warrant our Moll shall learn her part in a couple of days or so."

"If she learn it in a twelvemonth, 'twill be time enough."

"A twelvemonth," said Jack, going to his beaker again, for understanding. "Well, all's as one, so that we can get something in advance of our payment, to keep us through such a prodigious study."

"I will charge myself with your expenses," says Don Sanchez; and then, turning to me, he asks if I have any objection to urge.

"I take it, Señor, that you speak in metaphor," says I; "and that this 'comedy' is nought but a stratagem for getting hold of a fortune that doesn't belong to us."

Don Sanchez calmly assented, as if this had been the most innocent design in the world.

"Hang me," cries Dawson, "if I thought it was anything but a whimsey of your honour's."

"I should like to know if we may carry out this stratagem honestly," says I.

"Aye," cries Jack. "I'll not agree for cutting of throats or breaking of bones, for any money."

"I can tell you no more than this," says the Don. "The fortune we may take is now in the hands of a man who has no more right to it than we have."

"If that's so," says Jack, "I'm with you, Señor. For I'd as lief bustle a thief out of his gains as say my prayers, any day, and liefer."

"Still," says I, "the money must of right belong to some one."

"We will say that the money belongs to a child of the same age as Moll."

"Then it comes to this, Señor," says I, bluntly. "We are to rob that child of fifty thousand pounds."

"When you speak of robbing," says the Don, drawing himself up with much dignity, "you forget that I am to play a part in this stratagem — I, Don Sanchez del Castillo de Castelaña."

"Fie, Kit, han't you any manners?" cries Dick. "What's all this talk of a child? Hasn't the Señor told us we are but to bustle a cheat?"

"But I would know what is to become of this child, if we take her fortune, though it be withheld from her by another," says I, being exceeding obstinate and persistent in my liquor.

"I shall prove to your conviction," says the Don, "that the child will be no worse off, if we take this money, than if we leave it in the hands of that rascally steward. But I see," adds he, contemptuously, "that for all your brotherly love, 'tis no such matter to you whether poor little Molly comes to her ruin, as every maid must who goes to the stage, or is set beyond the reach of temptation and the goading of want."

"Aye, and be hanged to you, Kit!" cries Dawson.

"Tell me, Mr. Poet," continues Don Sanchez, "do you consider this steward who defrauds that child of a fortune is more unfeeling than you who, for a sickly qualm of conscience, would let slip this chance of making Molly an honest woman?"

"Aye, answer that, Kit," adds Jack, striking his mug on the table.

"I'll answer you to-morrow morning, Señor," says I. "And whether I fall in with the scheme or not is all as one, since my help is not needed; for if it be to Moll's good, I'll bid you farewell, and you shall see me never again."

"Spoken like a man!" says Don Sanchez, "and a wise one to boot. An enterprise of this nature is not to be undertaken without reflection, like the smoking of a pipe. If you put your foot forward, it must be with the understanding that you cannot go back. I must have that assurance, for I shall be hundreds of pounds out of pocket ere I can get any return for my venture."

"Have no fear of me or of Moll turning tail at a scarecrow," says Jack, adding with a sneer, "we are no poets."

"Reflect upon it. Argue it out with your friend here, whose scruples do not displease me, and let me know your determination when the last word is said. Business carries me to London to-morrow; but you shall meet me at night, and we will close the business — aye or nay — ere supper."

With that he opens the door and gives us our congee, the most noble in the world; but not offering to give us a bed, we are forced to go out of doors and grope our way through the snow to the cart-shed, and seek a shelter there from the wind, which was all the keener and more bitter for our leaving a good fire. And I believe the shrewd Spaniard had put us to this pinch as a foretaste of the misery we must endure if we rejected his design, and so to shape our inclinations to his.

Happily, the landlord, coming out with a lantern, and finding us by the chattering of our teeth, was moved by the consideration shown us by Don Sanchez to relax his severity; and so, unlocking the stable door, he bade us get up into the loft, which we did, blessing him as if he had been the best Christian in the world. And then, having buried ourselves in hay, Jack Dawson and I fell to arguing the matter in question, I sticking to my scruples (partly from vanity), and he stoutly holding t'other side; and I, being warmed by my own eloquence, and he not less heated by liquor (having taken best part of the last bowl to his share), we ran it pretty high, so that at one point Jack was for lighting a candle end he had in his pocket and fighting it out like men. But, little by little, we cooled down, and towards morning, each giving way something, we came to the conclusion that we would have Don Sanchez show us the steward, that we might know the truth of his story (which I misdoubted, seeing that it was but a roguish kind of game at best that he would have us take part in), and that if we found all things as he represented them, then we would accept his offer. And also we resolved to be down betimes and let him know our determination before he set out for London, to the end that we might not be left fasting all the day. But herein we miscalculated the potency of liquor and a comfortable bed of hay, for 'twas nine o'clock before either of us winked an eye, and when we got down, we learnt that Don Sanchez had been gone a full hour, and so no prospect of breaking our fast till nightfall.

Presently comes Moll, all fresh and pink from the house, and falls to exclaiming upon the joy of sleeping betwixt clean sheets in a feather bed, and could speak of nothing else, saying she would give all the world to sleep so well every day of her life.

"Eh," whispers her father in my ear, "you see how luxuries do tempt the poor child, and what kind of a bed she is like to lie in if our hopes miscarry."

On which, still holding to my scruples, I says to Moll:

"'Tis easy to say you would give the world, Moll, but I know full well you would give nothing for all the comfort possible that was not your own."

"Nay," says she, crossing her hands on her breast, and casting up her eyes with the look of a saint, "what are all the fruits of the earth to her who cannot take them with an easy conscience? Honesty is dearer to me than the bread of life."

Then, as Jack and I are looking at each other ruefully in the face at this dash to our knavish project, she bursts into a merry peal of laughter, like a set of Christmas bells chiming, whereupon we, turning about to find the cause of her merriment, she pulls another demure face, and, slowly lifting her skirt, shows us a white napkin tied about her waist, stuffed with a dozen delicacies she had filched from Don Sanchez's table in coming down from her room.

CHAPTER IV.

Of the several parts that we are appointed to play.

FINDING a sheltered secret corner, we made a very hasty breakfast of these stolen dainties, and since we had not the heart to restore them to our innkeeper, so we had not the face to chide Moll for her larceny, but made light of the business and ate with great content and some mirth.

A drizzly rain falling and turning the snow into slush, we kept under the shelter of the shed, and this giving us scope for the reflection Don Sanchez had counselled, my compunctions were greatly shaken by the consideration of our present position and the prospect of worse. When I thought of our breakfast that Moll had stolen, and how willingly we would all have eaten a dinner got by the same means, I had to acknowledge that certainly we were all thieves at heart; and this conclusion, together with sitting all day doing nothing in the raw cold, did make the design of Don Sanchez seem much less heinous to me than it appeared the night before, when I was warm and not exceedingly sober, and indeed towards dusk I came to regard it as no bad thing at all.

About six comes back our Don on a fine horse, and receives our salutations with a cool nod — we standing there of a row, looking our sweetest, like hungry dogs in expectation of a bone. Then in he goes to the house without a word, and now my worst fear was that he had thought better of his offer and would abandon it. So there we hang about the best part of an hour, now thinking the Don would presently send for us, and then growing to despair of everything but to be left in the cold forgotten; but in the end comes Master Landlord to tell us his worship in the Cherry room would see us. So, after the same formalities of cleansing ourselves as the night afore, upstairs we go at the heels of a drawer, carrying a roast pig, which to our senses was more delightful than any bunch of flowers.

With a gesture of his hands, after saluting us with great dignity, Don Sanchez bade us take our places at the table and with never a word of question as to our decision; but that was scarce necessary, for it needed no subtle observation to perceive that we would accept any conditions to get our share of that roast pig. This supper differed not greatly from the former, save that our Moll was taken with a kind of tickling at the throat which presently attracted our notice.

"What ails you, Molly, my dear?" asks Jack. "Has a bit of crackling gone down the wrong way?"

She put it off as if she would have us take no notice of it, but it grew worse and worse towards the end of the meal, and became a most horrid, tearing cough, which she did so natural as to deceive us all and put us in great concern, and especially Don Sanchez, who declared she must have taken a cold by being exposed all day to the damp weather.

"If I have," says she, very prettily, after wiping the tears from her eyes upon another fit, "'tis surely a most ungrateful return for the kindness with which you sheltered me last night, Señor."

"I shall take better care to shelter you in the future, my

poor child," replies the Don, ringing the bell. Then, the maid coming, he bids her warm a bed and prepare a hot posset against Moll was tucked up in the blankets. "And," says he, turning to Moll, "you shall not rise till noon, my dear; your breakfast shall be brought to you in your room, where a fire shall be made, and such treatment shown you as if you were my own child."

"Oh! what have I done that you should be so gentle to me?" exclaims Moll, smothering another cough. And with that she reaches out her leg under the table and fetches me a kick of the shin, looking all the while as pitiful and innocent as any painted picture.

"Would it be well to fetch in a doctor?" says Don Sanchez, when Moll was gone barking upstairs. "The child looks delicate, though she eats with a fairly good appetite."

"'Tis nothing serious," replies Jack, who had doubtless received the same hint from Moll she had given me. "I warrant she will be mended in a day or so, with proper care. 'Tis a kind of family complaint. I am taken that way at times," and with that he rasps his throat as a hint that he would be none of the worse for sleeping a night between sheets.

This was carrying the matter too far, and I thought it had certainly undone us; for stopping short, with a stare, in crossing the room, he turns and looks first at Dawson, then at me, with anything but a pleasant look in his eyes as finding his dignity hurt, to be thus bustled by a mere child. Then his dark eyebrows unbending with the reflection, maybe, that it was so much the better to his purpose that Moll could so act as to deceive him, he seats himself gravely, and replies to Jack:

"Your family wit may get you a night's lodging, but I doubt if you will ever merit it so well as your daughter."

"Well," says Jack, with a laugh, "what wit we have amongst us we are resolved to employ in your honour's service, so that you show us this steward-fellow is a rascal that deserves to be bounced, and we do no great injury to any one else."

"Good," says Don Sanchez. "We will proceed to that without delay. And now, as we have no matter to discuss, and must be afoot early to-morrow, I will ring for a light to take you to bed."

So we up presently to a good snug room with a bed to each of us fit for a prince. And there, with the blankets drawn up to our ears, we fell blessing our stars that we were now fairly out of our straits, and after that to discussing whether we should consult Moll's inclination to this business. First, Dawson was for telling her plump out all about our project, saying that being so young she had no conscience to speak of, and would like nothing better than to take part in any piece of mischief. But against this I protested, seeing that it would be dangerous to our design to let her know so much (she having a woman's tongue in her head), and also of a bad tendency to make her, as it were, at the very beginning of her life, a knowing active party to what looked like nothing more nor less than a piece of knavery. Therefore I proposed we should, when necessary, tell her just so much of our plan as was expedient, and no more. And this agreeing mightily with Jack's natural turn for taking of short cuts out of difficulties, he fell in with my views at once, and so, bidding God bless me, he lays the clothes over his head and was snoring the next minute.

In the morning we found the Don just as kind to us as the day before he had been careless, and so made us eat breakfast with him, to our great content. Also, he sent a maid up to Moll to enquire of her health, and if she could eat anything from our table, to which the baggage sends reply that she feels a little easier this morning and could fancy a dish of black puddings. These delicacies her father carried to her, being charged by the Don to tell her that we should be gone for a couple of days, and that in our absence she might command whatever she felt was necessary to her complete recovery against our return. Then I told Don Sanchez how we had resolved to tell Moll no more of our purpose than was necessary for the moment, which pleased him, I thought, mightily, he saying that our success or failure depended upon secrecy as much as anything, for which reason he had kept us in the dark as much as ever it was possible.

About eight o'clock three saddle nags were brought to the door, and we, mounting, set out for London, where we arrived about ten, the roads being fairly passable save in the marshy parts about Shoreditch, where the mire was knee-deep; so to Gracious Street, and there leaving our nags at the Turk inn, we walked down to the Bridge stairs, and thence with a pair of oars to Greenwich. Here, after our tedious chilly voyage, we were not ill-pleased to see the inside of an inn once more, and Don Sanchez, taking us to the King's posting-house, orders a fire to be lighted in a private room, and the best there was in the larder to be served us in the warm parlour. While we were at our trenchers Don Sanchez says:

"At two o'clock two men are coming hither to see me.

One is a master mariner named Robert Evans, the other a merchant adventurer of his acquaintance whom I have not yet seen. Now you are to mark these two men well, note all they say and their manner of speaking, for to-morrow you will have to personate these characters before one who would be only too glad to find you at fault."

"Very good, Señor," says Dawson; "but which of these parts am I to play?"

"That you may decide when you have seen the men, but I should say from my knowledge of Robert Evans that you may best represent his character. For in your parts to-day you are to be John and Christopher Knight, two needy cousins of Lady Godwin, whose husband, Sir Richard Godwin, was lost at sea seven years ago. I doubt if you will have to do anything in these characters beyond looking eager and answering merely yes and no to such questions as I may put."

Thus primed, we went presently to the sitting-room above, and the drawer shortly after coming to say that two gentlemen desired to see Don Sanchez, Jack and I seated ourselves side by side at a becoming distance from the Don, holding our hats on our knees as humbly as may be. Then in comes a rude, dirty fellow with a patch over one eye and a most peculiar bearish gait, dressed in a tarred coat, with a wool shawl about his neck, followed by a shrewd-visaged little gentleman in a plain cloth suit, but of very good substance, he looking just as trim and well-mannered as t'other was uncouth and rude.

"Well, here am I," says Evans (whom we knew at once for the master mariner), flinging his hat and shawl in a corner. "There's his excellency Don Sanchez, and here's

Mr. Hopkins, the merchant I spoke on yesterday; and who be these?" turning about to fix us with his one blue eye.

"Two gentlemen related to Mrs. Godwin, and very anxious for her return," replies the Don.

"Then we being met friends all, let's have up a bottle and heave off on this here business without more ado," says Evans; and with that he seats himself in the Don's chair, pokes up the fire with his boots, and spits on the hearth.

The Don graciously places a chair for Mr. Hopkins, rings the bell, and seats himself. Then after a few civilities while the bottle was being opened and our glasses filled, he says:

"You have doubtless heard from Robert Evans the purpose of our coming hither, Mr. Hopkins."

"Roughly," replies Mr. Hopkins, with a dry little cough. "But I should be glad to have the particulars from you, that I may judge more clearly of my responsibilities in this undertaking."

"Oh, Lord!" exclaims Evans, in disgust. "Here give us a pipe of tobacco if we're to warp out half a day ere we get a capful of wind."

CHAPTER V.

Don Sanchez puts us in the way of robbing with an easy conscience.

PROMISING to make his story as short as he possibly could, Don Sanchez began:

"On the coming of our present king to his throne, Sir Richard Godwin was recalled from Italy, whither he had been sent as embassador by the Protector. He sailed from Livorno with his wife and his daughter Judith, a child of nine years old at that time, in the Seahawk."

"I remember her," says Evans, "as stout a ship as ever was put to sea."

"On the second night of her voyage the Seahawk became parted from her convoy, and the next day she was pursued and overtaken by a pair of Barbary pirates, to whom she gave battle."

"Aye, and I'd have done the same," cries Evans, "though they had been a score."

"After a long and bloody fight," continues Don Sanchez, "the corsairs succeeded in boarding the Seahawk and overcoming the remnant of her company."

"Poor hearts! would I had been there to help 'em," says Evans.

"Exasperated by the obstinate resistance of these English and their own losses, the pirates would grant no mercy, but tying the living to the dead they cast all overboard save Mrs. Godwin and her daughter. Her lot was even worse; for her wounded husband, Sir Richard, was snatched from her arms and flung into the sea before her eyes, and he sank crying farewell to her."

"These Turks have no hearts in their bellies, you must understand," explains Evans. "And nought but venom in their veins."

"The Seahawk was taken to Alger, and there Mrs. Godwin and her daughter were sold for slaves in the public market-place."

"I have seen 'em sold by the score there," says Evans, "and fetch but an onion a head."

"By good fortune the mother and daughter were bought by Sidi ben Moula, a rich old merchant who was smitten by the pretty, delicate looks of Judith, whom he thenceforth treated as if she had been his own child. In this condition they lived with greater happiness than falls to the lot of most slaves, until the beginning of last year, when Sidi died, and his possessions fell to his brother, Bare ben Moula. Then Mrs. Godwin appeals to Bare for her liberty and to be sent home to her country, saying that what price (in reason) he chooses to set upon their heads she will pay from her estate in England — a thing which she had proposed before to Sidi, but he would not hear of it because of his love for Judith and his needing no greater fortune than he had. But this Bare, though he would be very well content, being also an old man, to have his household managed by Mrs. Godwin and to adopt Judith as his child, being of a more avaricious turn than his brother, at length consents to it, on condition that her ransoms be paid before she quits Barbary. And so, casting about how this may be done, Mrs. Godwin finds a captive whose price has been paid, about to be taken to Palma in the Baleares, and to him she entrusts two letters." Here Don Sanchez pulls two folded sheets of vellum from his pocket, and presenting one to me, he says:

"Mayhap you recognise this hand, Mr. Knight."

And I, seeing the signature Elizabeth Godwin, answers quickly enough: "Aye, 'tis my dear cousin Bess, her own hand."

"This," says the Don, handing the other to Evans, "you may understand."

"I can make out 'tis writ in the Moorish style," says Evans, "but the meaning of it I know not, for I can't tell great A from a bull's foot though it be in printed English."

"'Tis an undertaking on the part of Bare ben Moula," says the Don, "to deliver up at Dellys in Barbary the persons of Mrs. Godwin and her daughter against the payment of five thousand gold ducats within one year. The other writing tells its own story."

Mr. Hopkins took the first sheet from me and read it aloud. It was addressed to Mr. Richard Godwin, Hurst Court, Chislehurst in Kent, and after giving such particulars of her past as we had already heard from Don Sanchez, she writes thus: "And now, my dear nephew, as I doubt not you (as the nearest of my kindred to my dear husband after us two poor relicts) have taken possession of his estate in the belief we were all lost in our voyage from Italy, I do pray you for the love of God and of mercy to deliver us from our bondage by sending hither a ship with the money for our ransoms forthwith, and be assured by this that I shall not dispossess you of your fortune (more than my bitter circumstances do now require), so that I but come home to die in a Christian country and have my sweet Judith where she may be less exposed to harm than in this infidel country. I count upon your love,—being ever a dear nephew,—and am your most hopeful, trusting, and loving aunt, Elizabeth Godwin."

"Very well, sir," says Mr. Hopkins, returning the letter. "You have been to Chislehurst."

"I have," answers the Don, "and there I find the estate in the hands of a most curious Puritanical steward, whose honesty is rather in the letter than the spirit. For though I have reason to believe that not one penny's value of the estate has been misemployed since it has been in his hands, yet will he give nothing—no, not a maravedi to the redemption of his mistress, saying that the letter is addressed to Richard Godwin and not to him, etc., and that he hath no power to pay out monies for this purpose, even though he believed the facts I have laid before him—which for his own ends doubtless he fains to misdoubt."

"As a trader, sir," says Mr. Hopkins, "I cannot blame his conduct in that respect. For should the venture fall through, the next heir might call upon him to repay out of his own pocket all that he had put into this enterprise. But this Mr. Richard Godwin, what of him?"

"He is nowhere to be found. The only relatives I have been able to discover are these two gentlemen."

"Who," remarks Mr. Hopkins, with a shrewd glance at our soiled clothes, "are not, I venture to think, in a position to pay their cousin's ransom."

"Alas, no, sir," says Jack. "We are but two poor shopkeepers of London undone by the great fire."

"Well now, sir," says Mr. Hopkins, fetching an inkpot, a pen, and a piece of paper from his pocket. "I may conclude that you wish me to adventure upon the redemption of these two ladies in Barbary, upon the hazard of being repaid by Mrs. Godwin when she recovers her estate." And the Don making him a reverence, he continues, " We must first learn the extent of our liabilities. What sum is to be paid to Bare ben Moula?"

" Five thousand gold ducats—about two thousand pounds English."

" Two thousand," says Mr. Hopkins, writing. " Then, Robert Evans, what charge is yours for fetching the ladies from Dellys?"

" Master Hopkins, I have said fifteen hundred pounds," says he, " and I won't go from my word though all laugh at me for a madman."

" That seems a great deal of money," says Mr. Hopkins.

" Well, if you think fifteen hundred pounds too much for my carcase and a ship of twenty men, you can go seek a cheaper market elsewhere."

" You think there is very small likelihood of coming back alive?"

" Why, comrade, 'tis as if you should go into a den of lions and hope to get out whole; for though I have the Duke's pass, these Moors are no fitter to be trusted than a sackful of serpents. 'Tis ten to one our ship be taken, and we fools all sold into slavery."

" Ten to one," says Mr. Hopkins; " that is to say, you would make this voyage for the tenth part of what you ask were you sure of returning safe."

" I would go as far anywhere outside the straits for an hundred pounds with a lighter heart."

Mr. Hopkins nods his head, and setting down some figures on his paper, says:

"The bare outlay in hard money amounts to thirty-five hundred pounds. Reckoning the risk at Robert Evans' own valuation (which I take to be a very low one), I must see reasonable prospect of winning thirty-five thousand pounds by my hazard."

"Mrs. Godwin's estate I know to be worth double that amount."

"But who will promise me that return?" asks Mr. Hopkins. "Not you?" (The Don shook his head.) "Not you?" (turning to us, with the same result). "Not Mrs. Godwin, for we have no means of communicating with her. Not the steward — you have shown me that. Who then remains but this Richard Godwin who cannot be found? If," adds he, getting up from his seat, "you can find Richard Godwin, put him in possession of the estate, and obtain from him a reasonable promise that this sum shall be paid on the return of Mrs. Godwin, I may feel disposed to consider your proposal more seriously. But till then I can do nothing."

"Likewise, masters all," says Evans, fetching his hat and shawl from the corner, "I can't wait for a blue moon; and if so be we don't sign articles in a week, I'm off of my bargain, and mighty glad to get out of it so cheap."

"You see," says Don Sanchez, when they were gone out of the room, "how impossible it is that Mrs. Godwin and her daughter shall be redeemed from captivity. To-morrow I shall show you what kind of a fellow the steward is that he should have the handling of this fortune rather than we."

Then presently, with an indifferent, careless air, as if 'twas nought, he gives us a purse and bids us go out in the town to furnish ourselves with what disguise was necessary to our purpose. Therewith Dawson gets him some seaman's old clothes at a Jew's, and I a very neat, presentable suit of cloth, etc., and the rest of the money we take back to Don Sanchez without taking so much as a penny for our other uses; but he, doing all things very magnificent, would have none of it, but bade us keep it against our other necessities. And now having his money in our pockets, we felt 'twould be more dishonest to go back from this business than to go forward with it, lead us whither it might.

Next morning off we go betimes, Jack more like Robert Evans than his mother's son, and I a most seeming substantial man (so that the very stable lad took off his hat to me), and on very good horses a long ride to Chislehurst. And there coming to a monstrous fine park, Don Sanchez stayed us before the gates, and bidding us look up a broad avenue of great oaks to a most surprising brave house, he told us this was Hurst Court, and we might have it for our own within a year if we were so minded.

Hence, at no great distance we reach a square plain house, the windows all barred with stout iron, and the most like a prison I did ever see. Here Don Sanchez ringing a bell, a little grating in the door is opened, and after some parley we are admitted by a sturdy fellow carrying a cudgel in his hand. So we into a cold room, with not a spark of fire on the hearth but a few ashes, no hangings to the windows, nor any ornament or comfort at all, but only a table and half a dozen wooden stools, and a number of shelves against the wall full of account books and papers protected by a grating of stout wire secured with sundry padlocks. And here, behind a tableful of papers, sat our steward, Simon Stout-in-faith, a most withered, lean old man, clothed all in leather, wearing no wig but his own rusty grey hair falling lank on his shoulders, with a sour face of a very jaundiced complexion, and pale eyes that seemed to swim in a yellowish rheum, which he was for ever a-mopping with a rag.

"I am come, Mr. Steward," says Don Sanchez, "to conclude the business we were upon last week."

"Aye," cries Dawson, for all the world in the manner of Evans, "but ere we get to this dry matter let's have a bottle to ease the way, for this riding of horseback has parched up my vitals confoundedly."

"If thou art athirst," says Simon, "Peter shall fetch thee a jug of water from the well; but other liquor have we none in this house."

"Let Peter drown in your well," says Dawson, with an oath; "I'll have none of it. Let's get this matter done and away, for I'd as lief sit in a leaky hold as in this here place for comfort."

"Here," says Don Sanchez, "is a master mariner who is prepared to risk his life, and here a merchant adventurer of London who will hazard his money, to redeem your mistress and her daughter from slavery."

"Praise the Lord, Peter," says the steward. Whereupon the sturdy fellow with the cudgel fell upon his knees, as likewise did Simon, and both in a snuffling voice render thanks to Heaven in words which I do not think it proper to write here. Then, being done, they get up, and the steward, having dried his eyes, says:

"So far our prayers have been answered. Put me in

mind, friend Peter, that to-night we pray these worthy men prosper in their design."

"If they succeed," says Don Sanchez, "it will cost your mistress five-and-thirty thousand pounds."

The steward clutched at the table as if at the fortune about to turn from him; his jaw fell, and he stared at Don Sanchez in bewilderment, then getting the face to speak, he gasps out, "Thirty-five thousand pounds!" and still in a maze asks: "Art thou in thy right senses, friend?"

The Don hunches his shoulders and turns to me. Whereupon I lay forth in pretty much the same words as Mr. Hopkins used, the risk of the venture, etc., to all which this Simon listened with starting eyes and gaping mouth.

"Thirty-five thousand pounds!" he says again; "why, friend, 'tis half of all I have made of the estate by a life of thrift and care and earnest seeking."

"'Tis in your power, Simon," says Don Sanchez, "to spare your mistress this terrible charge, for which your fine park must be felled, your farms cut up, and your economies be scattered. The master here will fetch your mistress home for fifteen hundred pounds."

"Why, even that is an extortion."

"Nay," says Jack, "if you think fifteen hundred pounds too much for my carcase and a ship of twenty men, you may seek a cheaper market and welcome, for I've no stomach to risk my life and property for less."

"To the fifteen hundred pounds you must add the ransom of two thousand pounds. Thus Mrs. Godwin and her daughter may be redeemed for thirty-five hundred pounds to her saving of thirty-one thousand five hundred pounds," says the Don.

And here Dawson and I were secretly struck by his honesty in not seeking to affright the steward from an honest course, but rather tempting him to it by playing upon his parsimony and avarice.

"Three thousand five hundred," says Simon, putting it down in writing, that he might the better realise his position. "But you say, friend merchant, that the risk is as ten to one against seeing thy money again."

"I will run the risk for thirty-one thousand pounds, and no less," says I.

"But if it may be done for a tenth part, how then?"

"Why, 'tis your risk, sir, and not mine," says I.

"Yea, yea, my risk. And you tell me, friend sailor, that you stand in danger of being plundered by these infidels."

"Aye, more like than not."

"Why, then we may count half the estate gone; and the peril is to be run again, and thus all cast away for nought."

In this manner did Simon halt betwixt two ways like one distracted, but only he did mingle a mass of sacred words with his arguments which seemed to me nought but profanity, his sole concern being the gain of money. Then he falls to the old excuses Don Sanchez had told us of, saying he had no money of his own, and offering to show his books that we might see he had taken not one penny beyond his bare expenses from the estate, save his yearly wage, and that no more than Sir Richard had given him in his lifetime. And on Don Sanchez showing Mrs. Godwin's letter as a fitting authority to draw out this money for her use, he first feigns to doubt her hand, and then says he: "If an accident befalls these two women ere they return to justify me, how shall I answer to the next heir for this outlay?

Verily" (clasping his hands) "I am as one standing in darkness, and I dare not move until I am better enlightened; so prithee, friend, give me time to commune with my conscience."

Don Sanchez hunches up his shoulders and turns to us.

"Why, look here, Master," says Dawson. "I can't see as you need much enlightenment to answer yes or no to a fair offer, and as for me, I'm not going to hang in a hedge for a blue moon. So if you won't clap hands on the bargain without more ado, I throw this business overboard and shall count I've done the best day's work of my life in getting out of the affair."

Then I made as if I would willingly draw out of my share in the project.

"My friends," says Simon, "there can be scarce any hope at all if thou wilt not hazard thy money for such a prodigious advantage." Then turning to Peter as his last hope, he asks in despair, "What shall we do, my brother?"

"We can keep on a-praying, friend Simon," replies Peter, in a snivelling voice.

"A blessed thought!" exclaims the steward in glee. "Surely that is more righteous than to lay faith in our own vain effort. So do thou, friend" (turning to me), "put thy money to this use, for I will none."

"I cannot do that, sir," says I, "without an assurance that Mrs. Godwin's estate will bear this charge."

With wondrous alacrity Simon fetches a book with a plan of the estate, whereby he showed us that not a holding on the estate was untenanted, not a single tenant in arrear with his rent, and that the value of the property with all deductions made was sixty-five thousand pounds.

"Very good sir," says I. "Now you must give me a written note, stating what you have shown, with your sanction to my making this venture on Mrs. Godwin's behalf, that I may justify my claim hereafter."

But this Simon stoutly refused to do, saying his conscience would not allow him to sign any bond (clearly with the hope that he might in the end shuffle out of paying anything at all), until Don Sanchez, losing patience, declared he would certainly hunt all London through to find that Mr. Richard Godwin, who was the next of kin, hinting that he would certainly give us such sanction as we required if only to prove his right to the succession should our venture fail.

This put the steward to a new taking; but the Don holding firm, he at length agreed to give us this note, upon Don Sanchez writing another affirming that he had seen Mrs. Godwin and her daughter in Barbary, and was going forth to fetch them, that should Mr. Richard Godwin come to claim the estate he might be justly put off.

And so this business ended to our great satisfaction, we saying to ourselves that we had done all that man could to redeem the captives, and that it would be no harm at all to put a cheat upon the miserly steward. Whether we were any way more honest than he in shaping our conduct according to our inclinations is a question which troubled us then very little.

CHAPTER VI.

Moll is cast to play the part of a fine lady; doubtful promise for this undertaking.

ON our way back to Greenwich we stayed at an inn by the road to refresh ourselves, and there, having a snug parlour to ourselves, and being seated about a fine cheese with each a full measure of ale, Don Sanchez asks us if we are satisfied with our undertaking.

"Aye, that we are," replies Dawson, mightily pleased as usual to be a-feasting. "We desire nothing better than to serve your honour faithfully in all ways, and are ready to put our hands to any bond you may choose to draw up."

"Can you show me the man," asks the Don, lifting his eyebrows contemptuously, "who ever kept a treaty he was minded to break? Men are honest enough when nought's to be gained by breaking faith. Are you both agreed to this course?"

"Yes, Señor," says I, "and my only compunction now is that I can do so little to forward this business."

"Why, so far as I can see into it," says Dawson, "one of us must be cast for old Mrs. Godwin, if Moll is to be her daughter, and you're fitter to play the part than I, for I take it this old gentlewoman should be of a more delicate, sickly composition than mine."

"We will suppose that Mrs. Godwin is dead," says the Don, gravely.

"Aye, to be sure; that simplifies the thing mightily. But pray, Señor, what parts are we to play?"

"The parts you have played to-day. You go with me to fetch Judith Godwin from Barbary."

"This hangs together and ought to play well; eh, Kit?"

I asked Don Sanchez how long, in the ordinary course of things an expedition of this kind would take.

"That depends upon accidents of many kinds," answers he. "We may very well stretch it out best part of a year."

"A year," says Jack, scratching his ear ruefully, for I believe he had counted upon coming to live like a lord in a few weeks. "And what on earth are we to do in the meanwhile?"

"Teach Moll," answers the Don.

"She can read anything print or scrip," says Jack, proudly, "and write her own name."

"Judith Godwin," says the Don, reflectively, "lived two years in Italy. She would certainly remember some words of Italian. Consider this: it is not sufficient merely to obtain possession of the Godwin estate; it must be held against the jealous opposition of that shrewd steward and of the presumptive heir, Mr. Richard Godwin, who may come forward at any time."

"You're in the right, Señor. Well, there's Kit knows the language and can teach her a smattering of the Italian, I warrant, in no time."

"Judith would probably know something of music," pursues the Don.

"Why, Moll can play Kit's fiddle as well as he."

"But, above all," continues the Don, as taking no heed of this tribute to Moll's abilities, "Judith Godwin must be able to read and write the Moorish character and speak the tongue readily, answer aptly as to their ways and habits, and to do these things beyond suspect. Moll must live with these people for some months."

"God have mercy on us!" cries Jack. "Your honour is not for taking us to Barbary."

"No," answers the Don, dryly, passing his long fingers with some significance over the many seams in his long face, "but we must go where the Moors are to be found, on the hither side of the straits."

"Well," says Dawson, "all's as one whither we go in safety if we're to be out of our fortune for a year. There's nothing more for our Moll to learn, I suppose, Señor."

"It will not be amiss to teach her the manners of a lady," replies the Don, rising and knitting his brows together unpleasantly, "and especially to keep her feet under her chair at table."

With this he rings the bell for our reckoning, and so ends our discussion, neither Dawson nor I having a word to say in answer to this last hit, which showed us pretty plainly that in reaching round with her long leg for our shins, Moll had caught the Don's shanks a kick that night she was seized with a cough.

So to horse again and a long jog back to Greenwich, where Dawson and I would fain have rested the night (being unused to the saddle and very raw with our journey), but the Don would not for prudence, and therefore, after changing our clothes, we make a shift to mount once more, and thence another long horrid jolt to Edmonton very painfully.

Coming to the Bell (more dead than alive) about eight,

and pitch dark, we were greatly surprised that we could make no one hear to take our horses, and further, having turned the brutes into the stable ourselves, to find never a soul in the common room or parlour, so that the place seemed quite forsaken. But hearing a loud guffaw of laughter from below, we go downstairs to the kitchen, which we could scarce enter for the crowd in the doorway. And here all darkness, save for a sheet hung at the further end, and lit from behind, on which a kind of phantasmagory play of Jack and the Giant was being acted by shadow characters cut out of paper, the performer being hid by a board that served as a stage for the puppets. And who should this performer be but our Moll, as we knew by her voice, and most admirably she did it, setting all in a roar one minute with some merry joke, and enchanting 'em the next with a pretty song for the maid in distress.

We learnt afterwards that Moll, who could never rest still two minutes together, but must for ever be a-doing something new, had cut out her images and devised the show to entertain the servants in the kitchen, and that the guests above hearing their merriment had come down in time to get the fag end, which pleased them so vastly that they would have her play it all over again.

"This may undo us," says Don Sanchez, in a low voice of displeasure, drawing us away. "Here are a dozen visitors who will presently be examining Moll as a marvel. Who can say but that one of them may know her again hereafter to our confusion? We must be seen together no more than is necessary, until we are out of this country. I shall leave here in the morning, and you will meet me next at the Turk, in Gracious Street, to-morrow afternoon."

E

Therewith he goes up to his room, leaving us to shift for ourselves; and we into the parlour to warm our feet at the fire till we may be served with some victuals, both very silent and surly, being still sore, and as tired as any dogs with our day's jolting.

While we are in this mood, Moll, having finished her play, comes to us in amazing high spirits, and all aglow with pleasure shows us a handful of silver given her by the gentry; then, pulling up a chair betwixt us, she asks us a dozen questions of a string as to where we have been, what we have done, etc., since we left her. Getting no answer, she presently stops, looks first at one, then at the other, and bursting into a fit of laughter, cries: "Why, what ails you both to be so grumpy?"

"In the first place, Moll," says Jack, "I'll have you to know that I am your father, and will not be spoken to save with becoming respect."

"Why, I did but ask you where you have been."

"Children of your age should not ask questions, but do as they're bid, and there's an end of it."

"La, I'm not to ask any questions. Is there nothing else I am not to do?"

"Yes; I'll not have you playing of Galimaufray to cook wenches and such stuff. I'll have you behave with more decency. Take your feet off the hearth, and put 'em under your chair. Let me have no more of these galanty-shows. Why, 'twill be said I cannot give you a basin of porridge, that you must go a-begging of sixpences like this!"

"Oh, if you begrudge me a little pocket-money," cries she, springing up with the tears in her eyes, "I'll have none of it."

And with that she empties her pocket on the chair, and out roll her sixpences together with a couple of silver spoons.

"What," cries Jack, after glancing round to see we were alone. "You have filched a couple of spoons, Moll?"

"And why not?" asks she, her little nose turning quite white with passion. "If I am to ask no questions, how shall I know but we may have never a spoon to-morrow for your precious basin of porridge?"

CHAPTER VII.

Of our journey through France to a very horrid pass in the Pyraneans.

SKIPPING over many unimportant particulars of our leaving Edmonton, of our finding Don Sanchez at the Turk in Gracious Street, of our going thence (the next day) to Gravesend, of our preparation there for voyage, I come now to our embarking, the 10th March, in the Rose, for Bordeaux in France. Nor shall I dwell long on that journey, neither, which was exceedingly long and painful, by reason of our nearing the equinoctials, which dashed us from our course to that degree that it was the 26th before we reached our port and cast anchor in still water. And all those days we were prostrated with sickness, and especially Jack Dawson, because of his full habit, so that he declared he would rather ride a-horseback to the end of the earth than go another mile on sea.

We stayed in Bordeaux, which is a noble town, but dirty, four days to refresh ourselves, and here the Don lodged us in a fine inn and fed us on the best; and also he made us buy new clothes and linen (which we sadly needed after the pickle we had lain in a fortnight) and cast away our old; but no more than was necessary, saying 'twould be better to furnish ourselves with fresh linen as we needed it, than carry baggage, etc. "And let all you buy be good goods," says he, "for in this country a man is valued at what he seems, and the innkeepers do go in such fear of their seigneurs that they will charge him less for entertainment than if he were a mean fellow who could ill afford to pay."

So not to displease him we dressed ourselves in the French fashion, more richly than ever we had been clad in our lives, and especially Moll did profit by this occasion to furnish herself like any duchess; so that Dawson and I drew lots to decide which of us should present the bill to Don Sanchez, thinking he would certainly take exception to our extravagance; but he did not so much as raise his eyebrows at the total, but paid it without ever a glance at the items. Nay, when Moll presents herself in her new equipment, he makes her a low reverence and pays her a most handsome compliment, but in his serious humour and without a smile. He himself wore a new suit all of black, not so fine as ours, but very noble and becoming, by reason of his easy, graceful manner and his majestic, high carriage.

On the last day of March we set forth for Toulouse. At our starting Don Sanchez bade Moll ride by his side, and so we, not being bid, fell behind; and, feeling awkward in our new clothes, we might very well have been taken for their servants, or a pair of ill-bred friends at the best, for our Moll carried herself not a whit less magnificent than the Don, to the admiration of all who looked at her.

To see these grand airs of hers charmed Jack Dawson.

"You see, Kit," whispers he, "what an apt scholar the minx is, and what an obedient, dutiful, good girl. One word from me is as good as six months' schooling, for all this comes of that lecture I gave her the last night we were at Edmonton."

I would not deny him the satisfaction of this belief, but I felt pretty sure that had she been riding betwixt us in her old gown, instead of beside the Don as his daughter, all her father's preaching would not have stayed her from behaving herself like an orange wench.

We journey by easy stages ten days through Toulouse, on the road to Perpignan, and being favoured with remarkably fine weather, a blue sky, and a bright sun above us, and at every turn something strange or beautiful to admire, no pleasure jaunt in the world could have been more delightful. At every inn (which here they call hotels) we found good beds, good food, excellent wine, and were treated like princes, so that Dawson and I would gladly have given up our promise of a fortune to have lived in this manner to the end of our days. But Don Sanchez professed to hold all on this side of the Pyrenese Mountains in great contempt, saying these hotels were as nothing to the Spanish posadas, that the people here would rob you if they dared, whereas, on t'other side, not a Spaniard would take so much as the hair of your horse's tail, though he were at the last extremity, that the food was not fit for aught but a Frenchman, and so forth. And our Moll, catching this humour, did also turn up her nose at everything she was offered, and would send away a bottle of wine from the table because 'twas not ripe enough, though but a few weeks before she had been drinking penny ale with a relish, and that as sour as verjuice. And, indeed, she did carry it mighty high and artificial, wherever respect and humility were to be commanded. But it was pretty to see how she would unbend and become her natural self where her heart was touched by some tender sentiment. How she would empty her pockets to give to any one with a piteous tale, how she would get from her horse to pluck wild-flowers by the roadside, and how, one day, overtaking a poor woman carrying a child painfully on her back, she must have the little one up on her lap and carry it till we reached the hamlet where the woman lived, etc. On the fifteenth day we stayed at St. Denys, and going thence the next morning, had travelled but a couple of hours when we were caught in a violent storm of hailstones as big as peas, that was swept with incredible force by a wind rushing through a deep ravine in the mountains, so that 'twas as much as we could make headway through it and gain a village which lay but a little distance from us. And here we were forced to stay all day by another storm of rain, that followed the hail and continued till nightfall. Many others besides ourselves were compelled to seek refuge at our inn, and amongst them a company of Spanish muleteers, for it seems we were come to a pass leading through the mountains into Spain. These were the first Spaniards we had yet seen (save the Don), and for all we had heard to their credit, we could not admire them greatly, being a low-browed, coarse-featured, ragged crew, and more picturesque than cleanly, besides stinking intolerably of garlic. By nightfall there was more company than the inn could accommodate; nevertheless, in respect to our quality, we were given the best rooms in the house to ourselves.

About eight o'clock, as we were about to sit down to supper, our innkeeper's wife comes in to tell us that a Spanish grandee is below, who has been travelling for hours in the storm, and then she asked very humbly if our excellencies will permit her to lay him a bed in our room when we have done with it, as she can bestow him nowhere else (the muleteers filling her house to the very cock loft), and has not the heart to send him on to St. Denys in this pitiless driving rain. To this Don Sanchez replies, that a Spanish gentleman is welcome to all we can offer him, and therewith sends down a mighty civil message, begging his company at our table.

Moll has just time to whip on a piece of finery, and we to put on our best manners, when the landlady returns, followed by a stout, robust Spaniard, in an old coat several times too small for him, whom she introduced as Señor Don Lopez de Calvados.

Don Lopez makes us a reverence, and then, with his shoulders up to his ears and like gestures, gives us an harangue at some length, but this being in Spanish, is as heathen Greek to our ears. However, Don Sanchez explains that our visitor is excusing his appearance as being forced to change his wet clothes for what the innkeeper can lend him, and so we, grinning to express our amiability, all sit down to table and set to — Moll with her most finicking, delicate airs and graces, and Dawson and I silent as frogs, with understanding nothing of the Dons' conversation. This, we learn from Don Sanchez after supper, has turned chiefly on the best means of crossing into Spain, from which it appears there are two passes through the mountains, both leading to the same town, but one more circuitous than the other. Don Lopez has come by the latter, because the former is used by the muleteers, who are not always the most pleasant companions one can have in a dangerous road; and for this reason he recommends us to take his way, especially as we have a young lady with us, which will be the more practicable, as the same guides who conducted him will be only too glad to serve us on their return the next morning. To this proposition we very readily agree, and supper being ended, Don Sanchez sends for the guides, two hardy mountaineers, who very readily agree to take us this way the next morning, if the weather permits. And so we all, wishing Don Lopez a good-night, to our several chambers.

I was awoke in the middle of the night, as it seemed to me, by a great commotion below of Spanish shouting and roaring with much jingling of bells; and looking out of window I perceived lanterns hanging here and there in the courtyard, and the muleteers packing their goods to depart, with a fine clear sky full of stars overhead. And scarce had I turned into my warm bed again, thanking God I was no muleteer, when in comes the Don with a candle, to say the guide will have us moving at once if we would reach Ravellos (our Spanish town) before night. So I to Dawson's chamber, and he to Moll's, and in a little while we all shivering down to the great kitchen, where is never a muleteer left, but only a great stench of garlic, to eat a mess of soup, very hot and comforting. And after that out into the dark (there being as yet but a faint flush of green and primrose colour over towards the east), where four fresh mules (which Don Sanchez overnight had bargained to exchange against our horses, as being the only kind of cattle fit for this service) are waiting for us with other two mules, belonging to our guides, all very curiously trapped out with a network of wool and little jingling bells. Then when Don Sanchez had solemnly debated whether we should not awake Don Lopez to say farewell, and we had persuaded him that it would be kinder to let him sleep on, we mounted into our high, fantastic saddles, and set out towards the mountains, our guides leading, and we following close upon their heels as our mules could get, but by no guidance of ours, though we held the reins, for these creatures are very sagacious and so pertinacious and opiniastre that I believe though you pulled their heads off they would yet go their own way.

Our road at first lay across a rising plain, very wild and scrubby, as I imagine, by the frequent deviations of our beast, and then through a forest of cork oaks, which keep their leaves all the year through, and here, by reason of the great shade, we went, not knowing whither, as if blindfold, only we were conscious of being on rough, rising ground, by the jolting of our mules and the clatter of their hoofs upon stones; but after a wearisome, long spell of this business, the trees growing more scattered and a thin grey light creeping through, we could make out that we were all together, which was some comfort. From these oaks, we passed into a wood of chestnuts, and still going up and up, but by such devious, unseen ways, that I think no man, stranger to these parts, could pick it out for himself in broad daylight, we came thence into a great stretch of pine trees, with great rocks scattered amongst them, as if some mountain had been blown up and fallen in a huge shower of fragments.

And so, still for ever toiling and scambling upwards, we found ourselves about seven o'clock, as I should judge by the light beyond the trees and upon the side of the mountain, with the whole champaign laid out like a carpet under us on one side, prodigious slopes of rock on either hand, with only a shrub or a twisted fir here and there, and on the further side a horrid stark ravine with a cascade of water thundering down in its midst, and a peak rising beyond, covered with snow, which glittered in the sunlight like a monstrous heap of white salt.

After resting at this point half an hour to breathe our mules, the guides got into their saddles, and we did likewise, and so on again along the side of the ravine, only not of a cluster as heretofore, but one behind the other in a long line, the mules falling into this order of themselves as if they had travelled the path an hundred times; but there was no means of going otherwise, the path being atrociously narrow and steep, and only fit for wild goats, there being no landrail, coping, or anything in the world to stay one from being hurled down a thousand feet, and the mountain sides so inclined that 'twas a miracle the mules could find foothold and keep their balance. From the bottom of the ravine came a constant roar of falling water, though we could spy it only now and then leaping down from one chasm to another; and more than once our guides would cry to us to stop (and that where our mules had to keep shifting their feet to get a hold) while some huge boulder, loosened by the night's rain, flew down across our path in terrific bounds from the heights above, making the very mountain tremble with the shock. Not a word spoke we; nay, we had scarce courage at times to draw breath, for two hours and more of this fearful passage, with no encouragement from our guides save that one of them did coolly take out a knife and peel an onion as though he had been on a level, broad road; and then, reaching a flat space, we came to a stand again before an ascent that promised to be worse than that we had done. Here we got down, Moll clinging to our hands and looking around her with large, frighted eyes.

"Shall we soon be there?" she asked.

And the Don, putting this question in Spanish to the guides, they pointed upwards to a gap filled with snow, and answered that was the highest point. This was some consolation, though we could not regard the rugged way that lay betwixt us and that without quaking. Indeed, I thought that even Don Sanchez, despite the calm, unmoved countenance he ever kept, did look about him with a certain kind of uneasiness. However, taking example from our guides, we unloosed our saddle bags, and laid out our store of victuals with a hogskin of wine which rekindled our spirits prodigiously.

While we were at this repast, our guides, starting as if they had caught a sound (though we heard none save the horrid bursting of water), looked down, and one of them, clapping two dirty fingers in his mouth, made a shrill whistle. Then we, looking down, presently spied two mules far below on the path we had come, but at such a distance that we could scarce make out whether they were mounted or not.

"Who are they?" asks Don Sanchez, sternly, as I managed to understand.

"Friends," replies one of the fellows, with a grin that seemed to lay his face in two halves.

CHAPTER VIII.

How we were entertained in the mountains, and stand in a fair way to have our throats cut.

"WE will go on when you are ready," says Don Sanchez, turning to us.

"Aye," growled Jack in my ear, " with all my heart. For if these friends be of the same kidney as Don Lopez, we may be persuaded to take a better road, which God forbid if this be a sample of their preference."

So being in our saddles forth we set once more and on a path no easier than before, but worse — like a very housetop for steepness, without a tinge of any living thing for succour if one fell, but only sharp, jagged rocks, and that which now added to our peril was here and there a patch of snow, so that the mules must cock their ears and feel their way before advancing a step, now halting for dread, and now scuttling on with their tails betwixt their legs as the stones rolled under them.

But the longest road hath an end, and so at length reaching that gap we had seen from below, to our great content we beheld through an angle in the mountain a tract of open country below, looking mighty green and sweet in the distance. And at the sight of this, Moll clapt her hands and cried out with joy; indeed, we were all as mad as children with the thought that our task was half done. Only the Don kept his gravity. But turning to Moll, he stretches out his hand towards the plain and says with prodigious pride, "My country!"

And now we began the descent, which was actually more perilous than the ascent, but we made light of it, being very much enlivened by the high mountain air and the relief from dread uncertainty, shouting out our reflections one to another as we jolted down the rugged path.

"After all, Jack," says I to him at the top of my voice, being in advance and next to Don Sanchez; "after all, Don Lopez was not such a bad friend to us."

Upon which, the Don, stopping his mule at the risk of being cast down the abyss, turns in his saddle, and says:

" Fellow, Don Lopez is a Spaniard. A Castilian of noble birth — " but here his mule deciding that this was no fit place for halting, bundled onward at a trot to overtake the guides, and obliged his rider to turn his attention to other matters.

By the look of the sun it must have been about two in the afternoon when, rounding a great bluff of rock, we came upon a kind of tableland which commanded a wide view of the plain below, most dazzling to our eyes after the gloomy recesses of the pass; and here we found trees growing and some rude attempt at cultivation, but all very poor and stunted, being still very high and exposed to the bleak winds issuing from the gorges.

Our guides, throwing themselves on the ground, repaired once more to their store of onions, and we, nothing loath to follow their examples, opened our saddle bags, and with our cold meat and the hogskin of wine made another good repast and very merry. And the Don, falling into discourse with the guides, pointed out to us a little white patch on the plain below, and told us that was Ravellos, where we should find one of the best posadas in the world, which added to our satisfaction. "But" says he, "'tis yet four hours' march ere we reach it, so we had best be packing quickly."

Thereupon we finished our meal in haste, the guides still lying on the ground eating onions, and when we were prepared to start they still lay there and would not budge. On this ensued another discussion, very indignant and passionate on the part of Don Sanchez, and as cool and phlegmatic on the side of the guides, the upshot of which was, as we learned from Don, that these rascals maintained they had fulfilled their bargain in bringing us over into Spain, but as to carrying us to Ravellos they would by no means do that without the permission of their zefe, who was one of those they had whistled to from our last halting place, and whom they were now staying for.

Then, beginning to quake a bit at the strangeness of this treatment, we looked about us to see if we might venture to continue our journey alone. But Lord! one might as easily have found a needle in a bundle of hay as a path amidst this labyrinth of rocks and horrid fissures that environed us; and this was so obvious that the guides, though not yet paid for their service, made no attempt to follow or to stay us, as knowing full well we must come back in despair. So there was no choice but to wait the coming up of the zefe, the Don standing with his legs astride and his arms folded, with a very storm of passion in his face, in readiness to confront the tardy zefe with his reproaches for this delay and the affront offered to himself, we casting our eye longingly down at Ravellos, and the guides silently munching their onions. Thus we waited until the fine ear of our guides catching a sound, they rose to their feet muttering the word "zefe," and pull off their hats as two men mounted on mules tricked out like our own, came round the corner and pulled up before us. But what was our surprise to see that the foremost of these fellows was none other than the Don Lopez de Calvados we had entertained to supper the night before, and of whose noble family Don Sanchez had been prating so highly, and not a thread better dressed than when we saw him last, and full as dirty. That which gave us most uneasiness, however, was to observe that each of these " friends " carried an ugly kind of musket slung across his back, and a most unpleasant long sheath knife in his waist cloth.

Not a word says our Don Sanchez, but feigning still to believe him a man of quality, he returns the other Don's salutation with all the ceremony possible. Then Don Lopez, smiling from ear to ear, begs us (as I learnt afterwards) to pardon him for keeping us waiting, which had not happened, he assures us, if we had not suffered him to oversleep himself. He then informs us that we are now upon his domain, and begs us to accept such hospitality as his castillo will furnish, in return for our entertainment of last night. To this Don Sanchez replies with a thousand thanks that we are anxious to reach Ravellos before nightfall, and that, therefore, we will be going at once if it is all the same to him. With more bowing and scraping Don Lopez amiably but firmly declines to accept any refusal of his offer or to talk of business before his debt of gratitude is paid. With that he gives a sign to our guides, who at once lead off our mules at a brisk trot, leaving us to follow on foot with Don Lopez and his companion, whom he introduces as Don Ruiz del Puerto, — as arrant a cut-throat rascal to look at as ever I clapt eyes on.

So we with very dismal forebodings trudge on, having no other course to take, Don Sanchez, to make the best of it, warranting that no harm shall come to us while we are under the hospitable protection of a Spaniard, but to no great effect —our faith being already shaken in his valuation of Spaniards.

Quitting the tableland, ten minutes of leaping and scrambling brought us to a collection of miserable huts built all higgledy-piggledy along the edge of a torrent, overtopped by a square building of more consequence, built of grey stone and roofed with slate shingles, but with nothing but ill-shaped holes for windows; and this, Don Lopez with some pride told us was his castillo. A ragged crew of women and children, apprised of our coming by the guide, maybe, trooped out of the village to meet us and hailed our approach with shouts of joy, "for all the world like a pack of hounds at the sight of their keeper with a dish of bones," whispers Jack Dawson in my ear ominously. But it was curious to see how they did all fall back in two lines, those that had hats taking them off as Don Lopez passed, he bowing to them right and left, like any prince in his progress.

So we up to the castillo, where all the men of the village are assembled and all armed like Don Lopez, and they greet us with cries of "Hola!" and throwing up of hats. They making way for us with salutations on both sides, we enter the castillo, where we find one great ill-paved room with a step-ladder on one side leading to the floor above, but no furniture save a table and some benches of wood, all black and shining with grease and dirt. But indeed the walls, the ceiling, and all else about us was beyond everything for blackness, and this was easily to be understood, for a wench coming in with a cauldron lights a faggot of wood in a corner, where was no chimney to carry off the smoke, but only a hole in the wall with a kind of eaves over it, so that presently the place was so filled with the fumes 'twas difficult to see across it.

Don Lopez (always as gracious as a cat with a milkmaid) asks Moll through Don Sanchez if she would like to make her toilette, while dinner is preparing, and at this offer all of us jump—choosing anything for a change; so he takes us up the step-ladder to the floor above, which differs from that below in being cut up into half a dozen pieces by some low partition of planks nailed loosely together like cribs for cattle, with some litter of dry leaves and hay in each, but in other respects being just as naked and grimy, with a cloud of smoke coming up through the chinks in the floor.

"You will have the sole use of these chambers during your stay," says Don Lopez, "and for your better assurance you can draw the ladder up after you on retiring for the night."

But for the gravity of our situation and prospects I could have burst out laughing when Don Sanchez gave us the translation of this promise, for the idea of regarding these pens as chambers was not less ludicrous than the air of pride with which Don Lopez bestowed the privilege of using 'em upon us.

Don Lopez left us, promising to send a maid with the necessary appointments for Moll's toilette.

"A plague of all this finery!" growled Dawson. "How long may it be, think you, Señor, ere we can quit this palace and get to one of those posadas you promised us?"

NO RELISH FOR OUR MEAT.

Don Sanchez hunched his shoulders for all reply and turned away to hide his mortification. And now a girl comes up with a biggin of water on her head, a broken comb in her hand, and a ragged cloth on her arm that looked as if it had never been washed since it left the loom, and sets them down on a bench, with a grin at Moll; but she, though not over-nice, turns away with a pout of disgust, and then we to get a breath of fresh air to a hole in the wall on the windward side, where we stand all dumb with disappointment and dread until we are called down to dinner. But before going down Don Sanchez warns us to stand on our best behaviour, as these Spaniards, for all their rude seeming, were of a particularly punctilious, ticklish disposition, and that we might come badly out of this business if we happened to displease them.

"I cannot see reason in that, Señor," says Dawson; "for the less we please 'em, the sooner they are likely to send us hence, and so the better for us."

"As you please," replies the Don, "but my warning is to your advantage."

Down we go, and there stands Don Lopez with a dozen choice friends, all the raggedest, dirty villains in the world; and they saluting us, we return their civility with a very fair pretence and take the seats offered us—they standing until we are set. Then they sit down, and each man lugs out a knife from his waist-cloth. The cauldron, filled with a mess of kid stewed in a multitude of onions, is fetched from the fire, and, being set upon a smooth board, is slid down the table to our host, who, after picking out some tit-bits for us, serves himself, and so slides it back, each man in turn picking out a morsel on the end of his knife. Bearing in mind Don Sanchez's warning, we do our best to eat of this dish; but, Heaven knows! with little relish, and mighty glad when the cauldron is empty and that part of the performance ended. Then the bones being swept from the table, a huge skin of wine is set before Don Lopez, and he serves us each with about a quart in an odd-shaped vessel with a spout, which Don Sanchez and his countrymen use by holding it above their heads and letting the wine spurt into their mouths; but we, being unused to this fashion, preferred rather to suck it out of the spout, which seemed to them as odd a mode as theirs was to us. However, better wine, drink it how you may, there is none than the wine of these parts, and this reconciling us considerably to our condition, we listened with content to their singing of ditties, which they did very well for such rude fellows, to the music of a guitar and a tambourine. And so when our pots came to be replenished a second time, we were all mighty merry and agreeable save Jack Dawson, who never could take his liquor like any other man, but must fall into some extravagant humour, and he, I perceived, regarded some of the company with a very sour, jealous eye because, being warmed with drink, they fell to casting glances at Moll with a certain dregee of familiarity. Especially there was one fellow with a hook nose, who stirred his bile exceedingly, sitting with his elbows on the table and his jaws in his hands, and would scarcely shift his eyes from Moll. And since he could not make his displeasure understood in words, and so give vent to it and be done, Jack sat there in sullen silence watching for an opportunity to show his resentment in some other fashion. The other saw this well enough, but would not desist, and so these two sat fronting each other like two dogs ready to fly at each other's throats. At length, the hook-nosed rascal, growing bolder with his liquor, rises as if to reach for his wine pot, and stretching across the table, chucks Moll under the chin with his grimy fingers. At this Jack flinging out his great fist with all the force of contained passion, catches the other right in the middle of the face, with such effect that the fellow flies clean back over his bench, his head striking the pavement with a crash.

Then, in an instant, all his fellows spring to their feet, and a dozen long knives flash out from their sheaths.

CHAPTER IX.

Of the manner in which we escaped pretty fairly out of the hands of Señor Don Lopez and his brigands.

UP starts Jack Dawson, catching Moll by the arm and his joint stool by the leg, and stepping back a pace or two not to be taken in the flank, he swings his stool ready to dash the brains out of the first that nears him. And I do likewise, making the same show of valour with my stool, but cutting a poor figure beside Dawson's mighty presence.

Seeing their fellow laid out for dead on the floor, with his hook nose smashed most horridly into his face, the others had no stomach to meet the same fate, but with their Spanish cunning began to spread out that so they might attack us on all sides; and surely this had done our business but that Don Lopez, flinging himself before us with his knife raised high, cries out at the top of his voice, "Rekbah!"— a word of their own language, I am told, taken from the Moorish, and signifying that whosoever shall outrage the laws of hospitality under his roof shall be his enemy to the death. And at this word every man stood still as if by inchantment, and let fall his weapon. Then in the same high voice he gives them an harangue, showing them that Dawson was in the right to avenge an insult offered his daughter, and the other justly served for his offence to us. "For his offence to me as the host of these strangers," adds he, "Jose shall answer to me hereafter if he live; if he be dead, his body shall be flung to the vultures of the gorge, and his name be never uttered again beneath this roof."

"I bear no grudges, not I," says Dawson, when Don Sanchez gave him the English of this. "If he live, let his nose be set; and if dead, let him be buried decently in a churchyard. But hark ye, Señor, lest we fall out again and come out worse the next bout, do pray ask his worship if we may not be accommodated with a guide to take us on our way at once. We have yet two hours of daylight before us, there's not a cloud in the sky, and with such a moon as we had the night before last, we may get on well enough."

Poor Moll, who was all of a shake with the terror of another catastrophe, added her prayers to Dawson's, and Don Sanchez with a profusion of civilities laid the proposal before Don Lopez, who, though professing the utmost regret to lose us so soon, consented to gratify our wish, adding that his mules were so well accustomed to the road that they could make the journey as well in the dark as in broad day.

"Well, then," says Dawson, when this was told us, "let us settle the business at once, and be off."

And now, when Don Sanchez proposed to pay for the service of our guides, it was curious to see how every rascal at the table craned forward to watch the upshot. Don Lopez makes a pretence of leaving the payment to Don Sanchez's generosity; and he, not behindhand in courtesy, lugs out his purse and begs the other to pay himself. Whereupon, with more apologies, Don Lopez empties the money on the table and carefully counts it, and there being but about a score of gold pieces and some silver, he shakes his head and says a few words to Don Sanchez in a very reproachful tone of remonstrance, to which our Don replies by turning all the trifles out of his pocket, one after the other, to prove that he has no money.

"I thought as much," growls Jack in my ear. "A pretty nest of hornets we're fallen into."

The company, seeing there was no more to be got out of Don Sanchez, began to murmur and cast their eyes at us; whereupon Dawson, seeing how the land lay, stands up and empties his pockets on the table, and I likewise; but betwixt us there was no more than some French pennies and a few odds and ends of no value at all. Fetching a deep sigh, Don Lopez takes all these possessions into a heap before him, and tells Don Sanchez that he cannot believe persons of our quality could travel with so little, that he feels convinced Don Sanchez must have dropped a purse on the way, and that until it is found he can on no account allow us to leave the neighbourhood.

"This comes of being so mighty fine!" says Dawson, when Don Sanchez had explained matters. "Had we travelled as became our condition, this brigand would never have ensnared us hither. And if they won't believe your story, Señor, I can't blame 'em; for I would have sworn you had a thousand pounds to your hand."

"Do you reproach me for my generosity?" asks the Don.

"Nay, Master, I love you for being free with your money while you have it, but 'tis a queer kind of generosity to bring us into these parts with no means of taking us back again. Hows'ever, we'll say no more about that if we get out of this cursed smoke-hole; and as we are like to come off ill if these Jack-thieves keep us here a week or so and get nothing by it, 'twill be best to tell 'em the honest truth, and acquaint them that we are no gentle folk, but only three poor English mountebanks brought hither on a wild goose chase."

This was a bitter pill for Don Sanchez to swallow; however, seeing no other cure for our ills, he gulped it down with the best face he could put on it. But from the mockery and laughter of all who heard him, 'twas plain to see they would not believe a word of his story.

"What would you have me do now?" asks the Don, turning to us when the clamour had subsided, and he told us how he had tried to persuade them we were dancers he was taking for a show to the fair at Barcelona, which they, by our looks, would not believe, and especially that a man of such build as Jack Dawson could foot it, even to please such heavy people as the English.

"What!" cries Jack. "I can't dance! We will pretty soon put them to another complexion if they do but give us space and a fair trial. You can strum a guitar, Kit, for I've heard you. And Moll, my chick, do you dash the tears from your cheek and pluck up courage to show these Portugals what an English lass can do."

The brigands agreeing to this trial, the table is shoved back to give us a space in the best light, and our judges seat themselves conveniently. Moll brushes her eyes (to a little murmur of sympathy, as I thought), and I, striking out the tune, Jack, with all the magnificence of a king, takes her hand and leads her out to a French pavan; and sure no one in the world ever stepped it more gracefully than our poor little Moll (now put upon her mettle), nor more lightly than Dawson, so that every rascal in our audience was won to admiration, clapping hands and shouting

"Hola!" when it was done. And this warming us, we gave 'em next an Italian coranto, and after that, an English pillow dance; and, in good faith, had they all been our dearest friends, these dirty fellows could not have gone more mad with delight. And then Moll and her father sitting down to fetch their breath, a dispute arose among the brigands which we were at a loss to understand, until Don Sanchez explained that a certain number would have it we were real dancers, but that another party, with Don Lopez, maintained these were but court dances, which only proved the more we were of high quality to be thus accomplished.

"We'll convince 'em yet, Moll, with a pox of their doubts," cries Dawson, starting to his feet again. "Tell 'em we will give 'em a stage dance of a nymph and a wild man, Señor, with an excuse for our having no costume but this. Play us our pastoral, Kit. And sing you your ditty of 'Broken Heart,' Moll, in the right place, that I may get my wind for the last caper."

Moll nods, and with ready wit takes the ribbon from her head, letting her pretty hair tumble all about her shoulders, and then whipping up her long skirt, tucks one end under her girdle, thereby making a very dainty show of pink lining against the dark stuff, and also giving more play for her feet. And so thus they dance their pastoral, Don Sanchez taking a tambourine and tapping it lightly to the measure, up to Moll's song, which so ravished these hardy, stony men by the pathetic sweetness of her voice, — for they could understand nothing save by her expression, — that they would not let the dance go on until she had sung it through again. To conclude, Jack springs up as one enamoured to madness and flings out his last steps with such vigour and agility as to quite astound all.

And now the show being ended, and not one but is a-crying of " Hola ! " and " Animo ! " Moll snatches the tambourine from Don Sanchez's hand, and stepping before Don Lopez drops him a curtsey, and offers it for her reward. At this Don Lopez, glancing at the money on the table by his side, and looking round for sanction to his company (which they did give him without one voice of opposition), he takes up two of the gold pieces and drops them on the parchment. Thus did our Moll, by one clever hit, draw an acknowledgment from them that we were indeed no fine folks, but mere players, which point they might have stumbled over in their cooler moments.

But we were not quit yet; for on Don Sanchez's begging that we should now be set upon our road to Ravellos, the other replies that though he will do us this service with great pleasure, yet he cannot permit us to encounter the danger again of being taken for persons of quality. " Fine dress," says he, "may be necessary to the Señor and his daughter for their court dances, and they are heartily welcome to them for the pleasure they have given us, but for you and the musician who plays but indifferent well, meaner garb is more suitable; and so you will be good enough to step upstairs, the pair of you, and change your clothing for such as we can furnish from our store."

And upstairs we were forced to go, Don Sanchez and I, and there being stripped we were given such dirty foul rags and so grotesque, that when we came down, Jack Dawson and Moll fell a-laughing at us, as though they would burst. And, in truth, we made a most ludicrous spectacle, — especially the Don, whom hitherto we had seen only in the neatest and most noble of clothes, — looking more like a couple of scarecrows than living men.

Don Sanchez neither smiled nor frowned at this treatment, taking this misfortune with the resignation of a philosopher; only to quiet Dawson's merriment he told him that in the clothes taken from him was sewed up a bond for two hundred pounds, but whether this was true or not I cannot tell.

And now, to bring an end to this adventure, we were taken down the intricate passes of the mountain in the moonlight, as many of the gang as could find mules coming with us for escort, and brought at last to the main road, where we were left with nought but what we stood in (save Moll's two pieces), the robbers bidding us their adios with all the courtesy imaginable. But even then, robbed of all he had even to the clothes of his back, Don Sanchez's pride was unshaken, for he bade us note that the very thieves in Spain were gentlemen.

As we trudged along the road toward Ravellos, we fell debating on our case, as what we should do next, etc., Don Sanchez promising that we should have redress for our illtreatment, that his name alone would procure us a supply of money for our requirements, etc., to my great content. But Dawson was of another mind.

"As for seeking redress," says he, "I would as soon kick at a hive for being stung by a bee, and the wisest course when you've been once bit by a dog is to keep out of his way for the future. With respect of getting money by your honour's name, you may do as you please, and so may you, Kit, if you're so minded. But for my part, henceforth I'll pretend to be no better than I am, and the first suit of rags I can get will I wear in the fashion of this country. And so shall you, Moll, my dear; so make up your mind to lay aside your fine airs and hold up your nose no longer as if you were too good for your father."

"Why, surely, Jack," says I, "you would not quit us and go from your bargain."

"Not I, and you should know me well enough, Kit, to have no doubt on that score. But 'tis no part of our bargain that we should bustle anybody but Simon the steward."

"We have four hundred miles to go ere we reach Elche," says Don Sanchez. "Can you tell me how we are to get there without money?"

"Aye, that I can, and I warrant my plan as good as your honour's. How many tens are there in four hundred, Kit?"

"Forty."

"Well, we can walk ten miles a day on level ground, and so may do this journey in six weeks or thereabouts, which is no such great matter, seeing we are not to be back in England afore next year. We can buy a guitar and a tabor out of Moll's pieces; with them we can give a show wherever we stay for the night, and if honest men do but pay us half as much as the thieves of this country, we may fare pretty well."

"I confess," says Don Sanchez, "your scheme is the best, and I would myself have proposed it but that I can do so little for my share."

"Why, what odds does that make, Señor?" cries Jack. "You gave us of the best while you had aught to give, and 'tis but fair we should do the same now. Besides which, how could we get along without you for a spokesman, and I marked that you drummed to our dance very tunefully. Come, is it a bargain, friend?"

And on Don Sanchez's consenting, Jack would have us all shake hands on it for a sign of faith and good fellowship. Then, perceiving that we were arrived at the outskirts of the town, we ended our discussion.

CHAPTER X.

Of our merry journeying to Alicante.

WE turned into the first posada we came to — a poor, mean sort of an inn and general shop, to be sure, but we were in no condition to cavil about trifles, being fagged out with our journey and the adventures of the day, and only too happy to find a house of entertainment still open. So after a dish of sausages with very good wine, we to our beds and an end to the torment of fleas I had endured from the moment I changed my French habit for Spanish rags.

The next morning, when we had eaten a meal of goats' milk and bread and paid our reckoning, which amounted to a few rials and no more, Don Sanchez and I, taking what rested of Moll's two pieces, went forth into the town and there bought two plain suits of clothes for ourselves in the mode of the country, and (according to his desire) another of the same cut for Dawson, together with a little jacket and petticoat for Moll. And these expenditures left us but just enough to buy a good guitar and a tambourine — indeed, we should not have got them at all but that Don Sanchez higgled and bargained like any Jew, which he could do with a very good face now that he was dressed so beggarly. Then back to our posada, where in our room Jack and I were mighty merry in putting on our new clothes; but going below we find Moll still dressed in her finery, and sulking before the petticoat and jacket we had bought for her, which she would not put on by any persuasion until her father fell into a passion of anger. And the sight of him fuming in a short jacket barely covering his loins, and a pair of breeches so tight the seams would scarce hold together, so tickled her sense of humour that she fell into a long fit of laughter, and this ending her sulks she went upstairs with a good grace and returned in her hated petticoat, carrying her fine dress in a bundle. But I never yet knew the time when this sly baggage would not please herself for all her seeming yielding to others, and we were yet to have more pain from her than she from us in respect of that skirt. For ere we had got half way through the town she, dawdling behind to look first in this shop and then in that, gave us the slip, so that we were best part of an hour hunting the streets up and down in the utmost anxiety. Then as we were sweating with our exercise and trouble, lo! she steps out of a shop as calm as you please in a petticoat and jacket of her own fancy (and ten times more handsome than our purchase), a red shawl tied about her waist, and a little round hat with a bright red bob in it, set on one side of her head, and all as smart as a carrot.

"Da!" says she, "where have you been running all this time?"

And we, betwixt joy at finding her and anger at her impudence, could say nothing; and yet we were fain to admire her audacity too. But how, not knowing one word of the language, she had made her wants known was a mystery, and how she had obtained this finery was another, seeing that we had spent all there was of her two pieces. Certainly she had not changed her French gown and things for them, for these in a cumbrous bundle had her father been carrying up and down the town since we lost the minx.

"If you han't stole 'em," says Dawson, finding his tongue at last, "where did you find the money to pay for those trappings, slut?"

"In my pocket, sir," says she, with a curtsey, "where you might have found yours had you not emptied it so readily for the robbers yesterday. And I fancy," adds she slyly, "I may still find some left to offer you a dinner at midday if you will accept of it."

This hint disposed us to make light of our grievance against her, and we went out of Ravellos very well satisfied to know that our next meal depended not solely upon chance. And this, together with the bright sunlight and the sweet invigorating morning air, did beget in us a spirit of happy carelessness, in keeping with the smiling gay aspect of the country about us.

It was strange to see how easily Moll fell into our happy-go-lucky humour, she, who had been as stately as any Roman queen in her long gown, being now, in her short coloured petticoat, as frolicsome and familiar as a country wench at a fair; but indeed she was a born actress and could accommodate herself as well to one condition as another with the mere change of clothes. But I think this state was more to her real taste than the other, as putting no restraint upon her impulses and giving free play to her healthy, exuberant mirth. Her very step was a kind of dance, and she must needs fall a-carolling of songs like a lark when it flies. Then she would have us rehearse our old songs to our new music. So, slinging my guitar in front of me, I put it in tune, and Jack ties his bundle to his back that he may try his hand at the tambourine. And so we march along singing and playing as if to a feast, and stopping only to laugh prodigiously when one or other fell out of tune, — the most mad, light-hearted fools in the world;— but I speak not of Don Sanchez, who, feel what he might, never relaxed his high bearing or unbent his serious countenance.

One thing I remember of him on this journey. Having gone about five miles, we sat us down on a bridge to rest a while, and there the Don left us to go a little way up the course of the stream that flowed beneath, and he came back with a posey of sweet jonquils set off with a delicate kind of fern very pretty, and this he presents to Moll with a gracious little speech, which act, it seemed to me, was to let her know that he respected her still as a young gentlewoman in spite of her short petticoat, and Moll was not dull to the compliment neither; for, after the first cry of delight in seeing these natural dainty flowers (she loving such things beyond all else in the world), she bethought her to make him a curtsey and reply to his speech with another as good and well turned, as she set them in her waist scarf. Also I remember on this road we saw oranges and lemons growing for the first time, but full a mile after Moll had first caught their wondrous perfume in the air. And these trees, which are about the size of a crab tree, grew in close groves on either side of the road, with no manner of fence to protect them, so that any one is lief to pluck what he may without let, so plentiful are they, and curious to see how fruit and blossom grow together on the same bush, the lemons, as I hear, giving four crops in the year, and more delicious, full, and juicy than any to be bought in England at six to the groat.

We got a dinner of bread and cheese (very high) at a roadside house, and glad to have that, only no meat of any kind, but excellent good wine with dried figs and walnuts, which is the natural food of this country, where one may go a week without touching flesh and yet feel as strong and hearty at the end. And here very merry, Jack in his pertinacious, stubborn spirit declaring he would drink his wine in the custom of the country or none at all, and so lifting up the spouted mug at arm's length he squirts the liquor all over his face, down his new clothes and everywhere but into his mouth, before he could arrive to do it like Don Sanchez; but getting into the trick of it, he so mighty proud of his achievement that he must drink pot after pot until he got as drunk as any lord. So after that, finding a retired place, — it being midday and prodigious hot (though only now in mid-April), — we lay down under the orange trees and slept a long hour, to our great refreshment. Dawson on waking remembered nothing of his being drunk, and felt not one penny the worse for it. And so on another long stretch through sweet country, with here and there a glimpse of the Mediterranean, in the distance, of a surprising blueness, before we reached another town, and that on the top of a high hill. But it seems that all the towns in these parts (save those armed with fortresses) are thus built for security against the pirates, who ravage the seaboard of this continent incessantly from end to end. And for this reason the roads leading up to the town are made very narrow, tortuous, and difficult, with watch-towers in places, and many points where a few armed men lying in ambush may overwhelm an enemy ten times as strong. The towns themselves are fortified with gates, the streets extremely narrow and crooked, and the houses massed all together with secret passages one to another, and a network of little alleys leading whither only the inhabitants knew, so that if an enemy do get into them 'tis ten to one he will never come out alive.

It being market day in this town, here Jack and his daughter gave a show of dancing, first in their French suits, which were vastly admired, and after in their Spanish clothes; but then they were asked to dance a fandango, which they could not. However, we fared very well, getting the value of five shillings in little moneys, and the innkeepers would take nothing for our entertainment, because of the custom we had brought his house, which we considered very handsome on his part.

We set out again the next morning, but having shown how we passed the first day I need not dwell upon those which followed before we reached Barcelona, there being nothing of any great importance to tell. Only Moll was now all agog to learn the Spanish dances, and I cannot easily forget how, after much coaxing and wheedling on her part, she at length persuaded Don Sanchez to show her a fandango; for, surely, nothing in the world was ever more comic than this stately Don, without any music, and in the middle of the high road, cutting capers, with a countenance as solemn as any person at a burying. No one could be more quick to observe the ludicrous than he, nor more careful to avoid ridicule; therefore it said much for Moll's cajolery, or for the love he bore her even at this time, to thus expose himself to Dawson's rude mirth and mine in order to please her.

We reached Barcelona the 25th of April, and there we stayed till the 1st of May, for Moll would go no further before she had learnt a bolero and a fandango — which dances we saw danced at a little theatre excellently well, but in a style quite different to ours, and the women very fat and plain. And though Moll, being but a slight slip of a lass, in whom the warmer passions were unbegotten, could not give the bolero the voluptuous fervour of the Spanish dancers, yet in agility and in pretty innocent grace she did surpass them all to nought, which was abundantly proved when she danced it in our posada before a court full of Spaniards, for there they were like mad over her, casting their silk handkerchiefs at her feet in homage, and filling Jack's tambourine three times over with cigarros and a plentiful scattering of rials. And I believe, had we stayed there, we might have made more money than ever we wanted at that time — though not so much as Don Sanchez had set his mind on; wherefore he would have us jogging again as soon as Moll could be brought to it.

From Barcelona, we journeyed a month to Valencia, growing more indolent with our easier circumstances, and sometimes trudging no more than five or six miles in a day. And we were, I think, the happiest, idlest set of vagabonds in existence. But, indeed, in this country there is not that spur to exertion which is for ever goading us in this. The sun fills one's heart with content, and for one's other wants a few halfpence a day will suffice, and if you have them not 'tis no such great matter. For these people are exceeding kind and hospitable; they will give you a measure of wine if you are thirsty, as we would give a mug of water, and the poorest man will not sit down to table without making you an offer to share what he has. Wherever we went we were well received, and in those poor villages where they had no money to give they would pay us for our show in kind, one giving us bed, another board, and filling our wallets ere we left 'em with the best they could afford.

'Twas our habit to walk a few miles before dinner, to sleep in the shade during the heat of the day, and to reach a town (if possible) by the fall of the sun. There would we spend half the night in jollity, and lie abed late in the morning. The inns and big houses in these parts are built in the form of squares, enclosing an open court with a sort of arcade all round, and mostly with a grape-vine running over the sunnier side, and in this space we used to give our performance, by the light of oil lamps hung here and there conveniently, with the addition, maybe, of moonlight reflected from one of the white walls. Here any one was free to enter, we making no charge, but taking only what they would freely give. And this treatment engenders a feeling of kindness on both sides (very different to our sentiment at home, where we players as often as not dread the audience as a kind of enemy, ready to tear us to pieces if we fail to please), and ours was as great a pleasure to amuse as theirs to be amused. I can recall to mind nothing of any moment occurring on this journey, save that we spent some time every day in perfecting our Spanish dances, I getting to play the tunes correctly, which at first I made sad bungling of, and Dawson in learning of his steps. Also, he and Moll acquired the use of a kind of clappers, called costagnettes, which they play with their hands in these fandangos and boleros, with a very pleasing effect.

At Valencia we stayed a week and three days, lingering more than was necessary, in order to see a bull-fight. And this pastime they do not as we with dogs, but with men, and the bull quite free, and, save for the needless killing of horses, I think this a very noble exercise, being a fair trial of human address against brute force. And 'tis not nearly so beastly as seeing a prize fought by men, and not more cruel, I take it, than the shooting of birds and hares for sport, seeing that the agony of death is no greater for a sturdy bull than for a timid coney, and hath this advantage, that the bull, when exhausted, is despatched quickly, whereas the bird or hare may just escape capture, to die a miserable long death with a shattered limb.

From Valencia we travelled five weeks (growing, I think, more lazy every day), over very hilly country to Alicante, a seaport town very strongly protected by a castle on a great rock, armed with guns of brass and iron, so that the pirates dare never venture near. And here I fully thought we were to dawdle away another week at the least, this being a very populous and lively city, promising much entertainment. For Moll, when not playing herself, was mad to see others play, and she did really govern, with her subtle wiles and winning smiles, more than her father, for all his masterful spirit, or Don Sanchez with his stern authority. But seeing two or three English ships in the port, the Don deemed it advisable that we should push on at once for Elche, and, to our great astonishment, Moll consented to our speedy going without demur, though why, we could not then discover,' but did soon after, as I shall presently show.

CHAPTER XI.

Of our first coming to Elche and the strangeness of that city.

BEING resolved to our purpose overnight, we set out fairly early in the morning for Elche, which lies half a dozen leagues or thereabouts to the west of Alicante. Our way lay through gardens of oranges and spreading vineyards, which flourish exceedingly in this part, being protected from unkind winds by high mountains against the north and east; and here you shall picture us on the white, dusty road, Moll leading the way a dozen yards in advance, a tambourine slung on her back with streaming ribbons of many colours, taking two or three steps on one foot, and then two or three steps on t'other, with a Spanish twist of her hips at each turn, swinging her arms as she claps her costagnettes to the air of a song she had picked up at Barcelona, and we three men plodding behind, the Don with a guitar across his back, Dawson with our bundle of clothes, and I with a wallet of provisions hanging o' one side and a skin of wine on the other — and all as white as any millers with the dust of Moll's dancing.

"It might be as well," says Don Sanchez, in his solemn, deliberate manner, "if Mistress Moll were advised to practise her steps in our rear."

"Aye, Señor," replied Dawson, "I've been of the same mind these last ten minutes. But with your consent, Don Sanchez, I'll put her to a more serious exercise."

The Don consenting with a bow Jack continues:

"You may have observed that I haven't opened my lips since we left the town, and the reason thereof is that I've been turning over in my mind whether, having come thus far, it would not be advisable to let my Moll know of our project. Because, if she should refuse, the sooner we consider some other plan, the better, seeing that now she is in good case and as careless as a bird on the bough, and she is less tractable to our purposes than when she felt the pinch of hunger and cold and would have jumped at anything for a bit of comfort."

"Does she not know of our design?" asks the Don, lifting his eyebrows.

"No more than the man in the moon, Señor," answers Jack. "For, though Kit and I may have discoursed of it at odd times, we have been mighty careful to shut our mouths or talk of a fine day at her approach."

"Very good," says Don Sanchez. "You are her father."

"And she shall know it," says Jack, with resolution, and taking a stride or two in advance he calls to her to give over dancing and come to him.

"Have you forgot your breeding," he asks as she turns and waits for him, "that you have no more respect for your elders than to choke 'em with dust along of your shuffling?"

"What a thoughtless thing am I!" cries she, in a voice of contrition. "Why, you're floured as white as a shade!"

Then taking up a corner of her waist-shawl, she gently rubs away the dust from the tip of his nose, so that it stood out glowing red from his face like a cherry through a hole in a pie-crust, at which she claps her hands and rings out a peal of laughter.

"I counted to make a lady of you, Moll," says Jack, in sorrow, "but I see plainly you will ever be a fool, and so 'tis to no purpose to speak seriously."

"Surely, father, I have ever been what you wish me to be," answers she, demurely, curious now to know what he would be telling her.

"Then do you put them plaguy clappers away, and listen to me patiently," says he.

Moll puts her hands behind her, and drawing a long lip and casting round eyes at us over her shoulder, walks along very slowly by her father's side, while he broaches the matter to her. And this he did with some difficulty (for 'tis no easy thing to make a roguish plot look innocent), as we could see by his shifting his bundle from one shoulder to the other now and again, scratching his ear and the like; but what he said, we, walking a pace or two behind, could not catch, he dropping to a very low tone as if ashamed to hear his own voice. To all he has to tell she listens very attentively, but in the end she says something which causes him to stop dead short and turn upon her gaping like a pig.

"What!" he cries as we came up. "You knew all this two months ago?"

"Yes, father," answers she, primly, "quite two months."

"And pray who told you?" he asks.

"No one, father, since you forbade me to ask questions. But though I may be dumb to oblige you, I can't be deaf. Kit and you are for ever a-talking of it."

"Maybe, child," says Dawson, mightily nettled. "Maybe you know why we left Alicante this morning."

"I should be dull indeed if I didn't," answers she. "And if you hadn't said when we saw the ships that we might meet more Englishmen in the town than we might care to know hereafter, why, — well, maybe we should have been in Alicante now."

"By denying yourself that satisfaction," says Don Sanchez, "we may conclude that the future we are making for you is not unacceptable."

Moll stopped and says with some passion:

"I would turn back now and go over those mountains the way we came to ride through France in my fine gown like a lady."

"Brava! bravamente!" says the Don, in a low voice, as she steps on in front of us, holding her head high with the recollection of her former state.

"She was ever like that," whispers Dawson, with pride. "We could never get her to play a mean part willingly; could we, Kit? She was for ever wanting the part of a queen writ for her."

The next day about sundown, coming to a little eminence, Don Sanchez points out a dark patch of forest lying betwixt us and the mountains, and says:

"That is Elche, the place where we are to stay some months."

We could make out no houses at all, but he told us the town lay in the middle of the forest, and added some curious particulars as how, lying on flat ground and within easy access of the sea, it could not exist at all but for the sufferance of the Spaniards on one side and of the Barbary pirates on the other, how both for their own convenience respected it as neutral ground on which each could exchange his merchandise without let or hindrance from the other, how the sort of sanctuary thus provided was never violated either by

Algerine or Spaniard, but each was free to come and go as he pleased, etc., and this did somewhat reassure us, though we had all been more content to see our destination on the crest of a high hill.

From this point we came in less than half an hour to Santa Pola, a small village, but very bustling, for here the cart-road from Alicante ends, all transport of commodities betwixt this and Elche being done on mules; so here great commotion of carriers setting down and taking up merchandise, and the way choked with carts and mules and a very babel of tongues, there being Moors here as well as Spaniards, and all shouting their highest to be the better understood of each other. These were the first Moors we had seen, but they did not encourage us with great hopes of more intimate acquaintance, wearing nothing but a kind of long, ragged shirt to their heels, with a hood for their heads in place of a hat, and all mighty foul with grease and dirt.

Being astir betimes the next morning, we reached Elche before midday, and here we seemed to be in another world, for this region is no more like Spain than Spain is like our own country. Entering the forest, we found ourselves encompassed on all sides by prodigious high palm trees, which hitherto we had seen only singly here and there, cultivated as curiosities. And noble trees they are, standing eighty to a hundred feet high, with never a branch, but only a great spreading crown of leaves, with strings of dates hanging down from their midst. Beneath, in marshy places, grew sugar-canes as high as any haystack; and elsewhere were patches of rice, which grows like corn with us, but thrives well in the shade, curiously watered by artificial streams of water. And for hedges to their property, these Moors have agaves, with great spiky leaves which no man can penetrate, and other strange plants, whereof I will mention only one, they call the fig of Barbary, which is no fig at all, but a thing having large, fleshy leaves, growing one out of the other, with fruit and flower sprouting out of the edges, and all monstrous prickly. To garnish and beautify this formidable defence, nature had cast over all a network of creeping herbs with most extraordinary flowers, delightful both to see and smell, but why so prickly, no man can say.

"Surely, this must be paradise," cries Moll, staying to look around her.

And we were of the same thinking, until we came to the town, which, as I have said, lies in the midst of this forest, and then all our hopes and expectations were dashed to the ground. For we had looked to find a city in keeping with these surroundings, — of fairy palaces and stately mansions; in place whereof was nought but a wilderness of mean, low, squalid houses, with meandering, ill-paved alleys, and all past everything for unsavoury smells, — heaps of refuse lying before every door, stark naked brats of children screaming everywhere, and a pack of famished dogs snapping at our heels.

Don Sanchez leads the way, we following, with rueful looks one at the other, till we reach the market-place, and there he takes us into a house of entertainment, where a dozen Moors are squatting on their haunches in groups about sundry bowls of a smoking mess, called cuscusson, which is a kind of paste with a little butter in it and a store of spices. Their manner of eating it is simple enough: each man dips his hand in the pot, takes out a handful, and dances it about till it is fashioned into a ball, and then he eats it with all the gusto in the world. For our repast we were served with a joint of roast mutton, and this being cut up, we had to take up in our hands and eat like any savages,— their religion denying these Moors anything but the bare necessities of life. Also, their law forbids the drinking of wine, which did most upset Jack Dawson, he having for drink with his meat nothing but the choice of water and sour milk; but which he liked least I know not, for he would touch neither, saying he would rather go dry any day than be poisoned with such liquor.

Whilst we were at our meal, a good many Moors came in to stare at us, as at a raree show, and especially at Moll, whose bright clothes and loose hair excited their curiosity, for their women do rarely go abroad, except they be old, and wear only long dirty white robes, muffling the lower part of their faces. None of them smiled, and it is noticeable that these people, like our own Don, do never laugh, taking such demonstration as a sign of weak understanding and foolishness, but watching all our actions very intently. And presently an old Moor, with a white beard and more cleanly dressed than the rest, pushing the crowd aside to see what was forward, recognised Don Sanchez, who at once rose to his feet; we, not to be behind him in good manners, rising also.

"May Baba," says the old Moor; and repeating this phrase thrice (which is a sure sign of hearty welcome), he claps the Don's hand, without shaking it, and lays his own upon his breast, the Don doing likewise. Then Don Sanchez, introducing us as we understood by his gestures, the old Moor bends his head gravely, putting his right hand first to his heart, next to his forehead, and then kissing the two foremost fingers laid across his lips, we replying as best we could with a bowing and scraping. These formalities concluded, the Don and the old Moor walk apart, and we squat down again to our mutton bones.

After a lengthy discussion the old Moor goes, and Don Sanchez, having paid the reckoning, leads us out of the town by many crooked alleys and cross-passages; he speaking never a word, and we asking no questions, but marvelling exceedingly what is to happen next. And, following a wall overhung by great palms, we turn a corner, and find there our old Moor standing beside an open door with a key in his hand. The old Moor gives the key into Don Sanchez's hand, and with a very formal salutation, leaves us.

Then following the Don through the doorway, we find ourselves in a spacious garden, but quite wild for neglect; flower and weed and fruit all mingling madly together, but very beautiful to my eye, nevertheless, for the abundance of colour, the richness of the vegetables, and the graceful forms of the adjacent palms.

A house stood in the midst of this wilderness, and thither Don Sanchez picked his way, we at his heels still too amazed to speak. Beside the house was a well with a little wall about it, and seating himself on this, Don Sanchez opens his lips for the first time.

"My friend, Sidi ben Ahmed, has offered me the use of this place as long as we choose to stay here," says he. "Go look in the house and tell me if you care to live in it for a year."

CHAPTER X.I.

How Don Sanchez very honestly offers to free us of our bargain if we will; but we will not.

THE house, like nearly all Moorish houses of this class, was simply one large and lofty room, with a domed ceiling built of very thick masonry, to resist the heat of the sun. There was neither window nor chimney, the door serving to admit light and air, and let out the smoke if a fire were lighted within. One half of this chamber was dug out to a depth of a couple of feet, for the accommodation of cattle (the litter being thrown into the hollow as it is needed, and nought removed till it reaches the level of the other floor), and above this, about eight feet from the ground and four from the roof, was a kind of shelf (the breadth and length of that half), for the storage of fodder and a sleeping-place for the inhabitants, with no kind of partition, or any issue for the foul air from the cattle below.

"Are we to live a year in this hutch?" asks Moll, in affright.

"Have done with your chatter, Moll!" answers Jack, testily. "Don't you see I'm a-thinking? Heaven knows there's enough to swallow without any bugbears of your raising."

With that, having finished his inspection of the interior, he goes out and looks at it outside.

"Well," says Don Sanchez, "what think you of the house?"

"Why, Señor, 'tis no worse as I can see than any other in these parts, and hath this advantage, which they have not, of being in a sweet air. With a bit of contrivance we could make a shift to live here well enough. We should not do amiss neither for furniture, seeing that 'tis the custom of the country to eat off the floor and sit upon nothing. A pot to cook victuals in is about all we need in that way. But how we are to get anything to cook in it is one mystery, and" (clacking his tongue) "what we are going to drink is another, neither of which I can fathom. For, look you, Señor, if one may judge of men's characters by their faces or of their means by their habitations, we may dance our legs off ere ever these Moors will bestow a penny piece upon us, and as for their sour milk, I'd as lief drink hemlock, and liefer. Now, if this town had been as we counted on, like Barcelona, all had gone as merry as a marriage bell, for then might we have gained enough to keep us in jollity as long as you please; but here, if we die not of the colicks in a week, 'twill be to perish of starvation in a fortnight. What say you, Kit?"

I was forced to admit that I had never seen a town less likely to afford a subsistence than this.

Then Don Sanchez, having heard us with great patience, and waited a minute to see if we could raise any further objections, answers us in measured tones.

"I doubt not," says he, "that with a little ingenuity you may make the house habitable and this wilderness agreeable. My friend, Sidi ben Ahmed, has offered to provide us with what commodities are necessary to that end. I agree with you that it would be impossible to earn the meanest livelihood here by dancing; it would not be ad-

H

visable if we could. For that reason, my knowledge of various tongues making me very serviceable to Sidi ben Ahmed (who is the most considerable merchant of this town), I have accepted an office in his house. This will enable me to keep my engagement with you. You will live at my charge, as I promised, and you shall want for nothing in reason. If the Moors drink no wine themselves, they make excellent for those who will, and you shall not be stinted in that particular."

"Come, this sounds fair enough," cries Dawson. "But pray, Señor, are we to do nothing for our keep?"

"Nothing beyond what we came here to do," replies he, with a meaning glance at Moll.

"What!" cries poor Moll, in pain. "We are to dance no more!"

The Don shook his head gravely; and, remembering the jolly, vagabond, careless, adventurous life we had led these past two months and more, with a thousand pleasant incidents of our happy junketings, we were all downcast at the prospect of living in this place — though a paradise — for a year without change.

"Though I promised you no more than I offer," says the Don, "yet if this prospect displease you, we will cry quits and part here. Nay," adds he, taking a purse from his pocket, "I will give you the means to return to Alicante, where you may live as better pleases you."

It seemed to me that there was an unfeigned carelessness in his manner, as if he would as lief as not throw up this hazardous enterprise for some other more sure undertaking. And, indeed, I believe he was then balancing another alternative in his mind.

At this generous offer Moll dashed away the tears that had sprung to her eyes, brightening up wonderfully, but then, casting her eyes upon the Don, her face fell again as at the thought of leaving him. For we all admired him, and she prodigiously, for his great reserve and many good qualities which commanded respect, and this feeling was tinged in her case, I believe, with a kind of growing affection.

Seeing this sentiment in her eyes, the Don was clearly touched by it, and so, laying his hand gently on her shoulder, he says:

"My poor child, remember you the ugly old women we saw dancing at Barcelona? They were not more than forty; what will they be like in a few years? Who will tolerate them? who love them? Is that the end you choose for your own life — that the estate to which our little princess shall fall?"

"No, no, no!" cries she, in a passion, clenching her little hands and throwing up her head in disdain.

"And no, no, no, say I," cries Dawson. "Were our case ten times as bad, I'd not go back from my word. As it is, we are not to be pitied, and I warrant ere long we make ourselves to be envied. Come, Kit, rouse you out of your lethargies, and let us consult how we may improve our condition here; and do you, Señor, pray order us a little of that same excellent wine you spoke of, if it be but a pint, when you feel disposed that way."

The Don inclined his head, but lingered, talking to Moll very gravely, and yet tenderly, for some while, Dawson and I going into the house to see what we could make of it; and then, telling us we should see him no more till the next day, he left us. But for some time after he was gone Moll sat on the side of the well, very pensive and wistful, as one to whom the future was opened for the first time.

Anon comes a banging at our garden gate, which Moll had closed behind the Don; and, going to it, we find a Moorish boy with a barrow charged with many things. We could not understand a word he said, but Dawson decided these chattels were sent us by the Don, by perceiving a huge hogskin of wine, for which he thanked God and Don Sanchez an hundred times over. So these commodities we carried up to the house, marvelling greatly at the Don's forethought and generosity, for here were a score of things over and above those we had already found ourselves lacking; namely, earthen pipkins and wooden vessels, a bag of charcoal, a box of carpenters' tools (which did greatly like Dawson, he having been bred a carpenter in his youth), instruments for gardening (to my pleasure, as I have ever had a taste for such employment), some very fine Moorish blankets, etc. So when the barrow was discharged, Dawson gives the lad some rials out of his pocket, which pleased him also mightily.

Then, first of all, Dawson unties the leg of the hogskin, and draws off a quart of wine, very carefully securing the leg after, and this we drank to our great refreshment; and next Moll, being awoke from her dreams and eager to be doing, sets herself to sort out our goods, such as belong to us (as tools, etc.), on one side, and such as belong to her (as pipkins and the rest) on the other. Leaving her to this employment, Dawson and I, armed with a knife and bagging hook, betake ourselves to a great store of canes stacked in one corner of the garden, and sorting out those most proper to our purpose, we lopped them all of an equal length, and shouldering as many as we could carried them up to our house. Here we found Moll mighty jubilant in having got her work done, and admirably she had done it, to be sure. For, having found a long recess in the wall, she had brushed it out clean with a whisp of herbs, and stored up her crocks according to their size, very artificial, with a dish of oranges plucked from the tree at our door on one side, and a dish of almonds on the other, a pipkin standing betwixt 'em with a handsome posey of roses in it. She had spread a mat on the floor, and folded up our fine blankets to serve for cushions; and all that did not belong to her she had bundled out of sight into that hollowed side I have mentioned as being intended for cattle.

After we had sufficiently admired the performance, she told us she had a mind to give us a supper of broth. "But," says she, "the Don has forgotten that we must eat, and hath sent us neither bread nor flesh nor salt."

This put us to a stumble, for how to get these things we knew not; but Moll declared she would get all she needed if we could only find the money.

"Why, how?" asks Jack. "You know not their gibberish."

"'That may be," answers she, "but I warrant the same language that bought me this petticoat will get us a supper."

So we gave her what money we had, and she went off a-marketing, with as much confidence as if she were a born Barbary Moor. Then Jack falls to thanking God for blessing him with such a daughter, at the same time taking no small credit to himself for having bred her to such perfection, and in the midst of his encomiums, being down in the hollow searching for his hammer, he cries:

"Plague take the careless baggage! she has spilled all our nails, and here's an hour's work to pick 'em up!"

This accident was repaired, however, and Moll's transgression forgotten when she returned with an old woman carrying her purchases. Then were we forced to admire her skill in this business, for she had bought all that was needful for a couple of meals, and yet had spent but half our money. Now arose the difficult question how to make a fire, and this Jack left us to settle by our own devices, he returning to his own occupation. Moll resolved we should do our cooking outside the house, so here we built up a kind of grate with stones; and, contriving to strike a spark with the back of a jack-knife and a stone, upon a heap of dried leaves, we presently blew up a fine flame, and feeding this with the ends of cane we had cut and some charcoal, we at last got a royal fire on which to set our pot of mutton. And into this pot we put rice and a multitude of herbs from the garden, which by the taste we thought might serve to make a savoury mess. And, indeed, when it began to boil, the odour was so agreeable that we would have Jack come out to smell it. And he having praised it very highly, we in return went in to look at his handiwork and praise that. This we could do very heartily and without hypocrisy, for he had worked well and made a rare good job, having built a very seemly partition across the room, by nailing of the canes perpendicularly to that kind of floor that hung over the hollowed portion, thus making us now three rooms out of one. At one end he had left an opening to enter the cavity below and the floor above by the little ladder that stood there, and these canes were set not so close together but that air and light could pass betwixt them, and yet from the outer side no eye could see within, which was very commodious. Also upon the floor above, he had found sundry bundles of soft dried leaves, and these, opened out upon the surface of both chambers, made a very sweet, convenient bed upon which to lie. Then Dawson offering Moll her choice, she took the upper floor for her chamber, leaving us two the lower; and so, it being near sundown by this time, we to our supper in the sweet, cool air of evening, all mightily content with one another, and not less satisfied with our stew, which was indeed most savoury and palatable. This done, we took a turn round our little domain, admiring the many strange and wonderful things that grew there (especially the figs, which, though yet green, were wondrous pleasant to eat); and I laying out my plans for the morrow, how to get this wilderness into order, tear out the worthless herbs, dig the soil, etc., Dawson's thoughts running on the building of an outhouse for the accommodation of our wine, tools, and such like, and Moll meditating on dishes to give us for our repasts. And at length, when these divers subjects were no more to be discussed, we turned into our dormitories, and fell asleep mighty tired, but as happy as princes.

CHAPTER XIII.

A brief summary of those twelve months we spent at Elche.

THE surprising activity with which we attacked our domestic business at Elche lasted about two days and a half,— Dawson labouring at his shed, I at the cultivation of the garden, and Moll quitting her cooking and household affairs, as occasion permitted, to lend a helping hand first to her father and then to me. And as man, when this fever of enterprise is upon him, must for ever be seeking to add to his cares, we persuaded Don Sanchez to let us have two she-goats to stall in the shed and consume our waste herbage, that we might have milk and get butter, which they do in these parts by shaking the cream in a skin bag (a method that seems simple enough till you have been shaking the bag for twenty minutes in vain on a sultry morning) without cost. But the novelty of the thing wearing off, our eagerness rapidly subsided, and so about the third day (as I say), the heat being prodigious, we toiled with no spirit at all.

Dawson was the first to speak his mind. Says he, coming to me whilst I was still sweating over my shovel:

"I've done it, but hang me if I do more. There's a good piece of work worth thirty shillings of any man's money, but who'll give me a thank ye for it when we leave here next year?"

And then he can find nothing better to do than fall a-commenting on my labours, saying there was but precious little to show for my efforts, that had he been in my place he would have ordered matters otherwise, and begun digging t'other end, wagering that I should give up my job before it was quarter done, etc., all which was mighty discouraging and the more unpleasant because I felt there was a good deal of truth in what he said.

Consequently, I felt a certain malicious enjoyment the next morning upon finding that the goats had burst out one side of his famous shed, and got loose into the garden, which enabled me to wonder that two such feeble creatures could undo such a good thirty shillings' worth of work, etc. But ere I was done galling him, I myself was mortified exceedingly to find these mischievous brutes had torn up all the plants I had set by the trees in the shade as worthy of cultivation, which gave Jack a chance for jibing at me. But that which embittered us as much as anything was to have Moll holding her sides for laughter at our attempts to catch these two devilish goats, which to our cost we found were not so feeble, after all; for getting one up in a corner, she raises herself up on her hind legs and brings her skull down with such a smack on my knee that I truly thought she had broke my cramp-bone, whilst t'other, taking Dawson in the ankles with her horns, as he was reaching forward to lay hold of her, lay him sprawling in our little stream of water. Nor do I think we should ever have captured them, but that, giving over our endeavours from sheer fatigue, they of their own accord sauntered into the shed for shelter from the sun, where Moll clapt to the door upon them, and set her back against the gap in the side, until her father came with a hammer and some stout nails to secure the planks. So for the rest of that day Jack and I lay on our backs in the shade, doing nothing, but exceedingly sore one against the other for these mischances.

But our heart burnings ended not there; for coming in to supper at sundown, Moll has nothing to offer us but dry bread and a dish of dates, which, though it be the common supper of the Moors in this place, was little enough to our satisfaction, as Dawson told her in pretty round terms, asking her what she was good for if not to give us a meal fit for Christians, etc., and stating very explicitly what he would have her prepare for our dinner next day. Moll takes her upbraiding very humbly (which was ever a bad sign), and promises to be more careful of our comfort in the future. And so ended that day.

The next morning Dawson and I make no attempt at work, but after breakfast, by common accord, stretch us out under the palms to meditate; and there about half past ten, Don Sanchez, coming round to pay us a visit, finds us both sound asleep. A sudden exclamation from him aroused us, and as we stumbled to our feet, staring about us, we perceived Moll coming from the house, but so disfigured with smuts of charcoal all over her face and hands, we scarce knew her.

"God's mercy!" cries the Don. "What on earth have you been doing, child?"

To which Moll replies with a curtsey:

"I am learning to be a cook-wench, Señor, at my father's desire."

"You are here," answers the Don, with a frown, "to learn to be a lady. If a cook-wench is necessary, you shall have one" (this to us), "and anything else that my means may afford. You will do well to write me a list of your requirements; but observe," adds he, turning on his heel, "we may have to stay here another twelvemonth, if my economies are not sufficient by the end of the first year to take us hence."

This hint brought us to our senses very quickly, and overtaking him ere he reached our garden gate, Dawson and I assured the Don we had no need of any servant, and would be careful that Moll henceforth did no menial office; that we would tax his generosity no more than we could help, etc., to our great humiliation when we came to reflect on our conduct.

Thenceforth Dawson charged himself with the internal economy of the house, and I with that part which concerned the custody and care of the goats, the cultivation of potherbs and with such instruction of Moll in the Italian tongue as I could command. But to tell the truth, we neither of us did one stroke of work beyond what was absolutely necessary, and especially Dawson, being past everything for indolence, did so order his part that from having two dishes of flesh a day, we came, ere long, to getting but one mess a week; he forcing himself and us to be content with dates and bread for our repasts, rather than give himself the trouble of boiling a pot. Beyond browsing my goats, drawing their milk (the making of butter I quickly renounced), and watering my garden night and morn (which is done by throwing water from the little stream broadcast with a shovel on either side), I did no more than Dawson, but joined him in yawning the day away, for which my sole excuse is the great heat of this region, which doth beget most slothful humours in those matured in cooler climes.

With Moll, however, the case was otherwise; for she,

being young and of an exceeding vivacious, active disposition, must for ever be doing of something, and lucky for us when it was not some mischievous trick at our expense — as letting the goats loose, shaking lemons down on our heads as we lay asleep beneath it, and the like. Being greatly smitten with the appearance of the Moorish women (who, though they are not permitted to wander about at will like our women, are yet suffered to fetch water from the public fountains), she surprised us one morning by coming forth dressed in their mode. And this dress, which seems to be nought but a long sheet wound loosely twice or thrice about the body, buckled on the shoulder, with holes for the arms to be put through in the manner of the old Greeks, became her surprisingly; and we noticed then for the first time that her arms were rounder and fuller than when we had last seen them bare. Then, to get the graceful, noble bearing of the Moors, she practised day after day carrying a pitcher of water on her head as they do, until she could do this with perfect ease and sureness. In this habit the Don, who was mightily pleased with her looks, took her to the house of his friend and employer, Sidi ben Ahmed, where she ingratiated herself so greatly with the women of his household that they would have her come to them again the next day, and after that the next, — indeed, thenceforth she spent far more of her time with these new friends than with us. And here, from the necessity of making herself understood, together with an excellent memory and a natural aptitude, she learned to speak the Moorish tongue in a marvellously short space of time. Dawson and I were frequently asked to accompany Moll, and we went twice to this house, which, though nothing at all to look at outside, was very magnificently furnished within, and the entertainment most noble. But Lord! 'twas the most tedious, wearisome business for us, who could make out never a word of the civil speeches offered us without the aid of Don Sanchez and Moll, and then could think of no witty response, but could only sit there grinning like Gog and Magog. Still, it gave us vast pleasure to see how Moll carried herself with this company, talking as freely as they, yet holding herself with the dignity of an equal, and delighting all by her vivacity and sly, pretty ways.

I think no country in Europe can be richer than this Elche in fruits and vegetation, more beautiful in its surrounding aspects of plain and mountain, more blessed with constant, glorious sunlight; and the effect of these charms upon the quick, receptive spirit of our Molly was like a gentle May upon a nightingale, so that the days were all too short for her enjoyment, and she must need vent her happiness in song; but on us they made no more impression than on two owls in a tower, nay, if anything they did add to that weariness which arose from our lack of occupation. For here was no contrast in our lives, one day being as like another as two peas in a pod, and having no sort of adversities to give savour to our ease, we found existence the most flat, insipid, dull thing possible. I remember how, on Christmas day, Dawson did cry out against the warm sunshine as a thing contrary to nature, wishing he might stand up to his knees in snow in a whistling wind, and taking up the crock Moll had filled with roses (which here bloom more fully in the depth of winter than with us in the height of summer), he flung it out of the door with a curse for an unchristian thing to have in the house on such a day.

As soon as the year had turned, we began to count the days to our departure, and thenceforth we could think of nought but what we would do with our fortune when we got it; and, the evenings being long, we would set the bag of wine betwixt us after our supper of dates, and sit there for hours discussing our several projects. Moll being with us (for in these parts no womankind may be abroad after sundown), she would take part in these debates with as much gusto as we. For though she was not wearied of her life here as we were, yet she was possessed of a very stirring spirit of adventure, and her quick imagination furnished endless visions of lively pleasures and sumptuous living. We agreed that we would live together, and share everything in common as one family, but not in such an outlandish spot as Chislehurst. That estate we would have nothing to do with; but, selling it at once, have in its place two houses, — one city house in the Cheap, and a country house not further from town than Bednal Green, or Clerkenwell at the outside, to the end that when we were fatigued with the pleasures of the town, we might, by an easy journey, resort to the tranquillity of rural life, Dawson declaring what wines he would have laid down in our cellars, I what books should furnish our library, and Moll what dresses she would wear (not less than one for every month of the year), what coaches and horses we should keep, what liveries our servants should wear, what entertainments we would give, and so forth. Don Sanchez was not excluded from our deliberations; indeed, he encouraged us greatly by approving of all our plans, only stipulating that we would guard one room for him in each of our houses, that he might feel at home in our society whenever he chanced to be in our neighbourhood. In all these arguments, there was never one word of question from any of us as to the honesty of our design. We had settled that, once and for all, before starting on this expedition; and since then, little by little, we had come to regard the Godwin estate as a natural gift, as freely to be taken as a blackberry from the hedge. Nay, I believe Dawson and I would have contested our right to it by reason of the pains we were taking to possess it.

And now, being in the month of June, and our year of exile (as it liked us to call it) nigh at an end, Dawson one night put the question to Don Sanchez, which had kept us fluttering in painful suspense these past six months, whether he had saved sufficient by his labours, to enable us to return to England ere long.

"Yes," says he, gravely, at which we did all heave one long sigh of relief, "I learn that a convoy of English ships is about to sail from Alicante in the beginning of July, and if we are happy enough to find a favourable opportunity, we will certainly embark in one of them."

"Pray, Señor," says I, "what may that opportunity be; for 'tis but two days' march hence to Alicante, and we may do it with a light foot in one."

"The opportunity I speak of," answers he, "is the arrival, from Algeria, of a company of pirates, whose good service I hope to engage in putting us aboard an English ship under a flag of truce as redeemed slaves from Barbary."

"Pirates!" cry we, in a low breath.

"What, Señor!" adds Dawson, "are we to trust ourselves to the mercy and honesty of Barbary pirates on the open sea?"

"I would rather trust to their honesty," answers the Don, dropping his voice that he might not be heard by Moll, who was leading home the goats, "than to the mercy of an English judge, if we should be brought to trial with insufficient evidence to support our story."

Jack and I stared at each other aghast at this talk of trial, which had never once entered into our reckoning of probabilities.

"If I know aught of my fellow-men," continues the Don, surely and slow, "that grasping steward will not yield up his trust before he has made searching enquiry into Moll's claim, act she her part never so well. We cannot refuse to give him the name of the ship that brought us home, and, learning that we embarked at Alicante, jealous suspicion may lead him to seek further information there; with what result?"

"Why, we may be blown with a vengeance, if he come ferreting so nigh as that," says Dawson, "and we are like to rot in gaol for our pains."

"You may choose to run that risk; I will not," says the Don.

"Nor I either," says Dawson, "and God forgive me for overlooking such a peril to my Moll. But, do tell me plainly, Señor, granting these pirates be the most honest thieves in the world, is there no other risk to fear?"

The Don hunched his shoulders.

"Life itself is a game," says he, "in which the meanest stroke may not be won without some risk; but, played as I direct, the odds are in our favour. Picked up at sea from an Algerine boat, who shall deny our story when the evidence against us lies there" (laying his hand out towards the south), "where no man in England dare venture to seek it?"

"Why, to be sure," says Dawson; "that way all hangs together to a nicety. For only a wizard could dream of coming hither for our undoing."

"For the rest," continues the Don, thoughtfully, "there is little to fear. Judith Godwin has eyes the colour of Moll's, and in all else Simon must expect to find a change since he last saw his master's daughter. They were in Italy three years. That would make Judith a lisping child when she left England. He must look to find her altered. Why," adds he, in a more gentle voice, as if moved by some inner feeling of affection and admiration, nodding towards Moll, "see how she has changed in this little while. I should not know her for the raw, half-starved spindle of a thing she was when I saw her first playing in the barn at Tottenham Cross."

Looking at her now (browsing the goats amongst my most cherished herbs), I was struck also by this fact, which, living with her day by day, had slipped my observation somewhat. She was no longer a gaunt, ungainly child, but a young woman, well proportioned, with a rounded cheek and chin, brown tinted by the sun, and, to my mind, more beautiful than any of their vaunted Moorish women. But, indeed, in this country all things do mature quickly; and 'twas less surprising in her case because her growth had been checked before by privation and hardship, whereas since our coming hither it had been aided by easy circumstances and good living.

I

CHAPTER XIV.

Of our coming to London (with incidents by the way), and of the great address whereby Moll confounds Simon, the steward.

ON the third day of July, all things falling in pat with the Don's design, we bade farewell to Elche, Dawson and I with no sort of regret, but Moll in tears at parting from those friends she had grown to love very heartily. And these friends would each have her take away something for a keepsake, such as rings to wear on her arms and on her ankles (as is the Moorish fashion), silk shawls, etc., so that she had quite a large present of finery to carry away; but we had nothing whatever but the clothes we stood in, and they of the scantiest, being simply long shirts and "bernouses" such as common Moors wear. For the wise Don would let us take nought that might betray our sojourn in Spain, making us even change our boots for wooden sandals, he himself being arrayed no better than we. Nor was this the only change insisted on by our governor; for on Dawson bidding Moll in a surly tone to give over a shedding of tears, Don Sanchez turns upon him, and says he:

"It is time to rehearse the parts we are to play. From this day forth your daughter is Mistress Judith Godwin, you are Captain Robert Evans, and you" (to me), "Mr. Hopkins, the merchant. Let us each play our part with care, that we do not betray ourselves by a slip in a moment of unforeseen danger."

"You are in the right, Señor," answers Jack, "for I doubt it must be a hard task to forget that Mistress Judith is my daughter, as it is for a loving father to hold from chiding of his own flesh and blood; so I pray you, Madam" (to Moll), "bear that in mind and vex me no more."

We lay this lesson seriously to heart, Dawson and I, for the Don's hint that we might end our career in gaol did still rankle woundily in our minds. And so very soberly we went out of the forest of Elche in the night on mules lent us by Sidi ben Ahmed, with a long cavalcade of mules charged with merchandise for embarking on board the pirates' vessel, and an escort of some half-dozen fierce-looking corsairs armed with long firelocks and a great store of awesome crooked knives stuck in their waist-cloths.

After journeying across the plain, we came about midday to the seaboard, and there we spied, lying in a sheltered bay, a long galley with three masts, each dressed with a single cross-spar for carrying a leg-of-mutton sail, and on the shore a couple of ship's boats with a company of men waiting to transport our goods and us aboard. And here our hearts quaked a bit at the thought of trusting ourselves in the hands of these same murderous-looking pirates. Nevertheless, when our time came we got us into their boat, recommending ourselves very heartily to God's mercy, and so were rowed out to the galley, where we were very civilly received by an old Moor with a white beard, who seemed well acquainted with Don Sanchez. Then the merchandise being all aboard, and the anchor up, the men went to their oars, a dozen of each side, and rowed us out of the bay until, catching a little wind of air, the sails were run up, and we put out to sea very bravely.

"Señor," says Dawson, "I know not how I am to play this part of a sea-captain when we are sent on board an English ship, for if they ask me any questions on this business of navigating, I am done for a certainty."

"Rest easy on that score, Evans," replies the Don. "I will answer for you, for I see very clearly by your complexion that you will soon be past answering them yourself."

And this forecast was quickly verified; for ere the galley had dipped a dozen times to the waves, poor Dawson was laid low with a most horrid sickness like any dying man.

By sundown we sighted the island of Maggiore, and in the roads there we cast anchor for the night, setting sail again at daybreak; and in this latitude we beat up and down a day and a night without seeing any sail, but on the morning of the third day a fleet of five big ships appeared to the eastward, and shifting our course we bore down upon them with amazing swiftness. Then when we were near enough to the foremast to see her English flag and the men aboard standing to their deck guns for a defence, our old Moor fires a gun in the air, takes in his sails, and runs up a great white flag for a sign of peace. And now with shrewd haste a boat was lowered, and we were set in it with a pair of oars, and the old pirate bidding us farewell in his tongue, clapt on all sail and stood out before the wind, leaving us there to shift for ourselves. Don Sanchez took one oar, and I t'other, — Dawson lying in the bottom and not able to move a hand to save his life, — and Moll held the tiller, and so we pulled with all our force, crying out now and then for fear we should not be seen, till by God's providence we came alongside the Talbot of London, and were presently hoisted aboard without mishap. Then the captain of the Talbot and his officers gathering about us were mighty curious to know our story, and Don Sanchez very briefly told how we had gone in the Red Rose of Bristol to redeem two ladies from slavery; how we had found but one of these ladies living (at this Moll buries her face in her hands as if stricken with grief); how, on the eve of our departure, some of our crew in a drunken frolic had drowned a Turk of Alger, for which we were condemned by their court to pay an indemnity far and away beyond our means; how they then made this a pretext to seize our things, though we were properly furnished with the Duke's pass, and hold our men in bond; and how having plundered us of all we had, and seeing there was no more to be got, they did offer us our freedom for a written quittance of all they had taken for their justification if ever they should be brought to court; and finally, how, accepting of these conditions, we were shipped aboard their galley with nothing in the world but a few trifles, begged by Mistress Judith in remembrance of her mother.

This story was accepted without any demur; nay, Captain Ballcock, being one of those men who must ever appear to know all things, supported it in many doubtful particulars, saying that he remembered the Rose of Bristol quite well; that he himself had seen a whole ship's crew sold into slavery for no greater offence than breaking a mosque window; that the Duke's pass counted for nothing with these Turks; that he knew the galley we were brought in as well as he knew Paul's Church, having chased it a dozen times, yet never got within gunshot for her swift sailing, etc., which did much content us to hear.

But the officers were mighty curious to know what ailed Captain Robert Evans (meaning Dawson), fearing he might be ill of the plague; however, on the Don's vowing that he was only sick of a surfeit, Captain Ballcock declared he had guessed it the moment he clapt eyes on him, as he himself had been taken of the same complaint with only eating a dish of pease pudding. Nevertheless, he ordered the sick man to be laid in a part of the ship furthest from his quarters, and so great was the dread of pestilence aboard that (as his sickness continued) not a soul would venture near him during the whole voyage except ourselves, which also fell in very well with our wishes. And so after a fairly prosperous voyage we came up the Thames to Chatham, the third day of August.

We had been provided with some rough seamen's clothes for our better covering on the voyage; but now, being landed, and lodged in the Crown inn at Chatham, Don Sanchez would have the captain take them all back.

"But," says he, "if you will do us yet another favour, Captain, will you suffer one of your men to carry a letter to Mistress Godwin's steward at Chislehurst, that he may come hither to relieve us from our present straits?"

"Aye," answers he, "I will take the letter gladly, myself; for nothing pleases me better than a ramble in the country where I was born and bred."

So Moll writes a letter at once to Simon, bidding him come at once to her relief; and Captain Ballcock, after carefully enquiring his way to this place he knew so well (as he would have us believe), starts off with it, accompanied by his boatswain, a good-natured kind of lick-spittle, who never failed to back up his captain's assertions, which again was to our great advantage; for Simon would thus learn our story from his lips, and find no room to doubt its veracity.

As soon as these two were out of the house, Dawson, who had been carried from the ship and laid in bed, though as hale since we passed the Godwins as ever he was in his life before, sprang up, and declared he would go to bed no more, for all the fortunes in the world, till he had supped on roast pork and onions, — this being a dish he greatly loved, but not to be had at Elche, because the Moors by their religion forbid the use of swine's flesh, — and seeing him very determined on this head, Don Sanchez ordered a leg of pork to be served in our chamber, whereof Dawson did eat such a prodigious quantity, and drank therewith such a vast quantity of strong ale (which he protested was the only liquor an Englishman could drink with any satisfaction), that in the night he was seized with most severe cramp in his stomach. This gave us the occasion to send for a doctor in the morning, who, learning that Jack had been ill ever since we left Barbary, and not understanding his present complaint, pulled a very long face, and, declaring his case was very critical, bled him copiously, forbade him to leave his bed for another fortnight, and sent him in half a dozen bottles of physic. About midday he returns, and, finding his patient no better, administers a bolus; and while we are all standing about the bed, and Dawson the colour of death, and groaning, betwixt the nausea of the drug he had swallowed and the cramp in his inwards, in comes our Captain Ballcock and the little steward.

"There!" cries he, turning on Simon, "did not I tell you

that my old friend Evans lay at death's door with the treatment he hath received of these Barbary pirates? Now will you be putting us off with your doubts and your questionings? Shall I have up my ship's company to testify to the truth of my history? Look you, Madam," (to Moll), "we had all the trouble in the world to make this steward of yours do your bidding; but he should have come though we had to bring him by the neck and heels, and a pox to him — saving your presence."

"But this is not Simon," says Moll, with a pretty air of innocence. "I seem to remember Simon a bigger man than he."

"You must consider, Madam," says Don Sanchez, "that then you were very small, scarce higher than his waist, maybe, and so you would have to look up into his face."

"I did not think of that. And are you really Simon, who used to scold me for plucking fruit?"

"Yea, verily," answers he. "Doubt it not, for thou also hast changed beyond conception. And so it hath come to pass!" he adds, staring round at us in our Moorish garb like one bewildered. "And thou art my mistress now" (turning again to Moll).

"Alas!" says she, bowing her head and covering her eyes with her hand.

"Han't I told you so, unbelieving Jew Quaker!" growls Captain Ballcock, in exasperation. "Why will you plague the unhappy lady with her loss?"

"We will leave Evans to repose," says Moll, brushing her eyes and turning to the door. "You will save his life, Doctor, for he has given me mine."

The doctor vowed he would, if bleeding and boluses

could make him whole, and so, leaving him with poor groaning Dawson, we went into the next chamber. And there Captain Ballcock was for taking his leave; but Moll, detaining him, says:

"We owe you something more than gratitude — we have put you to much expense."

"Nay," cries he. "I will take nought for doing a common act of mercy."

"You shall not be denied the joy of generosity," says she, with a sweet grace. "But you must suffer me to give your ship's company some token of my gratitude." Then turning to Simon with an air of authority, she says, "Simon, I have no money."

The poor man fumbled in his pocket, and bringing out a purse, laid it open, showing some four or five pieces of silver and one of gold, which he hastily covered with his hand.

"I see you have not enough," says Moll, and taking up a pen she quickly wrote some words on a piece of paper, signing it "Judith Godwin." Then showing it to Simon, she says, "You will pay this when it is presented to you," and therewith she folds it and places it in the captain's hand, bidding him farewell in a pretty speech.

"A hundred pounds! a hundred pounds!" gasps Simon, under his breath, in an agony and clutching up his purse to his breast.

"I am astonished," says Moll, returning from the door, and addressing Simon, with a frown upon her brow, "that you are not better furnished to supply my wants, knowing by my letter how I stand."

"Mistress," replies he, humbly, "here is all I could raise upon such sudden notice" — laying his purse before her.

"What is this?" cries she, emptying the contents upon the table. "'Tis nothing. Here is barely sufficient to pay for our accommodation in this inn. Where is the money to discharge my debt to these friends who have lost all in saving me? You were given timely notice of their purpose."

"Prithee, be patient with me, gentle mistress. 'Tis true, I knew of their intent, but they were to have returned in six months, and when they came not at the end of the year I did truly give up all for lost; and so I made a fresh investment of thy fortune, laying it out all in life bonds and houses, to great worldly advantage, as thou shalt see in good time. Ere long I may get in some rents —"

"And in the meanwhile are we to stay in this plight — to beg for charity?" asks Moll, indignantly.

"Nay, mistress. Doubtless for your present wants this kind merchant friend —"

"We have lost all," says I, "Evans his ship, and I the lading in which all my capital was embarked."

"And I every maravedi I possessed," adds the Don.

"And had they not," cries Moll, "were they possessed now of all they had, think you that I with an estate, as I am told, of sixty thousand pounds would add to the debt I owe them by one single penny!"

"If I may speak in your steward's defence, Madam," says I, humbly, "I would point out that the richest estate is not always readily converted into money. 'Tis like a rich jewel which the owner, though he be starving, must hold till he find a market."

"Thee hearest him, mistress," cries Simon, in delight. "A man of business — a merchant who knows these things.

Explain it further, friend, for thine are words of precious wisdom."

"With landed property the case is even more difficult. Tenants cannot be forced to pay rent before it is due, nor can their messuages be sold over their heads. And possibly all your capital is invested in land—"

"Every farthing that could be scraped together," says Simon, "and not a rood of it but is leased to substantial men. Oh! what excellent discourse! Proceed further, friend."

"Nevertheless," says I, "there are means of raising money upon credit. If he live there still, there is a worthy Jew in St. Mary Axe, who upon certain considerations of interest—"

"Hold, friend," cries Simon. "What art thee thinking of? Wouldst deliver my simple mistress into the hands of Jew usurers?"

"Not without proper covenants made out by lawyers and attorneys."

"Lawyers, attorneys, and usurers! Heaven have mercy upon us! Verily, thee wouldst infest us with a pest, and bleed us to death for our cure."

"I will have such relief as I may," says Moll; "so pray, sir, do send for these lawyers and Jews at once, and the quicker, since my servant seems more disposed to hinder than to help me."

"Forbear, mistress; for the love of God, forbear!" cries Simon, in an agony, clasping his hands. "Be not misguided by this foolish merchant, who hath all to gain and nought to lose by this proceeding. Give me but a little space, and their claims shall be met, thy desires shall be satisfied, and yet half of thy estate be saved, which else must be all devoured betwixt these ruthless money-lenders and lawyers. I can make a covenant more binding than any attorney, as I have proved again and again, and " (with a gulp) "if money must be raised at once, I know an honest, a fairly honest, goldsmith in Lombard Street who will lend at the market rate."

"These gentlemen," answers Moll, turning to us, "may not choose to wait, and I will not incommode them for my own convenience."

"Something for our present need we must have, Madam," says the Don, with a significant glance at his outlandish dress; "but those wants supplied, *I* am content to wait."

"And you, sir?" says Moll to me.

"With a hundred or two," says I, taking Don Sanchez's hint, "we may do very well till Michaelmas."

"Be reasonable, gentlemen," implores Simon, mopping his eyes, which ran afresh at this demand. "'Tis but some five or six weeks to Michaelmas; surely fifty pounds—"

"Silence!" cries Moll, with an angry tap of her foot. "Will three hundred content you, gentlemen? Consider, the wants of our good friend, Captain Evans, may be more pressing than yours."

"He is a good, honest, simple man, and I think we may answer for his accepting the conditions we make for ourselves. Then, with some reasonable guarantee for our future payment—"

"That may be contrived to our common satisfaction, I hope," says Moll, with a gracious smile. "I owe you half my estate; share my house at Chislehurst with me till the rest is forthcoming. That will give me yet a little longer the pleasure of your company. And there, sir," turning to me, "you can examine my steward's accounts for your own satisfaction, and counsel me, mayhap, upon the conduct of my affairs, knowing so much upon matters of business that are incomprehensible to a simple, inexperienced maid. Then, should you find aught amiss in my steward's books, anything to shake your confidence in his management, you will, in justice to your friends, in kindness to me, speak your mind openly, that instant reformation may be made."

Don Sanchez and I expressed our agreement to this proposal, and Moll, turning to the poor, unhappy steward, says in her high tone of authority:

"You hear how this matter is ordered, Simon. Take up that purse for your own uses. Go into the town and send such tradesmen hither as may supply us with proper clothing. Then to your goldsmith in Lombard Street and bring me back six hundred pounds."

"Six — hundred — pounds!" cries he, hardly above his breath, and with a pause between each word as if to gain strength to speak 'em.

"Six hundred. Three for these gentlemen and three for my own needs; when that is done, hasten to Chislehurst and prepare my house; and, as you value my favour, see that nothing is wanting when I come there."

And here, lest it should be thought that Moll could not possibly play her part so admirably in this business, despite the many secret instructions given by the longheaded Don, I do protest that I have set down no more than I recollect, and that without exaggeration. Further, it must be observed that in our common experience many things happen which would seem incredible but for the evidence of our senses, and which no poet would have the hardihood to represent. 'Tis true that in this, as in other more surprising particulars to follow, Moll did surpass all common women; but 'tis only such extraordinary persons that furnish material for any history. And I will add that anything is possible to one who hath the element of greatness in her composition, and that it depends merely on the accident of circumstances whether a Moll Dawson becomes a great saint or a great sinner — a blessing or a curse to humanity.

CHAPTER XV.

Lay our hands on six hundred pounds and quarter ourselves in Hurst Court, but stand in a fair way to be undone by Dawson, his folly.

THE next day comes Simon with a bag of six hundred pounds, which he tells over with infinite care, groaning and mopping his eyes betwixt each four or five pieces with a most rueful visage, so that it seemed he was weeping over this great expenditure, and then he goes to prepare the Court and get servants against Moll's arrival. By the end of the week, being furnished with suitable clothing and equipment, Moll and Don Sanchez leave us, though Dawson was now as hale and hearty as ever he had been, we being persuaded to rest at Chatham yet another week, to give countenance to Jack's late distemper, and also that we might appear less like a gang of thieves.

Before going, Don Sanchez warned us that very likely Simon would pay us a visit suddenly, to satisfy any doubts that might yet crop up in his suspicious mind; and so, to be prepared for him, I got in a good store of paper and books, such as a merchant might require in seeking to reestablish himself in business, and Dawson held himself in readiness to do his share of this knavish business.

Sure enough, about three days after this, the drawer, who had been instructed to admit no one to my chamber without my consent, comes up to say that the little old man in leather, with the weak eyes, would see me; so I bade him in a high voice bid Mr. Simon step up, and setting myself before my table of paper, engage in writing a letter (already half writ), while Dawson slips out into the next room.

"Take a seat, Mr. Steward," says I, when Simon entered, cap in hand, and casting a very prying, curious look around. "I must keep you a minute or two"; and so I feign to be mighty busy, and give him scope for observation.

"Well, sir," says I, finishing my letter with a flourish, and setting it aside. "How do you fare?"

He raised his hands, and dropped them like so much lead on his knees, casting up his eyes and giving a doleful shake of his head for a reply.

"Nothing is amiss at the Court, I pray — your lady Mistress Godwin is well?"

"I know not, friend," says he. "She hath taken my keys, denied me entrance to her house, and left me no privilege of my office save the use of the lodge house. Thus am I treated like a faithless servant, after toiling night and day all these years, and for her advantage, rather than mine own."

"That has to be proved, Mr. Steward," says I, severely; "for you must admit that up to this present she has had no reason to love you, seeing that, had her fate been left in your hands, she would now be in Barbary, and like to end her days there. How, then, can she think but that you had some selfish, wicked end in denying her the service we, who are strangers, have rendered her?"

"Thee speakest truth, friend, and yet thee knowest that I observed only the righteous prudence of an honest servant."

"We will say no more on that head, but you may rest assured on my promise — knowing as I do the noble, generous nature of your mistress — that if she has done you wrong in suspecting you of base purpose, she will be the first to admit her fault and offer you reparation."

"I seek no reparation, no reward, nothing in the world but the right to cherish this estate," cries he, in passion; and, upon my looking at him very curiously, as not understanding the motive of such devotion, he continues: "Thee canst not believe me, and yet truly I am neither a liar nor a madman. What do others toil for? A wife — children — friends — the gratification of ambition or lust! I have no kith or kin, no ambition, no lust; but this estate is wife, child, everything, to me. 'Tis like some work of vanity, — a carved image that a man may give his whole life to making, and yet die content if he achieves but some approach to the creation of his soul. I have made this estate out of nothing; it hath grown larger and larger, richer and more rich, in answer to my skill; why should I not love it, and put my whole heart in the accomplishment of my design, with the same devotion that you admire in the maker of graven images?"

Despite his natural infirmities, Simon delivered this astonishing rhapsody with a certain sort of vehemence that made it eloquent; and indeed, strange as his passion was, I could not deny that it was as reasonable in its way as any nobler act of self-sacrifice.

"I begin to understand you, Mr. Steward," says I.

"Then, good friend, as thee wouldst help the man in peril of being torn from his child, render me this estate to govern; save it from the hands of usurers and lawyers, men of no conscience, to whom this Spanish Don would deliver it for the speedy satisfaction of his greed."

"Nay, my claim's as great as his," says I, "and my affairs more pressing" (with a glance at my papers). "I am undone, my credit lost, my occupation gone."

"Thee shalt be paid to the last farthing. Examine my books, enquire into the value of my securities, and thee wilt find full assurance."

"Well, one of these days mayhap," says I, as if to put him off.

"Nay, come at once, I implore thee; for until I am justified to my mistress, I stand like one betwixt life and death."

"For one thing," says I, still shuffling, "I can do nothing, nor you either, to the payment of our just claim, before the inheritance is safely settled upon Mistress Godwin."

"That shall be done forthwith. I understand the intricacies of the law, and know my way" (tapping his head and then his pocket), "to get a seal, with ten times the despatch of any attorney. I promise by Saturday thee shalt have assurance to thy utmost requirement. Say, good friend, thee wilt be at my lodge house on that day."

"I'll promise nothing," says I. "Our poor Captain Evans is still a prisoner in his room."

"Aye," says Dawson, coming in from the next room, in his nightgown, seeming very feeble and weak despite his blustering voice, "and I'm like to be no better till I can get a ship of my own and be to sea again. Have you brought my money, Mr. Quaker?"

"Thee shalt have it truly; wait but a little while, good friend, a little while."

"Wait a little while and founder altogether, eh? I know you land sharks, and would I'd been born with a smack of your cunning; then had I never gone of this venture, and lost my ship and twoscore men, that money'll ne'er replace. Look at me, a sheer hulk and no more, and all through lending ear to one prayer and another. I doubt you're minded to turn your back on poor old Bob Evans, as t'others have, Mr. Hopkins,— and why not? The poor old man's worth nothing, and cannot help himself." With this he fell a-snivelling like any girl.

"I vow I'll not quit you, Evans, till you're hale again."

"Bring him with thee o' Saturday," urged Simon. "Surely, my mistress can never have the heart to refuse you shelter at the Court, who owes her life to ye. Come and stay there till thy wage be paid, friend Evans."

"What! would ye make an honest sailor play bum-bailiff, and stick in a house, willy nilly, till money's found? Plague of your dry land! Give me a pitching ship and a rolling sea, and a gale whistling in my shrouds. Oh, my reins, my reins! give me a paper of tobacco, Mr. Hopkins, and a pipe to soothe this agony, or I shall grow desperate!"

I left the room as if to satisfy this desire, and Simon followed, imploring me still to come on Saturday to Chislehurst; and I at length got rid of him by promising to come as soon as Evans could be left or induced to accompany me.

I persuaded Dawson, very much against his gree, to delay our going until Monday, the better to hoodwink old Simon; and on that day we set out for Chislehurst, both clad according to our condition,— he in rough frieze, and

I in a very proper, seemly sort of cloth,—and with more guineas in our pockets than ever before we had possessed shillings. And a very merry journey this was; for Dawson, finding himself once more at liberty, and hearty as a lark after his long confinement and under no constraint, was like a boy let loose from school. Carolling at the top of his voice, playing mad pranks with all who passed us on the road, and staying at every inn to drink twopenny ale, so that I feared he would certainly fall ill of drinking, as he had before of eating; but the exercise of riding, the fresh, wholesome air, and half an hour's doze in a spinney, did settle his liquor, and so he reached Hurst Court quite sober, thanks be to Heaven, though very gay. And there we had need of all our self-command, to conceal our joy in finding those gates open to us, which we had looked through so fondly when we were last here, and to spy Moll, in a stately gown, on the fine terrace before this noble house, carrying herself as if she had lived here all her life, and Don Sanchez walking very deferential by her side. Especially Dawson could scarce bring himself to speak to her in an uncouth, surly manner, as befitted his character, and no sooner were we entered the house but he whips Moll behind a door, and falls a-hugging and kissing her like any sly young lover.

Whilst he was giving way to these extravagances, which Moll had not the heart to rebuff,— for in her full, warm heart she was as overjoyed to see him there as he her,— Don Sanchez and I paced up and down the spacious hall, I all of a twitter lest one or other of the servants might discover the familiarity of these two (which must have been a fine matter for curious gossip in the household and elsewhere), and the Don mighty sombre and grave (as foreseeing an evil outcome of this business), so that he would make no answer to my civilities save by dumb gestures, showing he was highly displeased. But truly 'twas enough to set us all crazy, but he, with joy, to be in possession of all these riches and think that we had landed at Chatham scarce a fortnight before without decent clothes to our backs, and now, but for the success of our design, might be the penniless strolling vagabonds we were when Don Sanchez lighted on us.

Presently Moll came out from the side room with her father, her hair all tumbled, and as rosy as a peach, and she would have us visit the house from top to bottom, showing us the rooms set apart for us, her own chamber, the state room, the dining-hall, the store closets for plate and linen, etc., all prodigious fine and in most excellent condition; for the scrupulous minute care of old Simon had suffered nothing to fall out of repair, the rooms being kept well aired, the pictures, tapestries, and magnificent furniture all preserved fresh with linen covers and the like. From the hall she led us out on to the terrace to survey the park and the gardens about the house, and here, as within doors, all was in most admirable keeping, with no wild growth or runaweeds anywhere, nor any sign of neglect. But I observed, as an indication of the steward's thrifty, unpoetic mind, that the garden beds were planted with onions and such marketable produce, in place of flowers, and that instead of deer grazing upon the green slopes of the park there was only such profitable cattle as sheep, cows, etc. And at the sight of all this abundance of good things (and especially the well-stored buttery), Dawson declared he could live here all his life and never worry. And with that, all unthinkingly, he lays his arm about Moll's waist.

Then the Don, who had followed us up and down stairs, speaking never one word till this, says, "We may count ourselves lucky, Captain Evans, if we are suffered to stay here another week."

CHAPTER XVI.

Prosper as well as any thieves may; but Dawson greatly tormented.

THE next morning I went to Simon at his lodge house, having writ him a note overnight to prepare him for my visit, and there I found him, with all his books and papers ready for my examination. So to it we set, casting up figures, comparing accounts, and so forth, best part of the day, and in the end I came away convinced that he was the most scrupulous, honest steward ever man had. And, truly, it appeared that by his prudent investments and careful management he had trebled the value of the estate, and more, in the last ten years. He showed me, also, that in all his valuations he had set off a large sum for loss by accident of fire, war, etc., so that actually at the present moment the estate, which he reckoned at seventy-five thousand pounds, was worth at the least one hundred and twenty-five thousand. But for better assurance on this head, I spent the remainder of the week in visiting the farms, messuages, etc., on his rent roll, and found them all in excellent condition, and held by good substantial men, nothing in any particular but what he represented it.

Reporting on these matters privily to Don Sanchez and Dawson, I asked the Don what we should now be doing.

"Two ways lie before us," says he, lighting a cigarro. "Put Simon out of his house — and make an enemy of him," adds he, betwixt two puffs of smoke, "seize his securities, sell them for what they will fetch, and get out of the country as quickly as possible. If the securities be worth one hundred and twenty-five thousand pounds, we may" (puff) "possibly" (puff) "get forty thousand for them" (puff), "about a third of their value — not more. That yields us ten thousand apiece. On ten thousand pounds a man may live like a prince — in Spain. The other way is to make a friend of Simon by restoring him to his office, suffer him to treble the worth of the estate again in the next ten years, and live like kings" (puff) "in England."

"Pray, which way do you incline, Señor?" says I.

"Being a Spaniard," answers he, gravely, "I should prefer to live like a prince in Spain."

"That would not I," says Dawson, stoutly. "A year and a half of Elche have cured me of all fondness for foreign parts. Besides, 'tis a beggarly, scurvy thing to fly one's country, as if we had done some unhandsome, dishonest trick. If I faced an Englishman, I should never dare look him straight in the eyes again. What say you, Mr. Hopkins?"

"Why, Evans," says I, "you know my will without telling. I will not, of my own accord, go from your choice, which way you will."

"Since we owe everything to Mistress Judith," observes the Don, "and as she is no longer a child, ought not her wishes to be consulted?"

"No," says Jack, very decidedly, and then, lowering his voice, he adds, "for was she Judith Godwin ten times told, and as old as my grandmother into the bargain, she is still my daughter, and shall do as I choose her to do. And if, as you say, we owe her everything, then I count 'twould be a mean, dirty return to make her live out of England and feel she has a sneaking coward for a father."

"As you please," says the Don. "Give me ten thousand of the sum you are to be paid at Michaelmas, and you are welcome to all the rest."

"You mean that, Señor," cries Jack, seizing the Don's hand and raising his left.

"By the Holy Mother," answers Don Sanchez, in Spanish.

"Done!" cries Dawson, bringing his hand down with a smack on the Don's palm. "Nay, I always believed you was the most generous man living. Ten from t'other. Master Hopkins," says he, turning to me, "what does that leave us?"

"More than a hundred thousand!"

"The Lord be praised for evermore!" cries Jack.

Upon this, Moll, by the advice of Don Sanchez, sends for Simon, and telling him she is satisfied with the account I have given of his stewardship, offers him the further control of her affairs, subject at all times to her decision on any question concerning her convenience, and reserving to herself the sole government of her household, the ordering of her home, lands, etc. And Simon grasping eagerly at this proposal, she then gives him the promise of one thousand pounds for his past services, and doubles the wages due to him under his contract with Sir R. Godwin.

"Give me what it may please thee to bestow that way," cries he. "All shall be laid out to enrich this property. I have no other use for money, no other worldly end in life but that."

And when he saw me next he was most slavish in his

thanks for my good offices, vowing I should be paid my claim by Michaelmas, if it were in the power of man to raise so vast a sum in such short space.

Surely, thinks I, there was never a more strange, original creature than this, yet it do seem to me that there is no man but his passion must appear a madness to others.

I must speak now of Moll, her admirable carriage and sober conduct in these new circumstances, which would have turned the heads of most others. Never once to my knowledge did she lose her self-possession, on the most trying occasion, and this was due, not alone to her own shrewd wit and understanding, but to the subtle intelligence of Don Sanchez, who in the character of an old and trusty friend was ever by her side, watchful of her interest (and his own), ready at any moment to drop in her ear a quiet word of warning or counsel. By his advice she had taken into her service a most commendable, proper old gentlewoman, one Mrs. Margery Butterby, who, as being the widow of a country parson, was very orderly in all things, and particularly nice in the proprieties. This notable good soul was of a cheery, chatty disposition, of very pleasing manners, and a genteel appearance, and so, though holding but the part of housekeeper, she served as an agreeable companion and a respectable guardian, whose mere presence in the house silenced any question that might have arisen from the fact of three men living under the same roof with the young and beautiful mistress of Hurst Court. Moreover, she served us as a very useful kind of mouthpiece; for all those marvellous stories of her life in Barbary, of the pirates we had encountered in redeeming her from the Turk, etc., with which Moll would beguile away any tedious half-hour, for the mere amusement of creating Mrs. Butterby's wonder and surprise, — as one will tell stories of fairies to children,— this good woman repeated with many additions of her own concerning ourselves, which, to reflect credit on herself, were all to our advantage. This was the more fitting, because the news spreading that the lost heiress had returned to Hurst Court excited curiosity far and wide, and it was not long before families in the surrounding seats, who had known Sir R. Godwin in bygone times, called to see his daughter. And here Moll's wit was taxed to the utmost, for those who had known Judith Godwin as an infant expected that she should remember some incident stored in their recollection; but she was ever equal to the occasion, feigning a pretty doubting innocence at first, then suddenly asking this lady if she had not worn a cherry dress with a beautiful stomacher at the time, or that gentleman if he had not given her a gold piece for a token, and it generally happened these shrewd shafts hit their mark: the lady, though she might have forgotten her gown, remembering she had a very becoming stomacher; the gentleman believing that he did give her a lucky penny, and so forth, from very vanity. Then Moll's lofty carriage and her beauty would remind them of their dear lost friend, Mrs. Godwin, in the heyday of her youth, and all agreed in admiring her beyond anything. And though Moll, from her lack of knowledge, made many slips, and would now and then say things uncustomary to women of breeding, yet these were easily attributed to her living so long in a barbarous country, and were as readily glanced over. Indeed, nothing could surpass Moll's artificial conduct on these occasions. She would lard her conversation with those scraps of Italian she learnt from me, and sometimes, affecting to have forgot her own tongue, she would stumble at a word, and turning to Don Sanchez, ask him the English of some Moorish phrase. Then one day, there being quite a dozen visitors in her state room, she brings down her Moorish dress and those baubles given her by friends at Elche, to show the ladies, much to the general astonishment and wonder; then, being prayed to dress herself in these clothes, she with some hesitation of modesty consents, and after a short absence from the room returns in this costume, looking lovelier than ever I had before seen, with the rings about her shapely bare arms and on her ankles, and thus arrayed she brings me a guitar, and to my strumming sings a Moorish song, swaying her arms above her head and turning gracefully in their fashion, so that all were in an ecstasy with this strange performance. And the talk spreading, the number of visitors grew apace, — as bees will flock to honey, — and yielding to their urgent entreaties, she would often repeat this piece of business, and always with a most winning grace, that charmed every one. But she was most a favourite of gentlemen and elderly ladies; for the younger ones she did certainly put their noses out of joint, since none could at all compare with her in beauty nor in manner, either, for she had neither the awkward shyness of some nor the boldness of others, but contrived ever to steer neatly betwixt the two extremes by her natural self-possession and fearlessness.

Of all her new friends, the most eager in courting her were Sir Harry Upton and his lady (living in the Crays), and they, being about to go to London for the winter, did press Moll very hard to go with them, that she might be presented to the king; and, truth to tell, they would not have had to ask her twice had she been governed only by her own inclination. For she was mad to go, — that audacious spirit of adventure still working very strong in her, — and she, like a winning gamester, must for ever be playing for higher and higher stakes. But we, who had heard enough of his excellent but lawless Majesty's court to fear the fate of any impulsive, beauteous young woman that came within his sway, were quite against this. Even Don Sanchez, who was no innocent, did persuade her from it with good strong argument, — showing that, despite his worldliness, he did really love her as much as 'twas in his withered heart to love any one. As for Dawson, he declared he would sooner see his Moll in her winding-sheet than in the king's company, adding that 'twould be time enough for her to think of going to court when she had a husband to keep her out of mischief. And so she refused this offer (but with secret tears, I believe). "But," says she to her father, "if I'm not to have my own way till I'm married, I shall get me a husband as soon as I can."

And it seemed that she would not have to look far nor wait long for one neither. Before a month was passed, at least half a dozen young sparks were courting her, they being attracted, not only by her wit and beauty, but by the report of her wealth, it being known to all how Simon had enriched the estate. And 'twas this abundance of suitors which prevented Moll from choosing any one in particular, else had there been but one, I believe the business would have been settled very quickly. For now she was in the very flush of life, and the blood that flowed in her veins was of no lukewarm kind.

But here (that I may keep all my strings in harmony) I must quit Moll for a space to tell of her father. That first hint of the Don's bringing him to his senses somewhat (like a dash of cold water), and the exuberance of his joy subsiding, he quickly became more circumspect in his behaviour, and fell into the part he had to play. And the hard, trying, sorrowful part that was, neither he nor I had foreseen. For now was he compelled for the first time in his life, at any length, to live apart from his daughter, to refrain from embracing her when they met in the morning, to speak to her in a rough, churlish sort when his heart, maybe, was overflowing with love, and to reconcile himself to a cool, indifferent behaviour on her side, when his very soul was yearning for gentle, tender warmth. And these natural cravings of affection were rather strengthened than stilled by repression, as one's hunger by starving. To add to this, he now saw his Moll more bewitching than ever she was before, the evidence of her wit and understanding stimulating that admiration which he dared not express. He beheld her loved and courted openly by all, whilst he who had deeper feeling for her than any, and more right to caress her, must at each moment stifle his desires and lay fetters on his inclinations, which constraint, like chains binding down a stout, thriving oak, did eat and corrode into his being, so that he did live most of these days in a veritable torment. Yet, for Moll's sake, was he very stubborn in his resolution; and, when he could no longer endure to stand indifferently by while others were enjoying her sprightly conversation, he would go up to his chamber and pace to and fro, like some she-lion parted from her cub.

These sufferings were not unperceived by Moll, who also had strong feeling to repress, and therefore could comprehend her father's torture, and she would often seize an opportunity, nay, run great risk of discovery, to hie her secretly to his room, there to throw herself in his arms and strain him to her heart, covering his great face with tender kisses, and whispering words of hope and good cheer (with the tears on her cheek). And one day when Jack seemed more than usual downhearted, she offered him to give up everything and return to her old ways, if he would. But this spurring his courage, he declared he would live in hell rather than she should fall from her high estate, and become a mere vagabond wench again, adding that 'twas but the first effort gave him so much pain, that with practice 'twould all be as nothing; that such sweet kisses as hers once a week did amply compensate him for his fast, etc. Then her tears being brushed away, she would quit him with noiseless step and all precautions, and maybe five minutes afterwards, whilst Jack was sitting pensive at his window pondering her sweetness and love, he would hear her laughing lightly below, as if he were already forgotten.

CHAPTER XVII.

How Dawson for Moll's good parts company with us, and goes away a lonely man.

ON the eve of Michaelmas day old Simon returned from London, whither he had gone two days before, to raise the money he had promised; and calling upon him in the afternoon I found him seated at his table, with a most woebegone look in his face, and his eyes streaming more copiously than usual. And with most abject humility he told me that doing the utmost that lay in his power, he had not been able to persuade his goldsmith to lend more than ten thousand pounds on the title deeds. Nor had he got that, he declared, but that the goldsmith knew him for an honest and trustworthy man whom he would credit beyond any other in the world; for the seal not yet being given to Judith Godwin's succession, there was always peril of dispute and lawsuits which might make these papers of no value at all (the king's ministers vying one with another to please their master by bringing money rightly or wrongly into the treasury), and this, indeed, may have been true enough.

"But," says he, "all will go well if thee wilt have but a little patience for a while. To-morrow my rents will come in, and I will exact to the last farthing; and there is a parcel of land I may sell, mayhap, for instant payment, though 'twill be at a fearsome loss" (mopping his eyes), "yet

I will do it rather than put thee to greater incommodity; and so, ere the end of the week, thee mayst safely count on having yet another three thousand, which together makes nigh upon half the sum promised. And this, dear good friend," adds he, slyly, "thee mayst well take on account of thine own share, — and none dispute thy right, for 'tis thy money hath done all. And from what I see of him, smoking of pipes in the public way and drinking with any low fellows in alehouses, this Captain Evans is but a paltry, mean man who may be easily put off with a pound or two to squander in his pleasures ; and as for the Spanish grandee, he do seem so content to be with our mistress that I doubt he needs no pretext for quitting her, added to which, being of a haughty, proud nature, he should scorn to claim his own, to the prejudice of a merchant who hath nought but his capital to live upon. And I do implore thee, good friend, to lay this matter before my mistress in such a way that she may not be wroth with me."

I told him I would do all he could expect of me in reason, but bade him understand that his chance of forgiveness for having broke his first engagement depended greatly upon his exactitude in keeping the second, and that he might count on little mercy from us if the other three thousand were not forthcoming as he promised So I took the money and gave him a quittance for it, signing it with my false name, James Hopkins, but, reflecting on this when I left him, I wished I had not. For I clearly perceived that by this forgery I laid myself open to very grievous consequences ; moreover, taking of this solid money, disguise it how I would, appeared to me nothing short of downright robbery, be it whose it might. In short, being now plunged

L

up to my neck in this business, I felt like a foolish lad who hath waded beyond his depth in a rapid current, hoping I might somehow get out of it safely, but with very little expectation. However, the sight of all this gold told up in scores upon the table in our closed room served to quiet these qualms considerably. Nevertheless, I was not displeased to remember our bargain with Don Sanchez, feeling that I should breathe more freely when he had taken this store of gold out of my hands, etc. Thus did my mind waver this way and that, like a weather-cock to the blowing of contrary winds.

'Twas this day that Moll (as I have said) dressed herself in her Moorish clothes for the entertainment of her new friends, and Dawson, hearing her voice, yet not daring to go into the state room where she was, must needs linger on the stairs listening to her song, and craning his neck to catch a glimpse of her through the open door below. Here he stands in a sort of ravishment, sucking in her sweet voice, and the sounds of delight with which her guests paid tribute to her performance, feeding his passion which, like some fire, grew more fierce by feeding, till he was well-nigh beside himself. Presently, out comes Moll from her state room, all glowing with exercise, flushed with pleasure, a rich colour in her cheek, and wild fire in her eyes, looking more witching than any siren. Swiftly she crosses the hall, and runs up the stairs to gain her chamber and reclothe herself, but half way up Dawson stops her, and clasping her about, cries hoarsely in a transport:

"Thou art my own Moll — my own sweet Moll!" adding, as she would break from him to go her way, "Nay, chick. You shall not go till you have bussed your old dad."

Then she, hesitating a moment betwixt prudence and her warmer feelings, suddenly yields to the impulse of her heart (her head also being turned maybe with success and delight), and flinging her arms about his neck gives him a hearty kiss, and then bursts away with a light laugh.

Jack watches her out of sight, and then, when the moment of escape is past, he looks below to see if there be any danger, and there he spies Don Sanchez, regarding him from the open door, where he stands, as if to guard it. Without a sign the Don turns on his heel and goes back into the room, while Dawson, with a miserable hangdog look, comes to me in my chamber, where I am counting the gold, and confesses his folly with a shamed face, cursing himself freely for his indiscretion, which at this rate must ruin all ere long.

This was no great surprise to me, for I myself had seen him many a time clip his dear daughter's hand, when he thought no one was by, and, more than once, the name of Moll had slipped out when he should have spoken of Mistress Judith.

These accidents threw us both into a very grave humour, and especially I was tormented with the reflection that a forgery could be proved against me, if things came to the worst. The danger thereof was not slight; for though all in the house loved Moll dearly and would willingly do her no hurt, yet the servants, should they notice how Mistress Judith stood with Captain Evans, must needs be prating, and there a mischief would begin, to end only the Lord knows where! Thereupon, I thought it as well to preach Jack a sermon, and caution him to greater prudence; and this he took in amazing good part — not bidding me tend my own business as he might at another time, but assenting very submissively to all my hints of disaster, and thanking me in the end for speaking my mind so freely. Then, seeing him so sadly downcast, I (to give a sweetmeat after a bitter draught) bade him take the matter not too much to heart, promising that, with a little practice, he would soon acquire a habit of self-restraint, and so all would go well. But he made no response, save by shaking of his head sorrowfully, and would not be comforted.

When all were abed that night, we three men met in my chamber, where I had set the bags of money on the table, together with a dish of tobacco and a bottle of wine for our refreshment, and then the Don, having lit him a cigarro, and we our pipes, with full glasses beside us, I proposed we should talk of our affairs, to which Don Sanchez consented with a solemn inclination of his head. But ere I began, I observed with a pang of foreboding, that Jack, who usually had emptied his glass ere others had sipped theirs, did now leave his untouched, and after the first pull or two at his pipe, he cast it on the hearth as though it were foul to his taste. Taking no open notice of this, I showed Don Sanchez the gold, and related all that had passed between Simon and me.

"Happily, Señor," says I, in conclusion, "here is just the sum you generously offered to accept for your share, and we give it you with a free heart, Evans and I being willing to wait for what may be forthcoming."

"Is it your wish both, that I take this?" says he, laying his hand on the money and looking from me to Dawson.

"Aye," says he, " 'tis but a tithe of what is left to us, and not an hundredth part of what we owe to you."

"Very good," says the Don. "I will carry it to London to-morrow."

"But surely, Señor," says I, "you will not quit us so soon."

Don Sanchez rolls his cigarro in his lips, looking me straight in the face and somewhat sternly, and asks me quietly if I have ever found him lacking in loyalty and friendship.

"In truth, never, Señor."

"Then why should you imagine I mean to quit you now when you have more need of a friend in this house" (with a sideward glance as towards Moll's chamber) "than ever you before had?" Then, turning towards Jack, he says, "What are you going to do, Captain Evans?"

Dawson pauses, as if to snatch one last moment for consideration, and then, nodding at me, "You'll not leave my Moll, Kit?" says he, with no attempt to disguise names.

"Why should I leave her; are we not as brothers, you and I?"

"Aye, I'd trust you with my life," answers he, "and more than that, with my — Moll! If you were her uncle, she couldn't love you more, Kit. And you will stand by her, too, Señor?"

The Don bowed his head.

"Then when you leave, to-morrow, I'll go with you to London," says Jack.

"I shall return the next day," says Don Sanchez, with significance.

"And I shall not, God help me!" says Jack, bitterly.

"Give me your hand," says the Don; but I could speak never a word, and sat staring at Jack, in a maze.

"We'll say nought of this to her," continues Jack; "there must be no farewells, I could never endure that. But it shall seem that I have gone with you for company, and have fallen in with old comrades who would keep me for a carousing."

"But without friends—alone—what shall you do there in London?" says I, heart-stricken at the thought of his desolation. The Don answers for Jack.

"Make the best of his lot with a stout heart, like any other brave man," says he. "There are natural hardships which every man must bear in his time, and this is one of them." Then lowering his voice, he adds, "Unless you would have her die an old maid, she and her father must part sooner or later."

"Why, that's true, and yet, Master," says Jack, "I would have you know that I'm not so brave but I would see her now and then."

"That may be ordered readily enough," says the Don.

"Then do you tell her, Señor, I have but gone a-junketing, and she may look to see me again when my frolic's over."

The Don closed his eyes as one in dubitation, and then says, lifting his eyebrows: "She is a clever woman — shrewd beyond any I have ever known; then why treat her as you would a foolish child? You must let me tell her the truth when I come back, and I warrant it will not break her heart, much as she loves you."

"As you will," says t'other. "'Twill be all as one to me," with a sigh.

"This falls out well in all ways," continues the Don, turning to me. "You will tell Simon, whose suspicion we have most to fear, that we have handed over four thousand of those pieces to Captain Evans as being most in need, we ourselves choosing to stay here till the rest of our claim is paid. That will account for Evans going away, and give us a pretext for staying here."

" I'll visit him myself, if you will," says Jack, "and wring his hand to show my gratitude. I warrant I'll make him wince, such a grip will I give him. And I'll talk of nothing else but seas and winds, and the manner of ship I'll have for his money."

The following morning before Moll was stirring, Don Sanchez and Dawson set forth on their journey, and I going with them beyond the park gates to the bend of the road, we took leave of each other with a great show of cheerfulness on both sides. But Lord! my heart lay in my breast like any lump of lead, and when Jack turned his back on me, the tears sprang up in my eyes as though indeed this was my brother and I was never to see him more. And long after he was out of sight I sat on the bank by the roadside, sick with pain to think of his sorrow in going forth like this, without one last loving word of parting from his dear Moll, to find no home in London, no friend to cheer him, and he the most companionable man in the world.

CHAPTER XVIII.

Of our getting a painter into the Court, with whom our Moll falls straightway in love.

BEING somewhat of a coward, I essayed to put Moll off with a story of her father having gone a-frolicking with Don Sanchez, leaving it to the Don to break the truth to her on his return. And a sorry, bungling business I made of it, to be sure. For, looking me straight in the eyes, whenever I dared lift them, she did seem to perceive that I was lying, from the very first, which so disconcerted me, though she interrupted me by never a word, that I could scarce stammer to the end of my tale. Then, without asking a single question, or once breaking her painful silence, she laid her face in her hands, her shoulders shook, and the tears ran out between her fingers, and fell upon her lap.

"I know, I know," says she, putting me away, when I attempted to speak. "He has gone away for my sake, and will come back no more; and 'tis all my fault, that I could not play my part better."

Then, what words of comfort I could find, I offered her; but she would not be consoled, and shut herself up in her room all that morning. Nevertheless, she ate more heartily than I at dinner, and fresh visitors coming in the afternoon, she entertained them as though no grief lay at her heart. Indeed, she recovered of this cruel blow much easier than I looked for; and but that she would at times sit pensive, with melancholy, wistful eyes, and rise from her seat with a troubled sigh, one would have said, at the end of the week, that she had ceased to feel for her father. But this was not so (albeit wounds heal quickly in the young and healthful), for I believe that they who weep the least do ache the most.

Then, for her further excuse (if it be needed), Don Sanchez brought back good tidings of her father,—how he was neatly lodged near the Cherry garden, where he could hear the birds all day and the fiddles all night, with abundance of good entertainment, etc. To confirm which, she got a letter from him, three days later, very loving and cheerful, telling how, his landlord being a carpenter, he did amuse himself mightily at his old trade in the workshop, and was all agog for learning to turn wood in a lathe, promising that he would make her a set of egg-cups against her birthday, please God. Added to this, the number of her friends multiplying apace, every day brought some new occupation to her thoughts; also, having now those three thousand pounds old Simon had promised us, Moll set herself to spending of them as quickly as possible, by furnishing herself with all sorts of rich gowns and appointments, which is as pretty a diversion of melancholy from a young woman's thoughts as any. And so I think I need dwell no longer on this head.

About the beginning of October, Simon comes, cap in hand, and very humble, to the Court to crave Moll's consent to his setting some men with guns in her park at night, to lie in ambush for poachers, telling how they had shot one man in the act last spring, and had hanged another the year before for stealing of a sheep; adding that a stranger had been seen loitering in the neighbourhood, who, he doubted not, was of their thieving crew.

"What makes you think that?" asks Moll.

"He has been seen lingering about here these three days," answers Simon. "Yet to my knowledge he hath not slept at either of the village inns. Moreover, he hath the look of a desperate, starving rascal, ripe for such work."

"I will have no man killed for his misfortunes."

"Gentle mistress, suffer me to point out that if thee lets one man steal with impunity, others, now innocent, are thereby encouraged to sin, and thus thy mercy tends to greater cruelty."

"No man shall be killed on my land,—there is my answer," says Moll, with passion. "If you take this poor, starved creature, it shall be without doing him bodily hurt. You shall answer for it else."

"Not a bone shall be broken, mistress. 'Tis enough if we carry him before Justice Martin, a godly, upright man, and a scourge to evil-doers."

"Nay, you shall not do that, neither, till I have heard his case," says Moll. "'Tis for me to decide whether he has injured me or not, and I'll suffer none to take my place."

Promising obedience, Simon withdrew before any further restrictions might be put upon him; but Moll's mind was much disturbed all day by fear of mischief being done despite her commands, and at night she would have me take her round the park to see all well. Maybe, she thought that her own father, stealing hither to see her privily, might fall a victim to Simon's ambushed hirelings. But we found no one, though Simon had certainly hidden these fellows somewhere in the thickets.

Whilst we were at table next morning, we heard a great commotion in the hall; and Mrs. Butterby coming in a mighty pucker, told how the robber had been taken in the park, and how Simon had brought him to the house in obedience to her lady's command.

"But do, pray, have a care of yourself, my dear lady," says she; "for this hardy villain hath struck Mr. Simon in the face and made most desperate resistance; and Heaven protect us from such wicked outlaws as have the villany to show themselves in broad daylight!"

Moll, smiling, said she would rather face a lion in the day than a mouse by night, and so bade the captive to be brought before her.

Then in comes Simon, with a stout band over one eye, followed by two sturdy fellows holding their prisoner betwixt them. And this was a very passionate man, as was evidenced by the looks of fury he cast from side to side upon his captors as they dragged him this way and that to make a show of their power, but not ill-looking. In his struggles he had lost his hat, and his threadbare coat and shirt were torn open, laying bare his neck and showing a very fair white skin and a good beard of light curling hair. There was nought mean or vile in his face, but rather it seemed to me a noble countenance, though woefully wasted, so that at a glance one might perceive he was no born rascal, but likely enough some ruined man of better sort driven to unlawful ways by his distress. He was of a fair height, but gaunt beyond everything, and so feeble that after one effort to free his arms his chin sank upon his breast as if his forces were all spent.

Seeing this, Moll bade the fellows unbind him, telling them sharply they might see there was no need of such rigour.

Being freed, our prisoner lifts his head and makes a slight reverence to Moll, but with little gratitude in his look, and places himself at the end of the table facing us, who are at the other end, Moll sitting betwixt Don Sanchez and me. And there, setting his hands for support upon the board, he holds his head up pretty proudly, waiting for what might come.

"Who are you?" asks Moll, in a tone of authority.

He waits a moment, as if deliberating with himself whether to speak fairly or not, then, being still sore with his ill-treatment, and angered to be questioned thus by a mere girl (he, as I take it, being a man of thirty or thereabouts), he answers:

"I do not choose to tell. Who I am, what I am, concerns you no more than who and what you are concerns me, and less since I may justly demand by what right these fellows, whom I take to be your servants, have thus laid hands on me."

"How do you answer this?" asks Moll, turning to Simon.

Then Simon told very precisely, as if he were before a magistrate, how this man, having been seen lingering about the Court several days, and being without home or occupation, had been suspected of felonious purposes; how, therefore, he had set a watch to lay wait for him; how that morning they had entrapped him standing within a covert of the park regarding the house; how he had refused to give his name or any excuse for his being there, and how he had made most desperate attempt to escape when they had lain hands on him.

"Is this true?" asks Moll of the prisoner.

"Yes," says he.

Moll regards him with incredulous eyes a moment, then, turning to Simon, " What arms had he for this purpose that you speak of?" says she.

" None, mistress; but 'twould be a dread villain verily who would carry the engines of his trade abroad in daylight to betray him." And then he told how 'tis the habit of these poachers to reconnoitre their ground by day, and keep their nets, guns, etc., concealed in some thicket or hollow tree convenient for their purpose. "But," adds he, "we may clearly prove a trespass against him, which is a punishable offence, and this assault upon me, whereof I have evidence, shall also count for something with Justice Martin, and so the wicked shall yet come by their deserts." And with that he gives his fellows a wink with his one eye to carry off their quarry.

"Stay," says Moll, "I would be further convinced—"

"If he be an honest man, let him show thee his hand," says Simon.

The man innocently enough stretches out his palm towards us, not perceiving Simon's end.

"There!" cries Simon. "What said I? Is that a hand that ever did a day's honest work?"

" 'Tis no worse than mine," says Moll, regarding the hand which in truth was exceeding smooth and well formed. "Come," adds she, still more kindly, "you see I am no harsh judge. I would not deny a fellow-creature the pleasure that is not grudged the coney that runs across my lawn. Tell me you were there but to gratify a passing caprice, and I'll forgive you as freely as I'll believe you."

This gentle appeal seemed to move the young man greatly, and he made as if he would do more than was demanded of him, and make that free confession which he had refused to force. But ere a word could leave his parted lips a deadly shade passed over his face, his knees gave under him, and staggering to save himself, he fell to the ground in a swoon.

Then, whilst all we men stood fixed in wonderment, Moll, with the quick, helpful impulse of her womanhood, ran swiftly from her place to his side, and dropping on her knees cried for water to be brought her.

"Dead of hunger," says Don Sanchez, in my ear. "Fetch a flask of brandy."

And then, laying hold of Simon by the shoulder, he pointed significantly to the open door. This hint Simon was not slow to take, and when I returned from the buttery with a case of strong waters, I found no one in the room but Don Sanchez, and Moll with the fainting man's head upon her lap, bathing his temples gently. Life had not come back, and the young man's face looked very handsome in death, the curls pushed back from his brow, and his long features still and colourless like a carved marble.

Then with a "lack-a-day" and "alas," in bustles Mrs. Butterby with a bottle of cordial in one hand and a bunch of burning feathers in the other.

"Fling that rubbish in the chimney," says the Don. "I know this malady — well enough," and pouring some hollands in a cup he put it to the dead man's parted lips.

In a few moments he breathed again, and hearing Moll's cry of joy, he opened his eyes as one waking from a dream and turned his head to learn what had happened. Then finding his head in Moll's lap and her small, soft, cool hand upon his brow, a smile played over his wasted face. And well, indeed, might he smile to see that young figure of justice turned to the living image of tender mercy.

Perceiving him out of danger, and recovering her own wits at the same time, Mrs. Butterby cries: "Lord! Madam, do let me call a maid to take your place; for, dear heart! you have quite spoiled your new gown with this mess of water, and all for such a paltry fellow as this!"

Truly, it must have seemed to her understanding an outrageous thing that a lady of her mistress' degree should be nursing such a ragged rascal; but to me, knowing Moll's helpful, impulsive disposition, 'twas no such extraordinary matter, for she at such a moment could not entertain those feelings which might have restrained a lady of more refined breeding.

The pretty speech of Mrs. Butterby, reaching the fallen man's ear, seemed instantly to quicken his spirits, and, casting off his lethargic humour, he quickly staggered to his feet, while we raised Moll. Then, resting one hand upon the table for support, he craved her pardon for giving so much trouble, but in a very faint, weak voice.

"I would have done as much for a dog," says Moll. "My friends will render you what further services are fit; and, if it appears that you have been unjustly used (as I do think you have), be sure you shall have reparation."

"I ask no more," says he, "than to be treated as I may merit in your esteem."

"Justice shall be done," says Don Sanchez, in his stern voice, and with that he conducts Moll to the door.

But Moll was not content with this promise of justice. For the quality of mercy begetteth love, so that one cannot moderate one's anger against an enemy, but it doth breed greater compassion and leniency by making one better content with oneself, and therefore more indulgent to others. And so, when she had left the room, she sends in her maid to fetch me, and taking me aside says with vivacity:

"I will have no punishment made upon that man."

"Nay," says I, "but if 'tis proved that his intent was to rob you—"

"What then!" says she. "Hath he not as much right to this estate as we? And are we one whit the better than he, save in the more fortunate issue of our designs? Understand me," adds she, with passion; "I will have nothing added to his unhappiness."

I found the young man seated at the table, and Don Sanchez gravely setting food before him. But he would take nothing but bread, and that he ate as though it were the sweetest meat in all the world. I lead the Don to the window, and there, in an undertone, told him of Moll's decision; and, whether her tone of supreme authority amused him or not, I cannot say, because of his impassive humour, but he answered me with a serious inclination of his head, and then we fell speaking of other matters in our usual tone, until the young man, having satisfied the cravings of nature, spoke:

"When you are at liberty, gentlemen," says he, "to question my conduct, I will answer you."

CHAPTER XIX.

Of the business appointed to the painter, and how he set about the same.

THE young man had risen and was standing by the table when we turned from the window; he seemed greatly refreshed, his face had lost its livid hue of passion and death, and looked the better for a tinge of colour. He met our regard boldly, yet with no braggart, insolent air, but the composure of a brave man facing his trial with a consciousness of right upon his side.

"I would ask you," says the Don, seating himself on t'other side the table, "why you refused to do that before?"

"Sir," answers he, "I have lost everything in the world save some small modicum of pride, which, being all I have, I do cherish, maybe, unduly. And so, when these unmannerly hinds took me by the throat, calling on me to tell my name and business, this spirit within me flaring up, I could not answer with the humility of a villain seeking to slink out of danger by submissive excuses."

"Be seated," says the Don, accepting this explanation with a bow. "How may we call you?"

"In Venice," replies the other, with some hesitation, "I was called Dario — a name given me by my fellow-scholars because my English name was not to their taste."

"Enough," says the Don. "I can understand a man of better fortune, as I perceive you have been, wishing in such a position as this to retain his incognito. There are no parks in Venice, to my knowledge, but surely, sir, you would not enter a palazzo there uninvited without some reasonable pretext."

"It would be sufficient that in such a house as this I thought I might find some employment for a painter."

"You are a painter?" says I.

"A poor one, as you see," replies Dario, with a significant glance at his clothes.

Don Sanchez turned to me, hunching his shoulders.

"'Tis clear," says he, "that Signor Dario has been grossly abused by our lady's over-zealous steward. You have but to tell us, sir, what reparation we can make you."

"I'll not refuse it," answers Dario, eagerly. "You shall grant me permission to prove the honesty of my story — and something more than that. Somewhere here," adds he, glancing around him, "I'd leave a tribute to the grace of that dear lady who brought me back to life."

Don Sanchez assents with a bow to this proposal, but with a rueful glance at the rich panels of the wall, as fearing this painter might be as poor in talent as in his clothes — the latter reflecting discredit on the former — and would disfigure the handsome walls with some rude daub.

"Ah!" cries Dario, casting his eye upon the ceiling, which was plastered in the Italian mode and embellished with a poor design of cherubs and clouds, "this ceiling is ill done. I could paint a fresco that would less disgrace the room."

"You will need materials," says the Don, laying his purse upon the table. "When you return with them, you may rely upon having our lady's consent to your wishes."

The painter took the purse with a bow of acknowledgment, and no more hesitation than one gentleman would show in receiving an obligation from another, and presently left us.

"Shall we see him again, think ye, Señor?" I asked when we were left to ourselves.

He nodded, but with such a reflective, sombre air, that I was impelled to ask him if he lacked confidence in the story told us by the painter.

"His story may be true enough, but whether Signor Dario be an honest man or not is another matter. A painter's but a man. A ruined gentleman will accommodate his principles to circumstances" (with a side glance that seemed to say, "I am a ruined gentleman")—"and my mind would be easier if I knew by what curious accident a painter in need should find himself in the heart of Kent, and why fixing on this house to seek employment he should linger to the point of starvation before he can pluck up courage to ask a simple question. We must keep our eyes open, Mr. Hopkins, and," adds he, dropping his voice, "our mouths shut."

I could not sleep that night for thinking of house-breakings and bloody struggles for dear life; for 'tis a matter of common report that this sort of robbers, ere they make attack, do contrive to get one of their number into the house that he may learn where good goods are stowed, which part is easiest of attack, etc.

I know not whether these quakings were shared by the Don, but certainly our misgivings never entered Moll's little head. Nay, rather, her romantic disposition did lead her (when she heard our narration) to conceive that this mysterious Dario might be some wandering genius, whose work upon our ceiling would make the Court for ever glorious. And while in this humour she bade me go to Simon, whose presence she would not tolerate in her house, and make him acquainted with her high displeasure, and furthermore, to command that he should make satisfactory apology to Dario upon his return. So to him I went, and he wringing his hands in anguish deplored that his best endeavours to serve his mistress served only to incense her the more against him. But for his apology he declared that has been made the moment he heard of the gentleman's release, at the same time that he restored to him his hat and a pocket-book which had fallen from his pocket.

This did somewhat reassure me, knowing full well that Simon would not have given up this book without first acquainting himself with its contents, and urging that had there been anything in it to incriminate him, he had certainly laid it before his mistress for his own justification.

A couple of days after this, as Don Sanchez and I were discoursing in the great avenue, Dario presents himself, looking all the better for a decent suit of clothes and a more prosperous condition, and Moll joining us at that moment, he makes her a very handsome obeisance and standing uncovered before her, begs to know if it is her will that he should paint the ceiling of her dining-hall.

As he spoke, the colour rose on his cheek, and a shaft of sunlight falling on his curling hair, which shone with the lustre of health, made him look as comely a man as ever I did see, and a good five years younger than when he stood before us in the extremity of distress.

"Sir," says Moll, "were you my debtor as much as I am yours, I could not ask for better payment."

Don Sanchez put an end to this pretty exchange of courtesies — which maybe he considered overmuch as between a lady of Moll's degree and one who might turn out to be no more than an indifferent painter at the best — by proposing that Dario should point out what disposition he would have made for his convenience in working. So he went within doors, and there Dario gave orders to our gardener, who was a handy sort of Jack-of-all-trades, what pieces of furniture should be removed, how the walls and floor should be protected, and how a scaffold should be set up for him to work on. And the gardener promising to carry out all these instructions in the course of the day, Dario took his leave of us in a very polished style, saying he would begin his business the next morning betimes.

Sure enough, we were awoke next day by a scraping below, and coming down, we found our painter in a scullcap and a smock that covered him to his heels, upon his scaffold, preparing the ceiling in a very workmanlike manner. And to see him then, with his face and beard thickly crusted over with a mess of dry plaster and paint, did I think somewhat dispel those fanciful illusions which our Moll had fostered — she, doubtless, expecting to find him in a very graceful attitude and beautiful to look at, creating a picture as if by inchantment. Her mortification was increased later in the day when, we having invited him on her insistence to dine at our table, he declined (civilly enough), saying he had brought his repast with him, and we presently found him seated astride one of his planks with a pocket knife in one hand and a thumb-piece of bread and bacon in the other, which he seemed to be eating with all the relish in the world.

"Why, he is nought but a common labourer," says Moll, disgusted to see him regaling himself in this fashion, as we returned to our room. "A pretty picture we are like to get for all this mess and inconvenience!"

And her idol being broken (as it were), and all her fond fancies dashed, she would not as much as look at him again nor go anigh the room, to be reminded of her folly.

However, on the third day Dario sent to ask if she would survey his outlines and decide whether the design pleased her or not. For this purpose he had pushed aside his scaffold, and here we saw a perspective done on the ceiling in charcoal, representing a vaulted roof with an opening to the sky in the middle, surrounded by a little balcony with trailing plants running over it, and flowers peeping out betwixt the balusters. And this, though very rough, was most artificial, making the room look twice its height, and the most admirable, masterly drawing that I did ever see.

And now Moll, who had prepared a courteous speech to cover the contempt she expected to feel for the work, could say nought for astonishment, but stood casting her eyes round at the work like one in a maze.

"If you would prefer an allegory of figures," says Dario, misconceiving her silence.

"Nay," answers she, "I would have nothing altered. 'Tis wonderful how such effect can be made with mere lines of black. I can scarce believe the ceiling is flat." And then she drops her eyes upon Dario, regarding him with wonder, as if doubting that such a dirty-looking man could have worked this miracle.

"You must have seen better designs in Rome," says he.

At this I took alarm, not thinking for the moment that he

might have picked up some particulars of Judith Godwin's history from Mrs. Butterby, or the curious servants who were ever prying in the room.

" 'Tis so long ago," says Moll, readily.

" I think I have seen something like it in the Holy City," observes the Don, critically.

" Probably. Nothing has been left undone in Rome — I am told. It has not been my good fortune to get so far."

This was good news; for otherwise he might have put some posers to Moll, which she had found it hard to answer without betraying her ignorance.

Having Moll's approval, Dario set to work forthwith to colour his perspective; and this he did with the sure firm hand of one who understands his business, and with such nice judgment, that no builder, whose design is ordered by fixed rule and line, could accomplish his work with greater truth and justice. He made it to appear that the lower part of his vaulted roof was wainscoted in the style of the walls, and to such perfection that 'twould have puzzled a conjurer to decide where the oaken panels ended and the painted ones began.

And now Moll suffers her fancies to run wild again, and could not sufficiently marvel over this poor painter and his work, of which she would discourse to such lengths, that both the Don and I at times had some ado to stifle our yawns. She would have it that he was no common man, but some great genius, compelled by misfortune or the persecution of rivals, to wander abroad in disguise, taking for evidence the very facts which had lately led her to condemn him, pointing out that, whereas those young gentlemen who courted her so persistently did endeavour, on all occasions, to make their estate and natural parts appear greater than they were, this Dario did not, proving that he had no such need of fictitious advancement, and could well afford to let the world judge of his worth by his works, etc. This point we did not contest, only we were very well content to observe that he introduced no one into the house, had no friends in the village (to our knowledge), and that nought was lacking from our store of plate.

She never tired of watching him at his work — having the hardihood to mount upon the scaffold where he stood, and there she would sit by the hour on a little stool, chatting like any magpie, when the nature of his occupation allowed his thoughts to wander, silent as a mouse when she perceived that his mind was absorbed in travail — ready at any moment to fetch this or hold t'other, and seizing every opportunity to serve him. Indeed, I believe she would gladly have helped him shift the heavy planks, when he would have their position altered, had he permitted her this rough usage of her delicate hands. One day, when he was about to begin the foliage upon his balcony, he brought in a spray of ivy for a model; then Moll told him she knew where much better was to be found, and would have him go with her to see it. And she, coming back from this expedition, with her arms full of briony and herbage, richly tinted by the first frost, I perceived that there was a new kind of beauty in her face, a radiance of great happiness and satisfaction which I had never seen there before.

Here was herbage enough for a week, but she must have fresh the next morning, and thenceforth every day they would go out ere the sun was high, hunting for new models.

To prepare for these early excursions, Mistress Moll,

though commonly disposed to lie abed late in the morning, must have been up by daybreak. And, despite her admiration of Dario's simplicity in dress, she showed no inclination to follow his example in this particular; but, on the contrary, took more pains in adorning her person at this time than ever she had done before; and as she would dress her hair no two mornings alike, so she would change the fashion of her dress with the same inconstancy until the sly hussy discovered which did most please Dario's taste; then a word of approval from him, nay, a glance, would suffice to fix her choice until she found that his admiration needed rekindling. And so, as if her own imagination was not sufficiently forcible, she would talk of nothing with her friends but the newest fashions at court, with the result that her maids were for ever a-brewing some new wash for her face (which she considered too brown), compounding charms to remove a little mole she had in the nape of her neck, cutting up one gown to make another, and so forth. One day she presented herself with a black patch at the corner of her lip, and having seen nought of this fashion before, I cried out in alarm:

"Lord, child! have you injured your face with that mess Betty was stewing yesterday?"

"What an absurd, old-fashioned creature you are!" answers she, testily. "Don't you know that 'tis the mode now for ladies to wear spots? Signor Dario," adds she, her eyes lighting up, "finds it mighty becoming."

When I saw her thus disfiguring her pretty face (as I considered it then, though I came to admire this embellishment later on) to please Signor Dario, I began to ask myself how this business was likely to end.

CHAPTER XX.

Of Moll's ill humour and what befel thereby.

FEELING, in the absence of Dawson, that I stood in the position of a guardian to his daughter, and was responsible for her welfare, my mind grew very uneasy about the consequences of her extravagant admiration for the painter; and, knowing that Don Sanchez, despite his phlegmatic humour, loved Moll very sincerely at heart, I took him aside one day, and asked him if he had observed nothing particular in Moll's behaviour of late.

"One would be blind," says he, "not to see that she is enamoured of Dario, if that's what you mean."

I admitted that my suspicions inclined that way, and, explaining my concern on her behalf, I asked him what he would do in my place.

"In my country," says he, "matters never would have been suffered to go so far, and Mistress Judith would have been shut up a prisoner in her room these past three weeks. But I doubt if our maidens are any the safer or better for such treatment, and I am quite sure that such treatment would be worse than useless for an English girl, and especially such an one as this. For, guard her how you might, she would assuredly find means to break her prison, and then no course is open to her but to throw herself in the arms of the man she loves, trusting to mere accident whether he abuses her devotion or not. You might as well strive to catch the wind and hold it as stay and stem the course of youthful passion."

"Aye, Señor," says I, "this may be all very true. But what should you do in my place?"

"Nothing," says he.

This was a piece of advice which set me scratching my head in dubitation.

"Beware," continues he, "how you suggest the thing you fear to one who needs but a hint to act. I have great faith in the natural modesty of women (and I do think no child more innocent than Mistress Judith), which, though it blind them to their danger, does, at the same time, safeguard them against secret and illicit courses of more fatal consequences. Let her discourse with him, openly, since it pleases her. In another fortnight or so Dario's work will be finished, he will go away, our young lady will shed secret tears and be downcast for a week. Then another swain will please her, and she'll smile again. That, as I take it, will be the natural order of events, unless," adds he, "that natural order is disturbed by some external influence."

Maugre this sage advice, my concern being unabated, I would step pretty frequently into the room where these young people were, as if to see how the work was going forward, and with such a quick step that had any interchange of amorous sentiments existed, I must at one time or another have discovered it. But I never detected any sign of this — no bashful silence, no sudden confusion, or covert interchange of glances. Sometimes they would be chatting lightly, at others both would be standing silent, she, maybe, holding a bunch of leaves with untiring steadfastness, for him to copy. But I observed that she was exceedingly jealous of his society, and no matter how glibly she was talking when I entered, or how indifferent the subject, she would quickly become silent, showing me very plainly by her manner that she would vastly prefer my room to my company.

Still, I was not displeased when I perceived this fresco drawing near to its completion.

"You are getting on apace," says I, very cheerfully one day. "I reckon you will soon have done."

"Yes," answers he, "in a week I shall have nought to do but to pack up my tools and go."

There was an accent of sorrow in his voice, despite himself, which did not escape me nor Moll neither, for I saw her cast her eyes upon his face, as if to read if there were sadness there. But she said never a word.

However, in the afternoon she comes to me, and says she:

"I am resolved I will have all the rooms in the house plastered, if Signor Dario will consent to paint them."

"All the rooms!" says I, in alarm. "Surely you have not counted the cost of what you propose."

"I suppose I have enough to keep my house in suitable condition."

"Without doubt, though I expect such work as Signor Dario's must command a high price."

"All I ask of you, then," says she, "is to bid my steward have five thousand pounds ready for my uses, and within a week, lest I should need it suddenly. Should he raise objections —"

"As assuredly he will," says I, who knew the crafty, subtle character of old Simon full well by this time. "A thousand objections, and not one you can pick a hole in."

"Then show him this and tell him I accept Mr. Goodman's offer unless he can find more profitable means of raising money."

With that she puts in my hand a letter she had that morning received from one Henry Goodman, a tenant, who having heard that she had disposed of a farm to his neighbour, now humbly prayed she would do him the same good turn by selling him the land he rented, and for which he was prepared to pay down in ready money the sum of five thousand pounds.

Armed with this letter, I sought Simon and delivered Moll's message. As I expected, the wily old man had good excuses ready for not complying with this request, showing me the pains he had taken to get the king's seal, his failures to move the king's officers, and the refusal of his goldsmith to furnish further supplies before the deed of succession was passed.

"These objections are all very just," says I, "so I see no way of pleasing our lady but by selling Mr. Goodman's farm, which she will have done at once if there be no alternative."

So I give him the letter, which he can scarce read for trembling with anguish.

"What," cries he, coming to the end, "I am to sell this land which I bought for nine hundred pounds and is now worth six thousand? I would rather my mistress had bid me have the last teeth torn from my head."

"We must have money," says I.

"Thee shalt have it in good time. Evans hath been paid, and thy debt shall be discharged; fear not."

"I spoke as representing our lady; for ourselves we are content to wait her better convenience." And I told him how his mistress would lay out her money in embellishing the Court with paintings, which put him to a new taking to think so much good money should be wasted in such vanities.

"But," says he, "this work must take time, and one pays for nothing ere 'tis done. By quarter day our rents will be coming in again —"

"No," says I, cutting him short, "the money must be found at once, or be assured that your lady will take the management of her affairs out of your hands."

This raised a fresh outcry and more lamentations, but in the end he promised to procure the money by collecting his rents in advance, if his mistress would refuse Mr. Goodman's offer and wait three weeks; and on Moll's behalf I agreed to these terms.

A few days after this, we were called into the dining-hall to see the finished ceiling, which truly deserved all the praise we could bestow upon it, and more. For now that the sky appeared through the opening, with a little pearly cloud creeping across it, the verdure and flowers falling over the marble coping, and the sunlight falling on one side and throwing t'other into shade, the illusion was complete, so that one could scarcely have been more astonished had a leaf fallen from the hanging flowers or a face looked over the balcony. In short, 'twas prodigious.

Nevertheless, the painter, looking up at his work with half-closed, critical eyes, seemed dissatisfied, and asking us if we found nothing lacking, we (not to appear behindhand in judgment) agreed that on one side there was a vacant place which might yet be adorned to advantage.

"Yes," says he, "I see what is wanted and will supply it. That," adds he, gently turning to Moll, "will give me still another day."

"Why, what charm can you add that is not there?" asks she.

"Something," says he, in a low voice, "which I must see whenever I do cast my eyes heavenwards."

And now Moll, big with her purpose, which she had hitherto withheld from Dario, begs him to come into her state room, and there she told how she would have this ceiling plastered over and painted, like her dining-hall, if he would undertake to do it.

Dario casts his eye round the room and over the ceiling, and then, shaking his head, says: "If I were in your place, I would alter nothing here."

"But I will have it altered," says she, nettled, because he did not leap at once at her offer, which was made rather to prolong their communion than to obtain a picture. "I detest these old-fashioned beams of wood."

"They are in keeping with the character of the room. I think," adds he, looking round him again with renewed admiration, "I think I have never seen a more perfect example of English art."

"What of that," cries she, "if it pleases me to have it otherwise?"

"Nothing," returns he, calmly. "You have as just a right to stand by your opinion as I by mine."

"And am I to understand that you will rather hold by your opinion than give me pleasure?"

"I pray you, do not press me to discourtesy," says he.

"Nay, but I would have a plain answer to my question," says she, haughtily.

"Then," says he, angering in his turn, "I must tell you that I would as soon chip an antique statue to suit the taste of a French modiste as disfigure the work of him who designed this room."

Now, whether Moll took this to be a reflection on her own figure, which had grown marvellous slim in the waist since she had her new stays from London, or not, I will not say; but certainly this response did exasperate her beyond all endurance (as we could see by her blanched cheek and flashing eye); so, dismissing him with a deep curtsey, she turns on her heel without another word.

This foolish business, which was not very creditable to our Moll's good sense (though I think she acted no worse than other maids in her condition,— for I have observed that young people do usually lose their heads at the same time that they lose their hearts), this foolish scene, I say, I would gladly omit from my history, but that it completely changed our destiny; for had these two parted with fair words, we should probably have seen no more of Dario, and Don Sanchez's prognostic had been realised. Such trifles as these do influence our career as greatly as more serious accidents, our lives being a fabric of events that hang together by the slenderest threads.

Unmoved from his design by Moll's displeasure, Dario replaced his scaffold before he left that day, and the next morning he came to put the last touch upon his work. Moll, being still in dudgeon, would not go near him, but sat brooding in a corner of her state room, ready, as I perceived, to fly out in passion at any one who gave her the occasion. Perceiving this, Don Sanchez prudently went forth for a walk after dinner; but I, seeing that some one must settle accounts with the painter for his work, stayed at home. And when I observed that he was collecting his materials to go, I went in to Moll.

"My dear," says I, "I believe Dario is preparing to leave us."

"My congratulations to him," says she, "for 'tis evident he is weary of being here."

"Nay, won't you come in and see his work now 'tis finished?"

"No; I have no desire to see it. If I have lost my taste for Italian art, 'tis through no fault of his."

"You will see him, surely, before he goes."

"No; I will not give him another opportunity to presume upon my kindness."

"Why, to be sure," says I, like a fool, "you have been a little over-familiar."

"Indeed," says she, firing up like a cracker. "Then I think 'twould have been kinder of you to give me a hint of it beforehand. However, 'tis a very good excuse for treating him otherwise now."

"Well, he must be paid for his work, at any rate."

"Assuredly. If you have not money enough, I will fetch it from my closet."

"I have it ready, and here is a purse for the purpose. The question is, how much to put in it. I should think such a perspective as that could not be handsomely paid under fifty guineas."

"Then you will give him a hundred, and say that I am exceedingly obliged to him."

I put this sum in the purse and went out into the hall where Dario was waiting, with his basket of brushes beside him. In a poor, bungling, stammering fashion, I delivered Moll's message, and made the best excuse I could for delivering it in her stead.

He waited a moment or two after I had spoken, and then, says he, in a low voice:

"Is that all?"

"Nay," says I, offering the purse, "we do beg you to take this as—"

He stopped me, pushing my hand aside.

"I have taken a purse from Don Sanchez," says he. "There was more in it than I needed—there are still some pieces left. But as I would not affront him by offering to return them, so I beg you will equally respect my feelings. I undertook the task in gratitude, and it hath been a work of love all through, well paid for by the happiness that I have found here."

He stood musing a little while, as if he were debating with himself whether he should seek to overcome Moll's resentment or not. Then, raising his head quickly, he says:

"'Tis best so, maybe. Farewell, sir" (giving me his hand). "Tell her," adds he, as we stand hand in hand at the door, "that I can never forget her kindness, and will ever pray for her happiness."

I found the door ajar and Moll pacing the room very white, when I returned. She checked me the moment I essayed to deliver Dario's message.

"You can save your breath," says she, passionately. "I've heard every word."

"More shame for you," says I, in a passion, casting my purse on the table. "'Tis infamous to treat an honest gentleman thus, and silly besides. Come, dear," altering my tone, "do let me run and fetch him back."

"You forget whom you are speaking to, Mr. Hopkins," cries she.

I saw 'twas impossible to move her whilst she was in this mood, for she had something of her father's obstinate, stubborn disposition, and did yet hope to bring Dario back to her feet, like a spaniel, by harsh treatment. But he came no more, though a palette he had overlooked could have given him the excuse, and for very vexation with Moll I was glad he did not.

He had not removed the scaffold, but when I went upon it to see what else he had put into his painting, the fading light only allowed me to make out a figure that seemed to be leaning over the balcony.

Moll would not go in there, though I warrant she was dying of curiosity; and soon after supper, which she could scarce force herself to touch, she went up to her own chamber, wishing us a very distant, formal good-night, and keeping her passionate, angry countenance.

But the next morning, ere I was dressed, she knocked at my door, and, opening it, I found her with swollen eyes and tears running down her cheeks.

"Come down," says she, betwixt her sobs, and catching my hand in hers. "Come down and see."

So we went downstairs together, — I wondering what now had happened, — and so into the dining-hall. And there I found the scaffold pushed aside, and the ceiling open to view. Then looking up, I perceived that the figure bending over the balcony bore Moll's own face, with a most sweet, compassionate expression in it as she looked down, such as I had observed when she bent over Dario, having brought him back to life. And this, thinks I, remembering his words, this is what he must ever see when he looks heavenwards.

CHAPTER XXI.

Of the strange things told us by the wise woman.

"TELL me I am wicked; tell me I'm a fool," says Moll, clinging to my arm.

But I had no feeling now but pity and forgiveness, and so could only try to comfort her, saying we would make amends to Dario when we saw him next.

"I will go to him," says she. "For nought in the world would I have him yield to such a heartless fool as I am. I know where he lodges."

"Well, when we have eaten—"

"Nay; we must go this moment. I cannot be at peace till I have asked him to forgive. Come with me, or I must go alone."

Yielding to her desire without further ado, I fetched my hat and cloak, and, she doing likewise, we sallied out forthwith. Taking the side path by which Dario came and went habitually, we reached a little wicket gate, opening from the path upon the highway; and here, seeing a man mending the road, we asked him where we should find Anne Fitch, as she was called, with whom the painter lodged. Pointing to a neat cottage that stood by the wayside, within a stone's throw, he told us the "wise woman" lived there. We crossed over and knocked at the door, and a voice within bidding us come in, we did so.

There was a very sweet, pleasant smell in the room from

the herbs that hung in little parcels from the beams, for this Anne Fitch was greatly skilled in the use of simples, and had no equal for curing fevers and the like in all the country round. (But, besides this, it was said she could look into the future and forecast events truer than any Egyptian.) There was a chair by the table, on which was an empty bowl and some broken bread; but the wise woman sat in the chimney corner, bending over the hearth, though the fire had burnt out, and not an ember glowed. And a strange little elf she looked, being very wizen and small, with one shoulder higher than the other, and a face full of pain.

When I told her our business, — for Moll was too greatly moved to speak, — the old woman pointed to the adjoining room.

"He is gone!" cries Moll, going to the open door, and peering within.

"Yes," answers Anne Fitch. "Alas!"

"When did he go?" asks Moll.

"An hour since," answers the other.

"Whither is he gone?"

"I am no witch."

"At least, you know which way he went."

"I have not stirred from here since I gave him his last meal."

Moll sank into the empty chair, and bowed her head in silence.

Anne Fitch, whose keen eyes had never strayed from Moll since she first entered the room, seeming as if they would penetrate to the most secret recesses of her heart, with that shrewd perception which is common to many whose bodily infirmity compels an extraordinary employment of their other faculties, rises from her settle in the chimney, and coming to the table, beside Moll, says:

"I am no witch, I say; yet I could tell you things would make you think I am."

"I want to know nothing further," answers she, dolefully, "save where he is."

"Would you not know whether you shall ever see him again, or not?"

"Oh! If you can tell me that!" cries Moll, quickly.

"I may." Then, turning to me, the wise woman asks to look at my hand, and on my demurring, she says she must know whether I am a friend or an enemy, ere she speaks before me. So, on that, I give my hand, and she examines it.

"You call yourself James Hopkins," says she.

"Why, every one within a mile knows that," says I.

"Aye," answers she, fixing her piercing eye on my face; "but every one knows not that some call you Kit."

This fairly staggered me for a moment.

"How do you answer that?" she asks, observing my confusion.

"Why," says I, recovering my presence of mind, "'tis most extraordinary, to be sure, that you should read this, for save one or two familiars, none know that my second name is Christopher."

"A fairly honest hand," says she, looking at my hand again. "Weak in some things, but a faithful friend. You may be trusted."

And so she drops my hand and takes up Moll's.

"'Tis strange," says she. "You call yourself Judith, yet here I see your name writ Moll."

Poor Moll, sick with a night of sorrow and terrified by the wise woman's divining powers, could make no answer; but soon Fitch, taking less heed of her tremble than of mine, regards her hand again.

"How were you called in Barbary?" asks she.

This question betraying a flaw in the wise woman's perception, gave Moll courage, and she answered readily enough that she was called "Lala Mollah"—which was true, "Lala" being the Moorish for lady, and "Mollah" the name her friends in Elche had called her as being more agreeable to their ear than the shorter English name.

"Mollah—Moll!" says Anne Fitch, as if communing with herself. "That may well be." Then, following a line in Moll's hand, she adds, "You will love but once, child."

"What is my sweetheart's name?" whispers Moll, the colour springing in her face.

"You have not heard it yet," replies the other, upon which Moll pulls her hand away impatiently. "But you have seen him," continues the wise woman, "and his is the third hand in which I have read another name."

"Tell me now if I shall see him again," cries Moll, eagerly—offering her hand again, and as quickly as she had before withdrawn it.

"That depends upon yourself," returns the other. "The line is a deep one. Would you give him all you have?"

Moll bends her head low in silence, to conceal her hot face.

"'Tis nothing to be ashamed of," says the old woman, in a strangely gentle tone. "'Tis better to love once than often; better to give your whole heart than part. Were I young and handsome and rich, I would give body and soul for such a man. For he is good and generous and exceeding kind. Look you, he hath lived here but a few weeks, and I feel for him, grieve for him, like a mother. Oh, I am no witch," adds she, wiping a tear from her cheek, " only a crooked old woman with the gift of seeing what is open to all who will read, and a heart that quickens still at a kind word or a gentle thought." (Moll's hand had closed upon hers at that first sight of her grief.) " For your names," continues she, recovering her composure, " I learnt from one of your maids who came hither for news of her sweetheart, that the sea captain who was with you did sometimes let them slip. I was paid to learn this."

" Not by him," says Moll.

" No ; by your steward Simon."

" *He* paid for that ! " says I, incredulous, knowing Simon's reluctance to spend money.

" Aye, and a good price, too. It seems you call heavily upon him for money, and do threaten to cut up your estate and sell the land he prizes as his life."

" That is quite true," says I.

" Moreover, he greatly fears that he will be cast from his office, when your title to it is made good. For that reason he would move heaven and earth to stay your succession by casting doubts upon your claim. And to this end he has by all the means at his command tried to provoke your cousin to contest your right."

" My cousin ! " cries Moll.

" Richard Godwin."

" My cousin Richard — why, where is he ? "

" Gone," says the old woman, pointing to the broken bread upon the table.

CHAPTER XXII.

How Moll and Mr. Godwin come together and declare their hearts' passion, and how I carry these tidings to Dawson.

"WHAT!" cries Moll, starting to her feet. "He whom I have treated thus is—" and here she checked herself, as if recoiling (and for the first time) from false pretence in a matter so near her heart.

"He is your cousin, Richard Godwin," says the wise woman. "Simon knew this from the first; for there were letters showing it in the pocket-book he found after the struggle in the park; but for his own ends he kept that knowledge secret, until it fitted his ends to speak. Why your cousin did not reveal himself to you may be more readily conceived by you than 'twas by me."

"Why, 'tis clear enough," says Moll. "Pressed by his necessities, he came hither to claim assistance of his kinsman; but finding he was dead and none here but me, his pride did shrink from begging of a mere maid that which he might with justice have demanded from a man. And then, for shame at being handled like a rogue—"

Surely there is something in the blood of a gentleman that tempers his spirit to a degree scarcely to be comprehended by men of meaner birth, thinks I.

"When did Simon urge him to dispute my rights?" asks Moll.

"On Sunday—in the wood out there. I knew by his

look he had some treacherous business in hand, and, matching my stealth with his, I found means to overhear him, creeping from thicket to thicket, as noiseless as a snake, to where they stood; for, be assured, I should not otherwise have learnt one word of this."

"How did *he* receive these hints at my ill doing?" asks Moll.

"Patiently, till the tale was told; then, taking your steward by the throat with sudden passion, he cries: 'Why should I not strangle you, rascal? 'Twould be a service to humanity. What have I done to deserve your love, or this lady your hate? Nothing. You would pit us one against the other merely to keep your hold upon these lands, and gratify your insensate love of possession. Go, get you gone, beast!' cries he, flinging him off; ''tis punishment enough for you to live and know you've failed. For, had you proved your case to my conviction, I'd not stir a hand against this lady, be she who she may. Nay,' adds he, with greater fury, 'I will not stay where my loyalty and better judgment may be affected by the contagion of a vile suspicion. Away while you may; my fingers itch to be revenged on you for sundering me from one who should have been my closest, dearest friend.'"

Moll claps her hands together with a cry of joy and pain mingled, even as the smile played upon her lips whilst tears filled her eyes.

"Sunday!" cries she, turning to me and dashing the tears that blinded her from her eyes; "Sunday, and it 'twas o' Monday he refused to stay. O, the brave heart!" Then, in impetuous haste, "He shall be found — we must overtake him."

"That may be done if you take horse," says Anne Fitch, "for he travels afoot."

"But which way shall we turn?"

"The way that any man would take, seeking to dispel a useless sorrow," answers the wise woman; "the way to London."

"God bless you!" cries Moll, clasping the withered old woman to her heaving breast and kissing her. Then the next moment she would be gone, bidding me get horses for our pursuit.

So, as quickly as I might, I procured a couple of nags, and we set out, leaving a message for Don Sanchez, who was not yet astir. And we should have gone empty, but that while the horses were a-preparing (and Moll, despite her mighty haste at this business too), I took the precaution to put some store of victuals in a saddle bag.

Reckoning that Mr. Godwin (as I must henceforth call him) had been set out two hours or thereabouts, I considered that we might overtake him in about three at an easy amble. But Moll was in no mood for ambling, and no sooner were we started than she put her nag to a gallop and kept up this reckless pace up hill and down dale, — I trailing behind and expecting every minute to be cast and get my neck broke, — until her horse was spent and would answer no more to the whip. Then I begged her for mercy's sake to take the hill we were coming to at a walk, and break her fast. "For," says I, "another such half-hour as the last on an empty stomach will do my business, and you will have another dead man to bring back to life, which will advance your journey nothing, and so more haste, less speed." Therewith I opened my saddle bag, and sharing its contents, we ate a rare good meal and very merry, and indeed it was a pleasure now to look at her as great as the pain had been to see her so unhappy a few hours before. For the exercise had brought a flood of rich colour into her face, and a lively hope sparkled in her eyes, and the sound of her voice was like any peal of marriage bells for gaiety. Yet now and then her tongue would falter, and she would strain a wistful glance along the road before us as fearing she did hope too much. However, coming to an inn, we made enquiry, and learnt that a man such as we described had surely passed the house barely an hour gone, and one adding that he carried a basket on his stick, we felt this must be our painter for certain.

Thence on again at another tear (as if we were flying from our reckoning) until, turning a bend of the road at the foot of a hill, she suddenly drew rein with a shrill cry. And coming up, I perceived close by our side Mr. Godwin, seated upon the bridge that crossed a stream, with his wallet beside him.

He sprang to his feet and caught in an instant the rein that had fallen from Moll's hand, for the commotion in her heart at seeing him so suddenly had stopped the current of her veins, and she was deadly pale.

"Take me, take me!" cries she, stretching forth her arms, with a faint voice. "Take me, or I must fall," and slipping from her saddle she sank into his open, ready arms.

"Help!" says Mr. Godwin, quickly, and in terror.

"Nay," says she; "I am better — 'tis nothing. But," adds she, smiling at him, "you may hold me yet a little longer."

The fervid look in his eyes, as he gazed down at her sweet

pale face, seemed to say: "Would I could hold you here for ever, sweetheart."

"Rest her here," says I, pointing to the little wall of the bridge, and he, complying (not too willingly), withdrew his arm from her waist, with a sigh.

And now the colour coming back to her cheek, Moll turns to him, and says:

"I thought you would have come again. And since one of us must ask to be forgiven, lo! here am I come to ask your pardon."

"Why, what is there to pardon, Madam?" says he.

"Only a girl's folly, which unforgiven must seem something worse."

"Your utmost folly," says he, "is to have been over-kind to a poor painter. And if that be an offence, 'tis my misfortune to be no more offended."

"Have I been over-kind?" says Moll, abashed, as having unwittingly passed the bounds of maiden modesty.

"As nature will be over-bounteous in one season, strewing so many flowers in our path that we do underprize them till they are lost, and all the world seems stricken with wintry desolation."

"Yet, if I have said or done anything unbecoming to my sex —"

"Nothing womanly is unbecoming to a woman," returns he. "And, praised be God, some still live who have not learned to conceal their nature under a mask of fashion. If this be due less to your natural free disposition than to an ignorance of our enlightened modish arts, then could I find it in my heart to rejoice that you have lived a captive in Barbary."

They had been looking into each other's eyes with the delight of reading there the love that filled their hearts, but now Moll bent her head as if she could no longer bear that searching regard, and unable to make response to his pretty speech, sat twining her fingers in her lap, silent, with pain and pleasure fluttering over her downcast face. And at this time I do think she was as near as may be on the point of confessing she had been no Barbary slave, rather than deceive the man who loved her, and profit by his faith in her, which had certainly undone us all; but in her passion, a woman considered the welfare of her father and best friends very lightly; nay, she will not value her own body and soul at two straws, but is ready to yield up everything for one dear smile.

A full minute Mr. Godwin sat gazing at Moll's pretty, blushing, half-hid face (as if for his last solace), and then, rising slowly from the little parapet, he says:

"Had I been more generous, I should have spared you this long morning ride. So you have something to forgive, and we may cry quits!" Then, stretching forth his hand, he adds, "Farewell."

"Stay," cries Moll, springing to her feet, as fearing to lose him suddenly again, "I have not eased myself of the burden that lay uppermost. Oh!" cries she, passionately, casting off all reserve, "I know all; who you are, and why you first came hither, and I am here to offer you the half of all I have."

"Half, sweet cousin?" answers he, taking her two hands in his.

"Aye; for if I had not come to claim it, all would have been yours by right. And 'tis no more than fair that, owing so much to Fortune, I should offer you the half."

"Suppose that half will not suffice me, dear?" says he.

"Why, then I'll give you all," answers she; "houses, gardens, everything."

"Then what will you do, coz?"

"Go hence, as you were going but just now," answers she, trembling.

"Why, that's as if you took the diamond from its setting, and left me nothing but the foil," says he. "Oh, I would order it another way: give me the gem, and let who will take what remains. Unless these little hands are mine to hold for ever, I will take nothing from them."

"They are thine, dear love," cries she, in a transport, flinging them about his neck, "and my heart as well."

At this conjuncture I thought it advisable to steal softly away to the bend of the road; for surely any one coming this way by accident, and finding them locked together thus in tender embrace on the king's highway, would have fallen to some gross conclusion, not understanding their circumstances, and so might have offended their delicacy by some rude jest. And I had not parted myself here a couple of minutes, ere I spied a team of four stout horses coming over the brow of the hill, drawing the stage waggon behind them which plies betwixt Sevenoaks and London. This prompting me to a happy notion, I returned to the happy, smiling pair, who were now seated again upon the bridge, hand in hand, and says I:

"My dear friends,— for so I think I may now count you, sir, as well as my Mistress Judith here,— the waggon is coming down the hill, by which I had intended to go to London this morning upon some pressing business. And so, Madam, if your cousin will take my horse and conduct you back to the Court, I will profit by this occasion and bid you farewell for the present."

This proposal was received with evident satisfaction on their part, for there was clearly no further thought of parting; only Moll, alarmed for the proprieties, did beg her lover to lift her on her horse instantly. Nevertheless, when she was in her saddle, they must linger yet, he to kiss her hands, and she to bend down and yield her cheek to his lips, though the sound of the coming waggon was close at hand.

Scarcely less delighted than they with this surprising strange turn of events, I left 'em there with bright, smiling faces, and journeyed on to London, and there taking a pair of oars at the Bridge to Greenwich, all eagerness to give these joyful tidings to my old friend, Jack Dawson. I found him in his workroom, before a lathe, and sprinkled from head to toe with chips, mighty proud of a bed-post he was a-turning. And it did my heart good to see him looking stout and hearty, profitably occupied in this business, instead of soaking in an alehouse (as I feared at one time he would) to dull his care; but he was ever a stout, brave fellow, who would rather fight than give in any day. A better man never lived, nor a more honest — circumstances permitting.

His joy at seeing me was past everything; but his first thought after our hearty greeting was of his daughter.

"My Moll," says he, "my dear girl; you han't brought her to add to my joy? She's not slinking behind a door to fright me with delight, hey?"

"No," says I; "but I've brought you great news of her."

"And good, I'll swear, Kit, for there's not a sad line in your face. Stay, comrade, wait till I've shook these chips off and we are seated in my parlour, for I do love to have a pipe of tobacco and a mug of ale beside me in times of pleasure. You can talk of indifferent things, though, for Lord! I do love to hear the sound of your voice again."

I told him how the ceiling of our dining-hall had been painted.

"Aye," says he. "I have heard of that; for my dear girl hath writ about that and nought else in her letters; and though I've no great fancy for such matters, yet I doubt not it is mighty fine by her long-winded praises of it. Come, Kit, let us in here and get to something fresher."

So we into his parlour, which was a neat, cheerful room, with a fine view of the river, and there being duly furnished with a mighty mug of ale and clean pipes, he bids me give him my news, and I tell him how Moll had fallen over head and ears in love with the painter, and he with her, and how that very morning they had come together and laid open their hearts' desire one to the other, with the result (as I believed) that they would be married as soon as they could get a parson to do their business.

"This is brave news indeed," cries he, "and easeth me beyond comprehension, for I could see clearly enough she was smitten with this painter, by her writing of nothing else; and seeing she could not get at his true name and condition, I felt some qualms as to how the matter might end. But do tell me, Kit, is he an honest, wholesome sort of man?"

"As honest as the day," says I, "and a nobler, handsomer man never breathed."

"God be praised for all things," says he, devoutly. "Tell me he's an Englishman, Kit — as Moll did seem to think he was, spite his foreign name — and my joy's complete."

"As true-born an Englishman as you are," says I.

"Lord love him for it!" cries he.

Then coming down to particulars, I related the events of the past few days pretty much as I have writ them here, showing in the end how Mr. Godwin would have gone away, unknown rather than profit by his claim as Sir Richard Godwin's kinsman, even though Moll should be no better than old Simon would have him believe, upon which he cries, "Lord love him for it, say I again! Let us drink to their health. Drink deep, Kit, for I've a fancy that no man shall put his lips to this mug after us."

So I drank heartily, and he, emptying the jug, flung it behind the chimney, with another fervent ejaculation of gratitude. Then a shade of sorrow falling on his face as he lay it in his hand, his elbow resting on the table:

"I'd give best half of the years I've got to live," says he, "to see 'em together, and grasp Mr. Godwin's hand in mine. But I'll not be tempted to it, for I perceive clearly enough by what you tell me that my wayward tongue and weakness have been undoing us all, and ruining my dear Moll's chance of happiness. But tell me, Kit" (straightening himself up), "how think you this marriage will touch our affairs?"

"Only to better them. For henceforth our prosperity is assured, which otherwise might have lacked security."

"Aye, to be sure, for now shall we be all in one family with these Godwins, and this cousin, profiting by the estate as much as Moll, will never begrudge her giving us a hundred or two now and then, for rendering him such good service."

"'Twill appease Moll's compunctions into the bargain," says I, heedlessly.

"What compunctions?"

"The word slipped me unintended," stammers I; "I mean nothing."

"But something your word must mean. Come, out with it, Kit."

"Well," says I, "since this fondness has possessed her, I have observed a greater compunction to telling of lies than she was wont to have."

"'Tis my fault," answers he, sadly. "She gets this leaning to honesty from me."

"This very morning," continues I, "she was, I truly believe, of two minds whether she should not confess to her sweetheart that she was not his cousin."

"For all the world my case!" cries he, slapping the table. "If I could only have five minutes in secret with the dear girl, I would give her a hint that should make her profit by my folly." And then he tells me how, in the heyday of courtship and the flush of confiding love, he did confess to his wife that he had carried gallantry somewhat too far with Sukey Taylor, and might have added a good half dozen other names beside hers but for her sudden outcry; and how, though she might very well have suspected other amours, she did never reproach him therewith, but was for ever to her dying day a-flinging Sukey Taylor in his teeth, etc.

"Lord, Kit!" cries he, in conclusion; "what would I give to save her from such torment! You know how obedient she is to my guiding, for I have ever studied to make her respect me; and no one in the world hath such empire over her. Could it not be contrived anyhow that we should meet for half an hour secretly?"

"Not secretly," says I. "But there is no reason why you should not visit her openly. Nay, it will create less surprise than if you stay away. For what could be more natural than your coming to the Court on your return from a voyage to see the lady you risked so much to save?"

"Now God bless you for a good, true friend!" cries he, clasping my hand. "I'll come, but to stay no great length. Not a drop will I touch that day, and a fool indeed I must be if I can't act my part without bungling for a few hours at a stretch, and I a-listening every night in the parlour of the 'Spotted Dog' to old seamen swearing and singing their songs. And I'll find an opportunity to give Moll a hint of my past folly, and so rescue her from a like pitfall. I'll abide by your advice, Kit, — which is the wisest I ever heard from your lips."

But I was not so sure of this, and, remembering the kind of obedience Moll had used to yield to her father's commands, my mind misgave me.

CHAPTER XXIII.

Don Sanchez proposes a very artful way to make Mr. Godwin a party to our knavery, etc.

I RETURNED to Hurst Court the following day in the forenoon, and there I found Mr. Godwin, with Moll clinging to his arm, in an upper room commanding a view of the northern slopes, discussing their future, and Moll told me with glee how this room was to be her husband's workroom, where he would paint pictures for the admiration of all the world, saying that he would not (nor would she have him) renounce his calling to lead the idle life of a country gentleman.

"If the world admire my pictures, the world shall pay to have them," says he, with a smile; then turning to her he adds very tenderly: "I will owe all my happiness to you, sweetheart; yet guard my independence in more material matters. No mercenary question shall ever cast suspicion on my love."

Seeing I was not wanted here, I left them to settle their prospectives, and sought Don Sanchez, whom I found reading in a room below, seated in a comfortable chair before a good fire of apple logs. To please me, he shut up his book and agreed to take a stroll in the park while dinner was a-dressing. So we clap on our hats and cloaks and set forth, talking of indifferent matters till we are come into a fair open glade (which sort of place the prudent Don did ever prefer to holes and corners for secret conference), and then he told me how Moll and Mr. Godwin had already decided they would be married in three weeks.

"Three weeks?" says I. "I would it were to be done in three days." To which desire the Don coincides with sundry grave nods, and then tells me how Moll would have herself cried in church, for all to know, and that nothing may be wanting to her husband's dignity.

"After all," says I, "three weeks is no such great matter. And now, Señor, do tell me what you think of all this."

"If you had had the ordering of your own destiny, you could not have contrived it better," answers he. "'Tis a most excellent game, and you cannot fail to win if" (here he pauses to blow his nose) "if the cards are played properly."

This somehow brought Dawson into my thoughts, and I told the Don of my visit to him, and how he did purpose to come down to see Moll; whereat the Don, stopping short, looked at me very curiously with his eyebrows raised, but saying nothing.

"'Tis no more than natural that a father should want to see what kind of man is to be his daughter's husband," says I, in excuse, "and if he *will* come, what are we to do?"

"I know what I should do in your place, Mr. Hopkins," says he, quietly.

"Pray, Señor, what is that?"

"Squeeze all the money you can out of old Simon before he comes," answers he. "And it wouldn't be amiss to make Mr. Godwin party to this business by letting him have a hundred or two for his present necessities at once."

Acting on this hint, when Moll left us after supper and we three men were seated before the fire, I asked Mr. Godwin if he would permit me to speak upon a matter which concerned his happiness no less than his cousin Judith's.

"Nay, sir," replies he, "I do pray you to be open with me, for otherwise I must consider myself unworthy of your friendship."

"Well, sir," says I, "my mind is somewhat concerned on account of what you said this morning; namely, that no pecuniary question shall ever be discussed betwixt you and your wife, and that you will owe nothing to her but happiness. This, together with your purpose of painting pictures to sell, means, I take it, that you will leave your wife absolute mistress of her present fortune."

"That is the case exactly, Mr. Hopkins," says he. "I am not indifferent to the world's esteem, and I would give no one reason to suspect that I had married my dear cousin to possess her fortune."

"Nevertheless, sir, you would not have it thought that she begrudged you an equal share of her possessions. Your position will necessitate a certain outlay. To maintain your wife's dignity and your own, you must dress well, mount a good horse, be liberal in hospitality, give largely to those in need, and so forth. With all due respect to your genius in painting, I can scarcely think that art will furnish you at once with supplies necessary to meet all these demands."

"All this is very true, Mr. Hopkins," says he, after a little reflection; "to tell the truth, I have lived so long in want that poverty has become my second nature, and so these matters have not entered into my calculations. Pray, sir, continue."

"Your wife, be she never so considerate, may not always

anticipate your needs; and hence at some future moment this question of supplies must arise — unless they are disposed of before your marriage."

"If that could be done, Mr. Hopkins," says he, hopefully.

"It may be done, sir, very easily. With your cousin's consent and yours, I, as her elected guardian, at this time will have a deed drawn up to be signed by you and her, settling one-half the estate upon you, and the other on your cousin. This will make you not her debtor, but her benefactor; for without this deed, all that is now hers becomes yours by legal right upon your marriage, and she could not justly give away a shilling without your permission. And thus you assure to her the same independence that you yourself would maintain."

"Very good," says Don Sanchez, in a sonorous voice of approval, as he lies back in his high chair, his eyes closed, and a cigarro in the corner of his mouth.

"I thank you with all my heart, Mr. Hopkins," says Mr. Godwin, warmly. "I entreat you have this deed drawn up — if it be my wife's wish."

"You may count with certainty on that," says I; "for if my arguments lacked power, I have but to say 'tis your desire, and 'twould be done though it took the last penny from her."

He made no reply to this, but bending forward he gazed into the fire, with a rapture in his face, pressing one hand within the other as if it were his sweetheart's.

"In the meantime," says I, "if you have necessity for a hundred or two in advance, you have but to give me your note of hand."

"Can you do me this service?" cries he, eagerly. "Can you let me have five hundred by to-morrow?"

"I believe I can supply you to the extent of six or seven."

"All that you can," says he; "for besides a pressing need that will take me to London to-morrow, I owe something to a friend here that I would fain discharge."

Don Sanchez waived his hand cavalierly, though I do believe the subtle Spaniard had hinted at this business as much for his own ends as for our assurance.

"I will have it ready against we meet in the morning," says I.

"You are so certain of her sanction?" he asks in delight, as if he could not too much assure himself of Moll's devotion.

"She has been guided by me in all matters relating to her estate, and will be in this, I am convinced. But here's another question, sir, which, while we are about business, might be discussed with advantage. My rule here is nearly at an end. Have you decided who shall govern the estate when I am gone?"

"Only that when I have authority that rascal Simon shall be turned from his office, neck and crop. He loves me as little as he loves his mistress, that he would set us by the ears for his own advantage."

"An honest man, nevertheless — in his peculiar way," observes the Don.

"Honest!" cries Mr. Godwin, hotly. "He honest who would have suffered Judith to die in Barbary! He shall go."

"Then you will take in your own hands the control of your joint estate?"

"I? Why, I know no more of such matters than the man in the moon."

"With all respect to your cousin's abilities, I cannot think her qualified for this office."

"Surely another steward can be found."

"Undoubtedly," says I. "But surely, sir, you'd not trust all to him without some supervision. Large sums of money must pass through his hands, and this must prove a great temptation to dishonest practices. 'Twould not be fair to any man."

"This is true," says he. "And yet from natural disinclination, ignorance, and other reasons, I would keep out of it." Then after some reflection he adds, "My cousin has told me how you have lost all your fortune in saving her, and that 'tis not yet possible to repay you. May I ask, sir, without offence, if you have any occupation for your time when you leave us?"

"I went to London when I left you to see what might be done; but a merchant without money is like a carpenter without tools."

"Then, sir, till your debt is discharged, or you can find some more pleasant and profitable engagement, would you not consent to govern these affairs? I do not ask you to stay here, though assuredly you will ever be a welcome guest; but if you would have one of the houses on the estate or come hither from time to time as it might fit your other purposes, and take this office as a matter of business, I should regard it as a most generous, friendly kindness on your part."

I promised him with some demur, and yet with the civility his offer demanded, to consider of this; and so our debate ended, and I went to bed, very well content with myself, for thus will vanity blind us to our faults.

CHAPTER XXIV.

I overcome Moll's honest compunctions, lay hold of three thousand pounds more, and do otherwise play the part of rascal to perfection.

I GOT together six hundred pounds (out of the sum left us after paying Don Sanchez his ten thousand), and delivered 'em to Mr. Godwin against his note of hand, telling him at the same time that, having slept upon his proposal, I was resolved to be his steward for three months, with freedom on both sides to alter our position, according to our convenience, at the end of that time, and would serve him and his lady to the best of my power. Thanking me very heartily for my friendly service to him (though, God knows, with little reason), he presently left us. And Moll, coming back from taking tender leave of him at her gates, appeared very downcast and pensive. However, after moping an hour in her chamber, she comes to me in her hood, and begs I will take her a walk to dispel her vapours. So we out across the common, it being a fine, brisk, dry morning and the ground hard with a frost. Here, being secure from observation, I showed her how I had settled matters with Mr. Godwin, dividing the estate in such a manner as would enable her to draw what funds she pleased, without let, hindrance, or any inconvenient question.

At this she draws a deep sigh, fixing her eyes sadly enough on the perspective, as if she were thinking rather of her absent lover than the business in hand. Somewhat nettled to find she prized my efforts on her behalf so lightly, I proceeded to show her the advantages of this arrangement, adding that, to make her property the surer, I had consented to manage both her affairs and Mr. Godwin's when they were married.

"And so," says I, in conclusion, "you may have what money you want, and dispose of it as you will, and I'll answer for it Mr. Godwin shall never be a penny the wiser."

"Do what you find is necessary," says she, with passion. "But for mercy's sake say no more on this matter to me. For all these hints do stab my heart like sharp knives."

Not reading rightly the cause of her petulance, I was at first disposed to resent it; but, reflecting that a maiden is no more responsible for her tongue than a donkey for his heels in this season of life (but both must be for ever a-flying out at some one when parted from the object of their affections), I held my peace; and so we walked on in sullen silence for a space; then, turning suddenly upon me, she cries in a trembling voice:

"Won't you say something to me? Can't you see that I am unhappy?"

And now, seeing her eyes full of tears, her lips quivering, and her face drawn with pain, my heart melted in a moment; so, taking her arm under mine and pressing it to my side, I bade her be of good cheer, for her lover would return in a day or two at the outside.

"No, not of him,—not of him," she entreats. "Talk to me of indifferent things."

So, thinking to turn her thoughts to another furrow, I told her how I had been to visit her father at Greenwich.

"My father," says she, stopping short. "Oh, what a heartless, selfish creature am I! I have not thought of him in my happiness. Nay, had he been dead I could not have forgot him more. You saw him — is he well?"

"As hearty as you could wish, and full of love for you, and rejoiced beyond measure to know you are to marry a brave, honest gentleman." Then I told how we had drunk to their health, and how her father had smashed his mug for a fancy. And this bringing a smile to her cheek, I went on to tell how he craved to see Mr. Godwin and grip his hand.

"Oh, if he could see what a noble, handsome man my Richard is!" cries she. "I do think my heart would ache for pride."

"Why, so it shall," says I, "for your father does intend to come hither before long."

"He is coming to see my dear husband!" says she, her face aglow with joy.

"Aye, but he does promise to be most circumspect, and appear as if, returning from a voyage, he had come but to see how you fare, and will stay no longer than is reasonably civil."

"Only that," says she, her countenance falling again, "we are to hide our love, pretend indifference, behave towards this dear father as if he were nought to me but a friend."

"My dear," says I, "'tis no new part you have to play."

"I know it," she answers hotly, "but that makes it only the worse."

"Well, what would you?"

"Anything" (with passion). "I would do anything but

cheat and cozen the man I love." Then, after some moments' silence o' both sides, "Oh, if I were really Judith Godwin!"

"If you were she, you'd be in Barbary now, and have neither father nor lover; is that what you want?" says I, with some impatience.

"Bear with me," says she, with a humility as strange in her as these new-born scruples of conscience.

"You may be sure of this, my dear," says I, in a gentler tone, "if you were anything but what you are, Mr. Godwin would not marry you."

"Why, then, not tell him what I am?" asks she, boldly.

"That means that you would be to-morrow what you're not to-day."

"If he told me he had done wrong, I could forgive him, and love him none the less."

"Your conditions are not the same. He is a gentleman by birth, you but a player's daughter. Come, child, be reasonable. Ponder this matter but a moment justly, and you shall see that you have all to lose and nought to gain by yielding to this idle fancy. Is he lacking in affection, that you would seek to stimulate his love by this hazardous experiment?"

"Oh, no, no, no!" cries she.

"Would he be happier knowing all?" (She shakes her head.) "Happier if you force him to give you up and seek another wife?" (She starts as if flicked with a whip.) "Would *you* be happier stripped of your possessions, cast out of your house, and forced to fly from justice with your father?" (She looks at me in pale terror.) "Why, then, there's nothing to be won, and what's to lose? the love of a noble, honest gentleman, the joy of raising him from penury."

"Oh, say no more," cries she, in passion. "I know not what madness possessed me to overlook such consequences. I kiss you for bringing me to my senses" (with that she catches up my hand and presses her lips to it again and again). "Look in my face," cries she, "and if you find a lurking vestige of irresolution there, I'll tear it out."

Indeed, I could see nothing but set determination in her countenance,— a most hard expression of fixed resolve, that seemed to age her by ten years, astonishing me not less than those other phases in her rapidly developing character.

"Now," says she, quickly, and with not a note of her repining tone, "what was that you spoke of lately,— you are to be our steward?"

"Yes," says I, "for Mr. Godwin has declared most firmly that the moment he has authority he will cast Simon out for his disloyalty."

"I will not leave that ungrateful duty to him," says she. "Take me to this wretch at once, and choose the shortest path."

I led her back across the common, and coming to Simon's lodge, she herself knocked loudly at the door.

Seeing who it was through his little grating, Simon quickly opens the door, and with fawning humility entreats her to step into his poor room, and there he stands, cringing and mopping his eyes, in dreadful apprehension, as having doubtless gathered from some about the house how matters stood betwixt Moll and Mr. Godwin.

"Where are your keys?" demands Moll, in a very hard, merciless voice.

Perceiving how the land lay, and finding himself thus beset, old Simon falls to his usual artifices, turning this way and that, like a rat in a pit, to find some hole for escape. First he feigns to misunderstand, then, clapping his hands in his pockets, he knows not where he can have laid them; after that fancies he must have given them to his man Peter, who is gone out of an errand, etc.; until Moll, losing patience, cut him short by declaring the loss of the keys unimportant, as doubtless a locksmith could be found to open his boxes and drawers without 'em.

"My chief requirement is," adds she, "that you leave this house forthwith, and return no more."

Upon this, finding further evasion impossible, the old man turns to bay, and asks upon what grounds she would dismiss him without writ or warrant.

"'Tis sufficient," returns she, "that this house is mine, and that I will not have you a day longer for my tenant or my servant. If you dispute my claim,—as I am told you do,—you may take what lawful means you please to dispossess me of my estate, and at the same time redress what wrong is done you."

Seeing his secret treachery discovered, Simon falls now to his whining arts, telling once more of his constant toil to enrich her, his thrift and self-denial; nay, he even carries it so far as to show that he did but incite Mr. Godwin to dispute her title to the estate, that thereby her claim should be justified before the law to the obtaining of her succession without further delay, and at the expense of her cousin, which did surpass anything I had ever heard of for artfulness. But this only incensed Moll the more.

"What!" cries she, "you would make bad blood between

two cousins, to the ruin and disgrace of one, merely to save the expense of some beggarly fees! I'll hear no more. Go at once, or I will send for my servants to carry you out by force."

He stood some moments in deliberation, and then he says, with a certain dignity unusual to him, "I will go." Then he casts his eye slowly round the room, with a lingering regard for his piles of documents and precious boxes of title deeds, as if he were bidding a last farewell to all that was dear to him on earth, and grotesque as his appearance might be, there was yet something pathetic in it. But even at this moment his ruling passion prevailed.

"There is no need," says he, "to burst these goodly locks by force. I do bethink me the keys are here" (opening a drawer, and laying them upon the table). Then dropping his head, he goes slowly to the door, but there he turns, lifting his head and fixing his rheumy eyes on Moll. "I will take nothing from this house, not even the chattels that belong to me, bought from the mean wage I have allowed myself. So shalt thou judge of my honesty. They shall stand here till I return, for that I shall return I am as fully persuaded as that a just God doth dispose of his creatures. Thee hast might on thy side, woman, but whether thee hast right as well, shall yet be proven — not by the laws of man, which are an invention of the devil to fatten rogues upon the substance of fools, but by the law of Heaven, to which I do appeal with all my soul" (lifting high his shaking hands). "Morning and night I will pray that God shall smite with heavy hand which of us two hath most wronged the other. Offer the same prayer if thee darest."

P

I do confess that this parting shot went home to my conscience, and troubled my mind considerably; for feeling that he was in the right of it as regarded our relative honesty, I was constrained to think that his prophecy might come true also to our shame and undoing. But Moll was afflicted with no such qualms, her spirit being very combative and high, and her conscience (such as it was) being hardened by our late discussion to resist sharper slaps than this. Nay, maintaining that Simon must be dishonest by the proof we had of his hypocrisy and double dealing, she would have me enter upon my office at once by sending letters to all her tenants, warning them to pay no rent to any one lately in her service, but only to me; and these letters (which kept my pen going all that afternoon) she signed with the name of Judith Godwin, which seemed to me a very bold, dangerous piece of business; but she would have it so, and did her signature with a strong hand and a flourish of loops beneath like any queen.

Nor was this all; for the next morning she would have me go to that Mr. Goodman, who had offered to buy her farm for ready money, and get what I could from him, seeing that she must furnish herself with fresh gowns and make other outlay for her coming marriage. So to him I go, and after much haggling (having learnt from Simon that the land was worth more than he offered for it), I brought him to give six thousand pounds instead of five, and this was clearly better business on his side than on mine at that, for that the bargain might not slip from his hands he would have me take three thousand pounds down as a handsell, leaving the rest to be paid when the deed of transference was drawn up.

And now as I jogged home with all this gold chinking in

my pockets, I did feel that I had thrust my head fairly into a halter, and no chance left of drawing it out. Look at it how I might, this business wore a most curst aspect, to be sure; nor could I regard myself as anything but a thorough-paced rogue.

"For," thinks I, "if old Simon's prayer be answered, what will become of this poor Mr. Goodman? His title deeds will be wrested from him, for they are but stolen goods he is paying for, and thus an innocent, honest man will be utterly ruined. And for doing this villany I may count myself lucky if my heels save my neck."

With this weight on my mind, I resolved to be very watchful and careful of my safety, and before I fell asleep that night I had devised a dozen schemes for making good my escape as soon as I perceived danger; nevertheless, I could dream of nothing but prisons, scourgings, etc., and in every vision I perceived old Simon in his leather skull-cap sitting on the top of Tyburn tree, with his handkercher a-hanging down ready to strangle me.

CHAPTER XXV.

A table of various accidents.

As your guide, showing you an exhibition of paintings, will linger over the first room, and then pass the second in hurried review to come the quicker to a third of greater interest, so I, having dwelt, may be, at undue length upon some secondary passages in this history, must economise my space by touching lightly on the events that came immediately before Moll's marriage, and so get to those more moving accidents which followed. Here, therefore, will I transcribe certain notes (forming a brief chronicle) from that secret journal which, for the clearer understanding of my position, I began to keep the day I took possession of Simon's lodge and entered upon my new office.

December 8. Very busy all this forenoon setting my new house in order, conveying, with the help of the gardener, all those domestic and personal goods that belong to Simon into the attick; but Lord! so few these things, and they so patched and worn, that altogether they are not worth ten shillings of anybody's money. I find the house wondrous neat and clean in every part, but so comfortless and prison-like, that I look forward with little relish to living here when the time comes for me to leave the Court. After this to examining books, papers, etc., and the more closely I look into these, the more assured I am that never was any servant more scrupulous, exact, and honest in his master's service than this old steward, which puts me to the hope that I may be only half as faithful to my trust as he, but I do fear I shall not.

Conversing privily with Don Sanchez after dinner, he gave me his opinion that we had done a very unwise thing in turning out old Simon, showing how by a little skill I might have persuaded Moll to leave this business to Mr. Godwin as the proper ruler of her estate; how by such delay Mr. Godwin's resentment would have abated and he willing to listen to good argument in the steward's favour; how then we should have made Simon more eager than ever to serve us in order to condone his late offence, and how by abusing our opportunities we had changed this useful servant to a dangerous enemy whose sole endeavour must be to undo us and recover his former position, etc. . . . " Why, what have we to fear of this miserable old man?" says I. "Unless he fetch Mrs. Godwin from Barbary, he cannot disprove Moll's right to the estate, and what else can he do?"

" There's the mischief of it," answers he. " 'Tis because you know not how he may attack you that you have no means of defending yourself. 'Tis ever the unseen trifle in our path which trips us up." And dismissing this part of the subject with a hunch of his shoulders, he advises me seriously to sell as many more farms as I may for ready money, and keep it in some secret convenient corner where I may lay hands on it at a moment's warning.

This discourse coming atop of a night's ill rest, depressed my mind to such a degree that I could take no interest in my work, but sat there in my naked room with my accounts before me, and no spirit to cast 'em up. Nor was I much happier when I gave up work and returned to the Court. For, besides having to wait an hour later than usual for dinner, Moll's treatment of me was none of the best,—she being particularly perverse and contrary, for having dressed herself in her best in expectation of her lover's return, and he not coming when at last she permitted supper to be dished. We were scarcely seated, however, when she springs up with a cry of joy and runs from the room, crying she hears her Richard's step, which was indeed true, though we had heard nothing more pleasant than the rattle of our plates. Presently they come in, all radiant with happiness, hand in hand, and thenceforth nought but sweetness and mirth on the part of Mistress Moll, who before had been all frown and pout. At supper Mr. Godwin tells us how his sweetheart hath certainly dispelled the clouds that have hung so long over him, he having heard in London that Sir Peter Lely, on seeing one of his pieces, desires to see him at Hatfield (where he is painting) on good business, and to Hatfield he will go to discharge this matter before his marriage; which joyeth Moll less than me, I being pleased to see he is still of the same, stout disposition to live an active life. In the evening he gives Moll a very beautiful ring for a troth token, which transports her with joy, so that she cannot enough caress her lover or this toy, but falls first to kissing one and then t'other in a rapture. In return, she gives him a ring from her finger. " 'Tis too small for my finger, love," says he; "but I will wear it against my heart as long as it beats." After that he finds another case and puts it in Moll's hand, and she, opening it, fetches her breath quickly and can say nothing for amazement; then, turning it in the light, she regards it with winking eyes, as if dazzled by some fierce brilliancy. And so closing the case as if it were too much for her, she lays her face upon Mr. Godwin's breast, he having his arm about her, murmuring some inarticulate words of passionate love. Recovering her energies presently, she starts up, and putting the case in her lover's hand, she bids him put on his gift, therewith pulling down her kerchief to expose her beautiful bare neck, whereupon he draws from the box a diamond collar and clasps it about her throat with a pretty speech. And truly this was a gift worthy of a princess, the most beautiful bauble I have ever seen, and must have cost him all he had of me to the last shilling.

December 10. Finding amongst Simon's quittances a bill for law expenses of one John Pearson, attorney, at Maidstone, I concluded this must be the most trustworthy man of his kind in the country; and so set forth early this morning to seek him,—a tedious, long journey, and the roads exceedingly foul. By good luck I found Mr. Pearson at home,—a very civil, shrewd man, as I think. Having laid my business before him, he tells me there will be no difficulty in dividing the estate according to the wish of Mr. Godwin and Moll, which may be done by a simple deed of agreement; and this he promises to draw up, and send to us for signature in a couple of days. But to get the seal to Moll's succession will not be such an easy matter, and, unless we are willing to give seven or eight hundred pounds in fees, we may be kept waiting a year, with the chance of being put to greater expense to prove our right; for he tells me the court and all about it are so corrupt that no minister is valued if he do not, by straight or crooked ways, draw money into the treasury, and that they will rather impede than aid the course of justice if it be to the king's interest, and that none will stir a hand to the advantage of any one but the king, unless it be secretly to his own, etc. And, though he will say nothing against Simon, save (by way of hint) that all men must be counted honest till they are proved guilty, yet he do apprehend he will do all in his power to obstruct the granting of this seal, which it is only reasonable to suppose he will. So, to close this discussion, I agree he shall spend as much as one thousand pounds in bribery, and he thinks we may certainly look to have it in a month at that price. Home late, and very sore.

December 11. Much astonished this morning on going to my house to find all changed within as if by inchantment — fine hangings to my windows, handsome furniture in every room, all arranged in due order (with a pair of pictures in my parlour), the linen press stocked with all that is needful and more, and even the cellar well garnished with wines, etc. And truly thus embellished my house looks no longer like a prison, but as cheerful and pleasant a dwelling-place as the heart of man could desire (in moderation), and better than any I have yet dreamt of possessing. And 'twas easy to guess whose hands had worked this transformation, even had I not recognised certain pieces of furniture as coming from the Court, for 'twas of a piece with Moll's loving and playful spirit to prepare this surprise for me while I was gone yesterday to Maidstone. I am resolved I will sleep here henceforth, — there being two bedrooms all properly furnished, — as being more in keeping with my new position.

December 13. This day a little before dinner time came Dawson to the Court, quite sober and looking as like a rough honest seaman as anything could be, but evidently with his best shore-going manners on. And when Moll very graciously offers him her hand, he whips out a red handkercher and lays it over her hand before kissing it, which was a piece of ceremony he must have observed at Greenwich, as also many odd phrases and sea expressions with which he garnished his conversation.

"Captain Evans," says Moll, taking her lover's hand, "this is Mr. Godwin, my cousin, and soon to be my husband."

Mr. Godwin holds forth his hand, but ere he would take it, Dawson looks him full in the face a good minute; then, taking it in his great grimy hand, and grasping it firmly, "Master," says Jack, "I see thou art an honest man, and none lives who hath ever sold me tar for pitch, be he never so double-faced, and so I wish you joy of your sweet wife. As for you, Mistress" (turning to Moll) "who have ever been kind to me beyond my deserts, I do wish you all the happiness in the world, and I count all my hardships well paid in bringing you safely to this anchorage. For sure I would sooner you were still Lala Mollah and a slave in Barbary than the Queen of Chiney and ill-mated; and so Lord love the both of you!"

After staying a couple of hours with us, he was for going (but not before he had given us the instructive history of the torment he had endured, by telling his wife, in an unguarded moment, of his gallantries with Sukey Taylor), nor would he be persuaded to sleep at the Court and leave next day, maintaining that whilst he had never a penny in the world he could very honestly accept Moll's hospitality, but that now being well-to-do, thanks to her bounty, he blessed Heaven he had sufficient good breeding, and valued himself well enough not to take advantage of her beneficence. However, hearing I had a house of my own, and could offer him a bed, he willingly agreed to be my guest for the night, regarding me as one of his own quality. We stayed to sup at the Court, where he entertained us with a lengthy account of his late voyage, and how being taken in a tempest, his masts had all been swept by the board, and his craft so damaged that 'twas as much as she would hold together till he brought her into Falmouth, where she must lie a-repairing a good two months ere he could again venture to sea in her. And this story he told with such an abundance of detail and so many nautical particulars, that no one in the world could have dreamt he was lying.

He explained to me later on that he had refused to lie at the Court, for fear a glass or two after supper might lead his tongue astray, telling me that he had touched nothing but penny ale all his long journey from London, for fear of losing his head; and on my asking why he had fabricated that long history of shipwreck he vowed I had put him to it by saying I had a house of my own where he could lie; "For," says he, "my ship being laid up will furnish me with a very good excuse for coming to spend a day or two with you now and then. So may I get another glimpse of my own dear Moll, and see her in the fulness of her joy."

He could not sufficiently cry up the excellence of Mr. Godwin, his noble bearing, his frank, honest countenance, his tenderness for Moll, etc., and he did truly shed tears of gratitude to think that now, whatever befell him, her welfare and happiness were assured; but this was when he had emptied his bottle and had got to that stage of emotion which usually preceded boisterous hilarity when he was in his cups.

And whilst I am speaking of bottles, it will not be amiss to note here, for my future warning, a grave imprudence of mine, which I discovered on leaving the room to seek more wine. On the flame of my candle blowing aside, I perceived that I had left my door unfastened, so that it now stood ajar. And, truly, this was as culpable a piece of oversight as I could well have committed; for here, had an enemy, or even an idle busybody, been passing, he might very well have entered the little passage and overheard that which had been our undoing to have made known.

CHAPTER XXVI.

How Moll Dawson was married to Mr. Richard Godwin; brief account of attendant circumstances.

December 14. Dawson left us this morning. In parting, Mr. Godwin graciously begged him to come to his wedding feast on Christmas day,— they having fixed upon Christmas eve to be married,— and Dawson promised he would; but he did assure me afterwards, as we were walking along the road to meet the stage waggon, that he would certainly feign some reason for not coming. "For," says he, "I am not so foolhardy as to jeopardise my Moll's happiness for the pleasure this feast would give me. Nay, Kit, I do think 'twould break my heart indeed, if anything of my doing should mar my Moll's happiness." And I was very well pleased to find him in this humour, promising him that we would make amends for his abstinence on this occasion by cracking many a bottle to Moll's joy when we could come together again secretly at my house. In the afternoon Mr. Pearson's clerk brought the deed of agreement for the settlement of the estate upon Moll and Mr. Godwin, which they signed, and so that is finished as we would have it. This clerk tells me his master hath already gone to London about getting the seal. So all things look mighty prosperous.

December 17. Fearing to displease Sir Peter Lely by longer delay, Mr. Godwin set out for Hatfield Tuesday, we — that is, Moll, Don Sanchez, and I — going with him as far as the borough, where Moll had a thousand things to buy against her wedding. And here we found great activity of commerce, and many shops filled with excellent good goods,— more than ever there were before the great fire drove out so many tradesmen from the city. Here Moll spends her money royally, buying whatever catches her eye that is rich and beautiful, not only for her own personal adornment, but for the embellishment of her house (as hangings, damasks, toys, etc.), yet always with a consideration of Mr. Godwin's taste, so that I think she would not buy a pair of stockings but she must ask herself whether he would admire 'em. And the more she had, the more eager she grew to have, buying by candle-light, which was an imprudence, and making no sort of bargain, but giving all the shopkeepers asked for their wares, which, to be sure, was another piece of recklessness. This business seemed to me the most wearisome in the world, but it served only to increase her energies, and she would not be persuaded to desist until, the shops closing, she could lay out no more money that night. Supped very well (but mighty late) at the Tabard inn, where we lay all night. And the next morning, Moll's fever still unabated, we set out again a-shopping, and no rest until we caught the stage (and that by a miracle) at four; and so home, dead beat.

December 18. Moll mad all day because the carrier hath brought but half her purchases, and they not what she wanted. By the evening waggon come three seamstresses she engaged yesterday morning, and they are to stay in the house till all is finished; but as yet nothing for them to do, which is less grievous to them than to poor Moll, who, I believe, would set 'em working all night for fear she shall not be fitted against her wedding.

December 19. Thank God, the carrier brought all our packages this morning, and they being all undone and laid out, there is no sitting down anywhere with comfort, but all confusion, and no regularity anywhere, so I was content to get my meals in the kitchen the best I could. And here I do perceive the wisdom of Don Sanchez, who did not return with us from London, and does intend (he told me) to stay there till the wedding eve.

December 20. Moll, bit by a new maggot, tells me this morning she will have a great feast on Christmas day, and bids me order matters accordingly. She will have a whole ox roasted before the house by midday, and barrels of strong ale set up, that there may be meat and drink for all who choose to take it; and at four she will have a supper of geese, turkeys, and plum puddings for all her tenants, their wives and sweethearts, with fiddles afterwards for dancing, etc. Lord knows how we shall come out of this madness; but I have got the innkeeper (a busy, capable man) to help me, and he does assure me all will go well enough, and I pray he be right.

December 21. Sick with fears that all must end ill. For the place is a very Babel for tradesmen and workpeople bringing in goods, and knowing not where to set them, servants hurrying this way and that, one charged with a dozen geese, another with silk petticoats, jostling each other, laughing, quarrelling, and no sort of progress, as it seems, anywhere, but all tumult and disorder.

December 22. Could not sleep a wink all last night for casting up accounts of all this feasting and finery will cost us, and finding it must eat up all that money we had of poor Mr. Goodman, and make a deep hole in our quarter's rents besides, I fell a speculating whether our tenants would pay me with the same punctuality they have used to pay old Simon, with grievous fears to the contrary. For, assuredly, Simon hath not been idle these past days, and will do us an ill turn if he can, by throwing doubts before these same tenants whether they should pay or not before Moll's succession is made sure. And I have good reason to fear they will not, for I observed yesterday when I called upon Farmer Giles to invite him to our feast, he seemed very jerky and ill at ease, which perplexed me greatly, until, on quitting, I perceived through a door that stood ajar old Simon seated in a side room. And 'tis but natural that if they find prudent excuse for withholding their rents they will keep their money in pocket, which will pinch us smartly when our bills come to be paid. Yet I conceived that this feast would incline our tenants to regard us kindly; but, on the other hand, thinks I, supposing they regard this as a snare, and do avoid us altogether! Then shall we be nipped another way; for, having no one to eat our feast but a few idle rogues, who would get beef and ale for nothing, we shall but lay ourselves open to mockery, and get further into discredit. Thus, betwixt one fear and another, I lay like a toad under a harrow, all night, in a mortal sweat and perturbation of spirit.

Nor has this day done much to allay my apprehension. For at the Court all is still at sixes and sevens, none of a very cheerful spirit, but all mighty anxious, save Moll, who throughout has kept a high, bold spirit. And she does declare they will work all night, but everything shall be in its place before her lover comes to-morrow. And, truly, I pray they may, but do think they will not. For such a mighty business as this should have been begun a full month back. But she will not endure me in the house (though God knows I am as willing as any to help), saying that I do hinder all, and damp their spirit for work with my gloomy countenance, which is no more than the truth, I fear. The sky very overcast, with wind in the south and the air very muggy, mild, and close, so that I do apprehend our geese will be all stinking before they are eat. And if it pour of rain on Christmas day how will the ox be roast, and what sort of company can we expect? This puts me to another taking for dread of a new fiasco.

December 23. Going to the Court about midday, I was dumbfounded to find no sign of the disorder that prevailed there yesterday, but all swept and garnished, and Moll in a brave new gown seated at her fireside, reading a book with the utmost tranquillity,— though I suspect she did assume something in this to increase my astonishment. She was largely diverted by my amazement, and made very light of her achievement; but she admitted that all had worked till daybreak, and she had slept but two hours since. Nevertheless, no one could have looked fresher and brighter than she, so healthy and vigorous are her natural parts. About one comes Mr. Godwin to cap her happiness and give fresh glory to her beauty. And sure a handsomer or better mated couple never was, Mr. Godwin's shapely figure being now set off to advantage by a very noble clothing, as becoming his condition. With him came also by the morning stage Don Sanchez, mighty fine in a new head, of the latest mode, and a figured silk coat and waistcoat. And seeing the brave show they made at table, I was much humbled to think I had gone to no expense in this particular. But I was yet more mortified when Don Sanchez presents Moll with a handsome set of jewels for a wedding gift, to see that I had nothing in the world to offer her, having as yet taken not a penny of her money, save for the use of others and my bare necessities. Moll, however, was too full of happiness to note this omission on my part; she could think of no one now but her dear husband, and I counted for nothing.

However, this little chagrin was no more than a little cloud on a summer's day, which harms no one and is quickly dispelled by generous heat; and the tender affection of these two for each other did impart a glow of happiness to my heart. 'Tis strange to think how all things to-night look bright and hopeful, which yesterday were gloomy and awesome. Even the weather hath changed to keep in harmony with our condition. A fresh wind sprang up from the north this morning, and to-night every star shines out sharp and clear through the frosty air, promising well for to-morrow and our Christmas feast. And smelling of the geese, I do now find them all as sweet as nuts, which contents me mightily, and so I shall go to bed this night blessing God for all things.

December 24. Now this blessed day hath ended, and Moll is sure and safely bound to Mr. Godwin in wedlock, thanks to Providence. Woke at daybreak and joyed to find all white without and covered with rime, sparkling like diamonds as the sun rose red and jolly above the firs; and so I thought our dear Moll's life must sparkle as she looked out on this, which is like to be the brightest, happiest day of her life. Dressed in my best with great care, and put on the favour of white ribbons given me by Moll's woman last night, and so very well pleased with my looks, to the Court, where Moll is still a-dressing, but Mr. Godwin and Don Sanchez, nobly arrayed, conversing before the fire. And here a great bowpot on the table (which Mr. Godwin had made to come from London this morning) of the most wondrous flowers I have ever seen at this time of the year, so that I could not believe them real at first, but they are indeed living; and Mr. Godwin tells me they are raised in houses of glass very artificially heated. Presently comes in Moll with her maids, she looking like any pearl, in a shining gown of white satin decked with rich lace, the collar of diamonds glittering about her white throat, her face suffused with happy blushes and past everything for sprightly beauty. Mr. Godwin offers his bowpot and takes her into his arms, and there for a moment she lay with closed eyes and a pallor spreading over her cheek as if this joy were more than her heart could bear; but recovering quickly, she was again all lively smiles and radiance.

Then comes a letter, brought by the night carrier, from her father (a most dirty, ill-written scrawl signed Robert Evans with his mark), praying he may be excused, as his masts are to be stepped o' Wednesday, and he must take the occasion of a ketch leaving Dartford for Falmouth this day, and at the same time begging her acceptance of a canister of China tea (which is, I learn, become a fashionable dish in London) as a marriage offering. Soon after this a maid runs in to say the church bells are a-ringing; so out we go into the crisp, fresh air, with not a damp place to soil Moll's pretty shoes — she and Mr. Godwin first, her maids next, carrying her train, and the Don and I closing the procession, very stately. In the churchyard stand two rows of village maids with baskets to strew rosemary and sweet herbs in our path, and within the church a brave show of gentlefolks, friends and neighbours, to honour the wedding.

But here was I put to a most horrid quaking the moment I passed the door, to perceive old Simon standing foremost in the throng about the altar, in his leather cap (which he would not remove for clerk or sexton, but threatened them, as I am told, with the law if they lay a finger on him). And seeing him there, I must needs conclude that he intended to do us an ill turn, for his face wore the most wicked, cruel, malicious look that ever thirst of vengeance could impart. Indeed, I expected nothing less than that he would forbid the marriage on such grounds as we had too good reason to fear; and with this dread I regarded Moll, who also could not fail to see him. Her face whitened as she looked at him, but her step never faltered, and this peril seemed but to fortify her courage and resolution; and indeed I do think by her high bearing and the defiance in her eye as she held her lover's arm that she was fully prepared to make good answer if he challenged her right to marry Mr. Godwin. But (the Lord be thanked!) he did not put her to this trial, only he stood there like a thing of evil omen to mar the joy of this day with fearful foreboding.

I can say nothing about the ceremony, for all my attention was fixed upon this hideous Simon, and I had no relief until 'twas safely ended and Moll's friends pressed forward to kiss the bride and offer their good wishes; nor did I feel really at ease until we were back again at the Court, and seated to a fine dinner, with all the friends who would join us, whereof there were as many as could sit comfortably to the long table. This feast was very joyous and merry, and except that the parson would be facetious over his bottle, nothing unseemingly or immodest was said. So we stayed at table in exceeding good fellowship till the candles were lit, and then the parson, being very drunk, we made a pretext of carrying him home to break up our company and leave the happy couple to their joy.

December 26. Down betimes yesterday morning to find the sky still clear, the air brisk and dry, and ample promise of a fair day. To the Court, and there perceive the great ox spitted on a stout fir pole, and the fire just kindling; John the gardener setting up the barrels of beer, and a famous crowd of boys and beggars already standing before the gates. And there they might have stayed till their dinner was cooked, ere I had let them in, but Moll coming down from the house with her husband, and seeing this shivering crew, their pinched cheeks yellow and their noses blue with cold, and so famished with hunger they could scarce find strength to cry, "God bless you, merry gentlefolks!" she would have them taste at once some of that happiness with which her heart was overflowing, and so did with her own hands unbolt the gates and set them wide, bidding the halting wretches come in and warm themselves. Not content with this, she sends up to the house for loaves and gives every one a hunch of bread and a mug of ale to stay his empty stomach. And Lord, 'twas a pleasure to see these poor folks' joy — how they spread their hands out to the flames; how they cockered up the fire here and there to brown their ox equally, with all hands now and then to turn him on the spit; how they would set their bread to catch the dropping gravy; and how they would lift their noses to catch the savoury whiffs that came from the roasting beef.

This is all very well, thinks I, but how about our geese and turkeys? will our tenants come, or shall we find that Simon hath spoilt their appetite, and so be left with nought but starved beggars for our company? However, before four o'clock an end was put to these doubts, for some in waggons, others on horse, with their wives or sweethearts on pillions behind, clasping their men tight, and the rest afoot, all came that were asked by me, and more, and pretty jolly already with ale on the road, and a great store of mistletoe amongst them for their further merriment. And what pleased me as much as anything was to find all mighty civil to Moll — nearly all offering her a Christmas box of fresh eggs, honey, and such homely produce, which she received with the most pretty, winning grace, that went home to every heart, so that the hardest faces were softened with a glow of contentment and admiration. Then down we sat to table, Moll at one end and her husband beside her; Don Sanchez and I at t'other; and all the rest packed as close as sprats in a barrel; but every lad squeezing closer to his lass to make room for his neighbour, we found room for all and not a sour look anywhere. Dear heart! what appetites they had, yet would waste nothing, but picked every one his bone properly clean (which did satisfy me nothing was amiss with our geese), and great cheering when the puddings and flap-dragons came in all aflame, and all as merry as grigs — flinging of lighted plums at each other, but most mannerly not to fling any at Moll or us. Then more shouting for joy when the bowls of wassail and posset come in, and all standing to give three times three for their new mistress and her husband. Hearing of which, the beggars without (now tired of dancing about the embers) troop up to the door and give three times three as well, and end with crying joy and long life to the wedded pair. When this tumult was ended and the door shut, Mr. Godwin gave a short oration, thanking our tenants for their company and good wishes; and then he told them how his dear wife and he, wishing others to share their joy and remember this day, had resolved to forgive every tenant one-half of his quarter's rent. "And so, Mr. Hopkins," says he, addressing me, "you will think of this to-morrow."

At first I was disposed to begrudge this munificence — thinking of my accounts and the bills I should have to pay ere rent day came again; but on second thoughts it rejoiced me much as being a counterblast to anything Simon could do against us. For no tenant, thinks I, will be fool enough to withold payment when he may get his quittance to-morrow for half its value. And herein was I not mistaking; for to-day every tenant hath paid with a cheerful countenance. So that this is very good business, and I am not in any way astonished to find that our subtle Spaniard was at the bottom of it, for indeed it was Don Sanchez who (knowing my fears on this head and thinking them well-grounded) suggested this act of generosity to Moll, which she, in her fulness of heart, seized on at once. (Truly, I believe she would give the clothes off her back, no matter what it cost her, to any one in need, so reckless is she in love and pity.)

December 27. Don Sanchez took leave of us this day, he setting forth for Spain to-morrow, with the hope to reach his friends there, for their great feast of the New Year. And we are all mighty sorry to lose him; for not only hath he been a rare good friend to us, but also he is a most seemly gentleman (to keep us in countenance), and a very good staunch and reliable companion. But this comprises not all our loss, he having, as I confess, more wit in his little finger than we in all our bodies, and being ever ready with an expedient in the hour of need; and I know not why, but I look on his going as a sign of coming evil; nor am I greatly comforted by his telling me privily that when we want him he shall be found by a letter sent to the Albego Puerto del Sole, Toledo, in Spain. And I pray Heaven we have no occasion to write to him.

To-night at supper I find Moll all cock-a-hoop with a new delight, by reason of her dear husband offering to take her to London for a month to visit the theatres and other diversions, which put me to a new quirk for fear Moll should be known by any of our former playhouse companions. But this I now perceive is a very absurd fear; for no one in the world who had seen Moll three years ago — a half-starved, long-legged, raw child — could recognise her now, a beautiful, well-proportioned young woman in her fine clothes; and so my mind is at ease on this head. When Moll was retired, Mr. Godwin asked if I could let him have a few hundreds upon his account, and I answered very willingly he shall. And now setting aside enough to pay all bills and furnish our wants till next quarter day, I am resolved to give him every farthing left of the rents paid yesterday, and shall be most hearty glad to be rid of it, for this money do seem to scar my hands every time I touch it; nor can I look at it but my heart is wrung with pity for those poor tenants who paid so gleefully yesterday, for surely their quittances will hold good for no more than spoilt paper if ever our roguery is discovered.

December 28. This day Moll and Mr. Godwin set out for London, all smiles and gladness, and Moll did make me promise to visit them there, and share their pleasures. But if I have no more appetite for gaiety than I feel at this moment, I shall do better to stay here and mind my business; though I do expect to find little pleasure in that, and must abide by a month of very dull, gloomy days.

CHAPTER XXVII.

Of the great change in Moll, and the likely explanation thereof.

A WEEK before the promised month was up, Moll and her husband came back to the Court, and lest I should imagine that her pleasures had been curtailed by his caprice, she was at great pains to convince me that he had yielded to her insistence in this matter, declaring she was sick of theatres, ridottos, masquerades, and sight-seeing, and had sighed to be home ere she had been in London a week. This surprised me exceedingly, knowing how passionate fond she had ever been of the playhouse and diversions of any kind, and remembering how eager she was to go to town with her husband; and I perceived there was more significance in the present distaste for diversion than she would have known. And I observed further (when the joy of return and ordering her household subsided) that she herself had changed in these past three weeks, more than was to be expected in so short a time. For, though she seemed to love her husband more than ever she had loved him as her lover, and could not be happy two minutes out of his company, 'twas not that glad, joyous love of the earlier days, but a yearning, clinging passion, that made me sad to see; for I could not look upon the strained, anxious tenderness in her young face without bethinking me of my poor sister, as she knelt praying by her babe's cot for God to spare its frail life.

Yet her husband never looked more hearty and strong, and every look and word of his bespoke increasing love. The change in her was not unperceived by him, and often he would look down into her wistful, craving eyes as if he would ask of her, "What is it, love? tell me all." And she, as understanding this appeal, would answer nothing, but only shake her head, still gazing into his kind eyes as if she would have him believe she had nought to tell.

These things made me very thoughtful and urgent to find some satisfactory explanation. To be sure, thinks I, marriage is but the beginning of a woman's real life, and so one may not reasonably expect her to be what she was as a thoughtless child. And 'tis no less natural that a young wife should love to be alone with her husband, rather than in the midst of people who must distract his thoughts from her; as also it is right and proper she should wish to be in her own home, directing her domestic affairs and tending to her husband — showing him withal she is a good and thoughtful housewife. But why these pensive tristful looks, now she hath her heart's desire? Then, finding I must seek some better explanation of her case, I bethought me she must have had a very hard, difficult task in London to conceal from one, who was now a part of herself, her knowledge of so many things it was unbefitting she should reveal. At the playhouse she must feign astonishment at all she saw, as having never visited one before, and keep constant guard upon herself lest some word slipped her lips to reveal her acquaintance with the players and their art. At the ridotto she must equally feign ignorance of modish dancing — she whose nimble feet had tripped to every measure since she could stand alone. There was scarcely a subject on which she would dare to speak without deliberation, and she must check her old habit of singing and be silent, lest she fall by hazard to humming some known tune. Truly, under such continuous strain (which none but such a trained actress could maintain for a single day) her spirit must have wearied. And if this part was hard to play in public, where we are all, I take it, actors of some sort and on the alert to sustain the character we would have our own, how much more difficult must it be in private when we drop our disguise and lay our hearts open to those we love! And here, as it seemed to me, I did hit rightly at the true cause of her present secret distress; for at home as abroad she must still be acting a part, weighing her words, guarding her acts — for ever to be hiding of something from her dearest friend — ever denying him that confidence he appealed for — ever keeping a cruel, biting bond upon the most generous impulse of her heart, closing that heart when it was bursting to open to her dear mate.

Soon after their return Mr. Godwin set to work painting the head of a Sybil, which the Lord of Hatfield House had commanded, on the recommendation of Sir Peter Lely, taking Anne Fitch for his model, and she sitting in that room of the Court house he had prepared for his workshop. Here he would be at it every day, as long as there was light for his purpose, Moll, near at hand, watching him, ready to chat or hold her peace, according to his inclination — just as she had done when he was a-painting of the ceiling, only that now her regard was more intent upon him than his work, and when he turned to look at her, 'twas with interchange of undisguised love in their fond eyes. She ever had a piece of work or a book in her lap, but she made not half a dozen stitches or turned a single page in the whole day, for he was the sole occupation of her mind; the living book, ever yielding her sweet thoughts.

This persevering, patient toil on his part did at first engender in my mind suspicion that some doubting thoughts urged him to assume his independence against any accident that might befall the estate; but now I believe 'twas nothing but a love of work and of his art, and that his mind was free from any taint of misgiving, as regards his wife's honesty. 'Tis likely enough, that spite her caution, many a word and sign escaped Moll, which an enemy would have quickly seized on to prove her culpable; but we do never see the faults of those we love (or, seeing them, have ready at a moment excuse to prove them no faults at all), and at this time Mr. Godwin's heart was so full of love, there was no place for other feeling. Venom from a rose had seemed to him more possible than evil, from one so natural, sweet, and beautiful as Moll.

CHAPTER XXVIII.

Moll plays us a mad prank for the last time in her life.

ABOUT once in a fortnight I contrived to go to London for a couple of days on some pretext of business, and best part of this time I spent with Dawson. And the first visit I paid him after the return of Moll and her husband, telling him of their complete happiness, Moll's increasing womanly beauty, and the prosperous aspect of our affairs (for I had that day positive assurance our seal would be obtained within a month), I concluded by asking if his mast might not now be stepped, and he be in a position to come to Chislehurst and see her as he had before.

" No, Kit, thanking ye kindly," says he, after fighting it out with himself in silence a minute or two, " better not. I am getting in a manner used to this solitude, and bar two or three days a week when I feel a bit hangdog and hipped a-thinking there's not much in this world for an old fellow to live for when he's lost his child, I am pretty well content. It would only undo me. If you had a child — your own flesh and blood — part of your life — a child that had been to you what my sweet Moll hath been to me, you would comprehend better how I feel. To pretend indifference when you're longing to hug her to your heart, to talk of fair weather and foul when you're thinking of old times, and then to bow and scrape and go away without a single desire of your aching heart satisfied, — 'tis more than a man with a spark of warmth in his soul can bear." And then he proceeded to give a dozen other reasons for declining the tempting bait,—the sum of all proving to my conviction that he was dying to see Moll, and I feared he would soon be doing by stealth that which it were much safer he should do openly.

About a week after this I got a letter from him, asking me to come again as soon as I might, he having cut his hand with a chisel, "so that I cannot work my lathe, and having nothing to occupy my mind, do plague myself beyond endurance."

Much concerned for my old friend, I lose no time in repairing to Greenwich, where I find him sitting idle before his lathe, with an arm hanging in a handkerchief, and his face very yellow; but this, I think, was of drinking too much ale. And here he fell speedily discoursing of Moll, saying he could not sleep of nights for thinking of the pranks she used to play us, our merry vagabond life together in Spain ere we got to Elche, etc., and how he missed her now more than ever he did before. After that, as I anticipated, he came in a shuffling, roundabout way (as one ashamed to own his weakness) to hinting at seeing Moll by stealth, declaring he would rather see her for two minutes now and again peering through a bush, though she should never cast a glance his way, than have her treat him as if she were not his child and ceased to feel any love for him. But seeing the peril of such ways, I would by no means consent to his hanging about the Court like a thief, and told him plainly that unless he would undo us all and ruin Moll, he must come openly as before or not at all.

Without further demur he consents to be guided by me, and then, very eagerly, asks when it will be proper for him to come; and we agree that if he come in a week's time, there will be no thought in anybody's mind of our having conspired to this end.

As the fates would have it, Mr. Godwin finished his painting on the Saturday following (the most wonderful piece of its kind I ever saw, or any one else, in my belief), and being justly proud of his work and anxious Sir Peter Lely should see it soon, he resolved he would carry it to Hatfield on Monday. Moll, who was prouder of her husband's piece than if it were of her own doing, was not less eager it should be seen; yet the thought that she must lose him for four days (for this journey could not well be accomplished in less time) cast down her spirits exceedingly. 'Twas painful to see her efforts to be cheerful despite of herself. And, seeing how incapable she was of concealing her real feeling from him whom she would cheer, she at length confessed to him her trouble. " I would have you go, and yet I'd have you stay, love," says she.

" 'Tis but a little while we shall be parted," says he.

" A little while?" says she, trembling and wringing one hand within the other. " It seems to me as if we were parting for ever."

"Why, then," returns he, laughing, "we will not part at all. You shall come with me, chuck. What should prevent you?"

She starts with joy at this, then looks at him incredulous for a moment, and so her countenance falling again, she shakes her head as thinking, I take it, that if it were advisable she should go with him, he would have proposed it before.

" No," says she, " 'twas an idle fancy, and I'll not yield to it. I shall become a burden, rather than a helpmate, if you cannot stir from home without me. Nay," adds she, when he would override this objection, "you must not tempt me to be weak, but rather aid me to do that which I feel right."

And she would not be persuaded from this resolution, but bore herself most bravely, even to the moment when she and her husband clasped each for the last time in a farewell embrace.

She stood where he had left her for some moments after he was gone. Suddenly she ran a few paces with parted lips and outstretched hands, as if she would call him back; then, as sharply she halts, clasping her hands, and so presently turns back, looking across her shoulder, with such terror in her white face, that I do think her strong imagination figured some accusing spirits, threatening the end of all her joys.

I followed her into the house, but there I learnt from Mrs. Butterby that her mistress was gone to her own chamber.

As I was sitting in my office in the afternoon, Jack Dawson came to me in his seaman's dress, his hand still wrapped up, but his face more healthful for his long ride and cheerful thoughts.

"Why, this could not have fallen out better," says I, when we had exchanged greetings; "for Moll is all alone, and down in the dumps by reason of her husband having left her this morning on business, that will hold him absent for three or four days. We will go up presently and have supper with her."

"No, Kit," says he, very resolutely, "I'll not. I am

resolved I won't go there till to-morrow, for this is no hour to be a-calling on ladies, and her husband being away 'twill look as if we had ordered it of purpose. Besides, if Moll's in trouble, how am I to pretend I know nothing of the matter and care less, and this Mother Butterby and a parcel of sly, observant servants about to surprise one at any moment? Say no more — 'tis useless — for I won't be persuaded against my judgment."

"As you will," says I.

"There's another reason, if other's needed," says he, "and that's this plaguey thirst of mine, which seizes me when I'm doleful or joyful, with a force there's no resisting. And chiefly it seizes me in the later part of the day; therefore, I'd have you take me to the Court to-morrow morning betimes, ere it's at its worst. My throat's like any limekiln for dryness now; so do pray, Kit, fasten the door snug, and give me a mug of ale."

This ended our discussion; but, as it was necessary I should give some reason for not supping with Moll, I left Dawson with a bottle, and went up to the house to find Moll. There I learnt that she was still in her chamber, and sleeping, as Mrs. Butterby believed; so I bade the good woman tell her mistress when she awoke that Captain Evans had come to spend the night with me, and he would call to pay her his devoirs the next morning.

Here, that nothing may be unaccounted for in the sequence of events, I must depart from my train of present observation to speak from after-knowledge.

I have said that when Moll started forward, as if to overtake her husband, she suddenly stopped as if confronted by some menacing spectre. And this indeed was the case;

for at that moment there appeared to her heated imagination (for no living soul was there) a little, bent old woman, clothed in a single white garment of Moorish fashion, and Moll knew that she was Mrs. Godwin (though seeing her now for the first time), come from Barbary to claim her own, and separate Moll from the husband she had won by fraud.

She stood there (says Moll) within her gates, with raised hand and a most bitter, unforgiving look upon her wasted face, barring the way by which Moll might regain her husband; and as the poor wife halted, trembling in dreadful awe, the old woman advanced with the sure foot of right and justice. What reproach she had to make, what malediction to pronounce, Moll dared not stay to hear, but turning her back fled to the house, where, gaining her chamber, she locked the door, and flung herself upon her husband's bed; and in this last dear refuge, shutting her eyes, clasping her ears, as if by dulling her senses to escape the phantom, she lay in a convulsion of terror for the mere dread that such a thing might be.

Then, at the thought that she might never again be enfolded here in her husband's arms, an agony of grief succeeded her fit of maddening fear, and she wept till her mind grew calm from sheer exhaustion. And so, little by little, as her courage revived, she began to reason with herself as how 'twas the least likely thing in the world that if Mrs. Godwin were in England, she should come to the Court unattended and in her Moorish clothes; and then, seeing the folly of abandoning herself to a foolish fancy, she rose, washed the tears from her face, and set herself to find some occupation to distract her thoughts. And what employment is nearer to her thoughts or dearer to her heart than making things straight for her husband; so she goes into the next room where he worked, and falls to washing his brushes, cleaning his paint-board, and putting all things in order against his return, that he may lose no time in setting to work at another picture. And at dinner time, finding her face still disfigured with her late emotions and ashamed of her late folly, she bids her maid bring a snack to her room, under the pretence that she feels unwell. This meal she eats, still working in her husband's room; for one improvement prompting another, she finds plenty to do there: now bethinking her that the hangings of her own private room (being handsomer) will look better on these walls, whereas t'others are more fit for hers, where they are less seen; that this corner looks naked, and will look better for her little French table standing there, with a china image atop, and so forth. Thus, then, did she devote her time till sundown, whereabouts Mrs. Butterby raps at her door to know if she will have a cup of warm caudle to comfort her, at the same time telling her that Mr. Hopkins will not sup with her, as he has Captain Evans for his guest at the lodge.

And now Moll, by that natural succession of extremes which seems to be a governing law of nature (as the flow the ebb, the calm the storm, day the night, etc.), was not less elated than she had been depressed in the early part of the day, — but still, I take it, in a nervous, excitable condition. And hearing her father, whom she has not seen so long, is here, a thousand mad projects enter her lively imagination. So, when Mrs. Butterby, after the refusal of her warm caudle, proposes she shall bring Madam a tray of victuals, that she may pick something in bed, Moll, stifling a merry thought, asks, in a feeble voice, what there is in the larder.

"Why, Madam," says Mrs. Butterby, from the outside, "there's the partridges you did not eat at breakfast, there's a cold pigeon pasty and a nice fresh ham, and a lovely hasty pudding I made with my own hands, in the pot."

"Bring 'em all," says Moll, in the same aching voice; "and I'll pick what tempts me."

Therewith, she silently slips the bolt back, whips on her nightgown, and whips into bed.

Presently, up comes Mrs. Butterby, carrying a wax candle, followed by a couple of maids charged with all the provisions Moll had commanded. Having permission to enter, the good woman sets down her candle, puts on her glasses, and, coming to the bedside, says she can see very well by her poor looks, that her dear mistress has got a disorder of the biliaries on her, and prays Heaven it may not turn to something worse.

"Nay," says Moll, very faintly, "I shall be well again when I am relieved of this headache, and if I can only fall asleep,—as I feel disposed to,—you will see me to-morrow morning in my usual health. I shan't attempt to rise this evening" ("For mercy's sake, don't," cries Mrs. Butterby), "and so, I pray you, order that no one shall come near my room to disturb me" ("I'll see that no one so much as sets a foot on your stair, Madam, poor dear!" says t'other), "and you will see that all is closed carefully. And so good-night, mother, and good-night to you, Jane and Betsy—oh, my poor head!"

With a whispered "Good-night, dear madam," Mrs. Butterby and the maids leave the room a-tiptoe, closing the door behind them as if 'twere of gingerbread; and no sooner are they gone than Moll, big with her mad design, nips out of bed, strips off her nightgown, and finding nothing more convenient for her purpose, puts the ham, pasty, and partridges in a clean pillow-slip. This done, she puts on her cloak and hood, and having with great caution set the door open and seen all safe and quiet below, she takes up her bag of victuals, blows out the candle, and as silent as any mouse makes her way to the little private staircase at the end of the stairs. And now, with less fear of encountering Mrs. Godwin than Black Bogey, she feels her way down the dark, narrow staircase, reaches the lower door, unbolts it, and steps out on the path at the back of the house.

There is still a faint twilight, and this enables her to find her way to the wicket gate opposite Anne Fitch's cottage. Not a soul is to be seen; and so, with her hood drawn well over her head, she speeds on, and in five minutes reaches my house. Here finding the door fastened, she gives a couple of knocks, and on my opening she asks meekly in a feigned voice, which for the life of me I should not have known for hers, if I am minded to buy a couple of partridges a friend has sent and she has no use for.

"Partridges!" cries Dawson, from within. "Have 'em, Kit, for your bread and cheese is mighty every-day fare."

"Let me see 'em, good woman," says I.

"Yes, sir," answers she, meekly, putting her pillow-slip in my hand, which perplexed me vastly by its weight and bulk.

"They seem to be pretty big birds by the feel of 'em," says I. "You can come in and shut the door after you."

Moll shuts the door and shoots the bolt, then tripping behind me into the light she casts back her hood and flings her arms round her father's neck with a peal of joyful laughter.

"What!" cries I. "Why, what can have brought you here?"

"Why, I knew you'd have nothing to give my poor old dad but mouldy cheese, so I've brought you a brace of partridges, if you please, sir," says she, concluding in her feigned voice, as she emptied the ham, pasty, and partridges all higgledy-piggledy out of the slip on to the table.

"But, Mrs. Godwin—" says I, in alarm.

"Oh, call me Moll," cries she, wildly. "Let me be myself for this one night."

CHAPTER XXIX.

Of the subtile means whereby Simon leads Mr. Godwin to doubt his wife.

AGAIN must I draw upon matter of after-knowledge to show you how all things came to pass on this fatal night.

When Mr. Godwin reached London, he went to Sir Peter Lely's house in Lincoln's Inn, to know if he was still at Hatfield, and there learning he was gone hence to Hampton, and no one answering for certainty when he would return, Mr. Godwin, seeing that he might linger in London for days to no purpose, and bethinking him how pale and sorrowful his dear wife was when they parted, concludes to leave his picture at Sir Peter Lely's and post back to Chislehurst, counting to give his wife a happy surprise.

About eight o'clock he reaches the Court, to find all shut and barred by the prudent housekeeper, who, on letting him in (with many exclamations of joy and wonder), falls presently to sighing and shaking her head, as she tells how her mistress has lain abed since dinner, and is sick of the biliaries.

In great concern, Mr. Godwin takes the candle from Mrs. Butterby's hand, and hastes up to his wife's room. Opening the door softly, he enters, to find the bed tumbled, indeed, but empty. He calls her in a soft voice, going into the next room, and, getting no reply, nor finding her there, he calls again, more loudly, and there is no response. Then, as he stands irresolute and amazed, he hears a knock at the door below, and concluding that 'tis his wife, who has had occasion to go out, seeking fresh air for her comfort maybe, he runs swiftly down and opens, ere a servant can answer the call. And there he is faced, not by sweet Moll, but the jaundiced, wicked old Simon, gasping and panting for breath.

"Dost thee know," says he, fetching his breath at every other word, "dost thee know where the woman thy wife is?"

"Where is she?" cries Mr. Godwin, in quick alarm, thinking by this fellow's sweating haste that some accident had befallen his dear wife.

"I will show thee where she is; aye, and what she is," gasps the old man, and then, clasping his hands, he adds, "Verily, the Lord hath heard my prayers and delivered mine enemies into my hand."

Mr. Godwin, who had stepped aside to catch up his hat from the table, where he had flung it on entering, stopped short, hearing this fervent note of praise, and turning about, with misgivings of Simon's purpose, cries:

"What are your enemies to me?"

"Everything," cries Simon. "Mine enemies are thine, for as they have cheated me so have they cheated thee."

"Enough of this," cries Mr. Godwin. "Tell me where my wife is, and be done with it."

"I say I will show thee where she is and what she is."

"Tell me where she is," cries Mr. Godwin, with passion.

"That is my secret, and too precious to throw away."

"I comprehend you, now," says Mr. Godwin, bethinking him of the fellow's greed. "You shall be paid. Tell me where she is and name your price."

"The price is this," returns the other, "thy promise to

be secret, to catch them in this trap, and give no opening for escape. Oh, I know them; they are as serpents, that slip through a man's fingers and turn to bite. They shall not serve me so again. Promise — "

"Nothing. Think you I'm of your own base kind, to deal with you in treachery? You had my answer before, when you would poison my mind, rascal. But," adds he, with fury, "you shall tell me where my wife is."

"I would tear the tongue from my throat ere it should undo the work of Providence. If they escape the present vengeance of Heaven, thee shalt answer for it, not I. Yet I will give thee a clue to find this woman who hath fooled thee. Seek her where there are thieves and drunkards to mock at thy simplicity, to jeer at their easy gull, for I say again thy wife never was in Barbary, but playing the farded, wanton — "

The patience with which Mr. Godwin had harkened to this tirade, doubting by his passion that Simon was stark mad, gave way before this vile aspersion on his wife, and clutching the old man by the throat he flung him across the threshold and shut the door upon him.

But where was his wife? That question was still uppermost in his thoughts. His sole misgiving was that accident had befallen her, and that somewhere in the house he should find her lying cold and insensible.

With this terror in his mind, he ran again upstairs. On the landing he was met by Mrs. Butterby, who (prudent soul), at the first hint of misconduct on her mistress's part, had bundled the gaping servants up to their rooms.

"Mercy on us, dear master!" says she. "Where can our dear lady be? For a surety she hath not left the house, for I locked all up, as she bade me when we carried up her supper, and had the key in my pocket when you knocked. 'See the house safe,' says she, poor soul, with a voice could scarce be heared, 'and let no one disturb me, for I do feel most heavy with sleep.'"

Mr. Godwin passed into his wife's room and then into the next, looking about him in distraction.

"Lord! here's the sweet thing's nightgown," exclaims Mrs. Butterby, from the next room, whither she had followed Mr. Godwin. "But dear heart o' me, where's the ham gone?"

Mr. Godwin, entering from the next room, looked at her as doubting whether he or all the world had taken leave of their wits.

"And the pigeon pasty?" added Mrs. Butterby, regarding the table laid out beside her mistress's bed.

"And the cold partridge," adds she, in redoubled astonishment. "Why, here's nought left but my pudding, and that as cold as a stone."

Mr. Godwin, with the candle flaring in his hand, passed hastily by her, too wrought by fear to regard either the ludicrous or incomprehensible side of Mrs. Butterby's consternation; and so, going down the corridor away from the stairs, he comes to the door of the little back stairs, standing wide open, and seeming to bid him descend. He goes quickly down, yet trembling with fear that he may find her at the bottom, broken by a fall; but all he discovers is the bolt drawn and the door ajar. As he pushes it open a gust of wind blows out the light, and here he stood in the darkness, eager to be doing, yet knowing not which way to turn or how to act.

Clearly, his wife had gone out by this door, and so far this gave support to Simon's statement that he knew where she was; and with this a flame was kindled within him that seemed to sear his very soul. If Simon spoke truth in one particular, why should he lie in others? Why had his wife refused to go with him to Hatfield? Why had she bid no one come near her room? Why had she gone forth by this secret stair, alone? Then, cursing himself for the unnamed suspicion that could thus, though but for a moment, disfigure the fair image that he worshipped, he asked himself why his wife should not be free to follow a caprice. But where was she? Ever that question surged upwards in the tumult of his thoughts. Where should he seek her? Suddenly it struck him that I might help him to find her, and acting instantly upon this hope he made his way in breathless haste to the road, and so towards my lodge.

Ere he has gone a hundred yards, Simon steps out of the shadow, and stands before him like a shade in the dimness.

"I crave thy pardon, Master," says he, humbly. "I spoke like a fool in my passion."

"If you will have my pardon, tell me where to find my wife; if not, stand aside," answers Mr. Godwin.

"Wilt thee hear me speak for two minutes if I promise to tell thee where she is and suffer thee to find her how thee willst. 'Twill save thee time."

"Speak," says Mr. Godwin.

"Thy wife is there," says Simon, under his breath, pointing towards my house. "She is revelling with Hopkins and Captain Evans, — men that she did tramp the country with as vagabond players, ere the Spaniard taught them more profitable wickedness. Knock at the door, —

which thee mayst be sure is fast,—and while one holds thee in parley the rest will set the room in order, and find a plausible tale to hoodwink thee afresh. Be guided by me, and thee shalt enter the house unknown to them, as I did an hour since, and there thee shalt know, of thine own senses, how thy wife doth profit by thy blindness. If this truth be not proved, if thee canst then say that I have lied from malice, envy, and evil purpose, this knife," says he, showing a blade in his hand, "this knife will I thrust into my own heart, though I stand the next instant before the Eternal Judge, my hands wet with my own blood, to answer for my crime."

"Have you finished?" asks Mr. Godwin.

"No, not yet; I hold thee to thy promise," returns Simon, with eager haste. "Why do men lie? for their own profit. What profit have I in lying, when I pray thee to put my word to the proof and not take it on trust, with the certainty of punishment even if the proof be doubtful. Thee believest this woman is what she pretends to be; what does that show?—your simplicity, not hers. How would women trick their husbands without such skill to blind them by a pretence of love and virtue?"

"Say no more," cries Mr. Godwin, hoarsely, "or I may strangle you before you pass trial. Go your devilish way, I'll follow."

"Now God be praised for this!" cries Simon. "Softly, softly!" adds he, creeping in the shade of the bank towards the house.

But ere he has gone a dozen paces Mr. Godwin repents him again, with shame in his heart, and stopping, says:

"I'll go no further."

"Then thee doubtest my word no longer," whispers Simon, quickly. "'Tis fear that makest thee halt,— the fear of finding thy wife a wanton and a trickster."

" No, no, by God !"

" If that be so, then art thee bound to prove her innocent, that I may not say to all the world, thee mightest have put her honour to the test and dared not — choosing rather to cheat thyself and be cheated by her, than know thyself dishonoured. If thee dost truly love this woman and believe her guiltless, then for her honour must thee put me — not her — to this trial."

"No madman could reason like this," says Mr. Godwin. " I accept this trial, and Heaven forgive me if I do wrong."

CHAPTER XXX.

How we are discovered and utterly undone.

"WHAT!" cries Dawson, catching his daughter in his arms and hugging her to his breast, when the first shock of surprise was past. "My own sweet Moll — come hither to warm her old father's heart?"

"And my own," says she, tenderly, "which I fear hath grown a little wanting in love for ye since I have been mated. But, though my dear Dick draws so deeply from my well of affection, there is still somewhere down here" (clapping her hand upon her heart) "a source that first sprang for you and can never dry."

"Aye, and 'tis a proof," says he, "your coming here where we may speak and act without restraint, though it be but for five minutes."

"Five minutes!" cries she, springing up with her natural vivacity, "why, I'll not leave you before the morning, unless you weary of me." And then with infinite relish and sly humour, she told of her device for leaving the Court without suspicion.

I do confess I was at first greatly alarmed for the safe issue of this escapade; but she assuring me 'twas a dirty night, and she had passed no one on the road, I felt a little reassured. To be sure, thinks I, Mr. Godwin by some accident may return, but finding her gone, and hearing Captain Evans keeps me to my house, he must conclude she has come hither, and think no harm of her for that neither — seeing we are old friends and sobered with years, for 'tis the most natural thing in the world that, feeling lonely and dejected for the loss of her husband, she should seek such harmless diversion as may be had in our society.

However, for the sake of appearances I thought it would be wise to get this provision of ham and birds out of sight, for fear of misadventure, and also I took instant precaution to turn the key in my street door. Being but two men, and neither of us over-nice in the formalities, I had set a cheese, a loaf, and a bottle betwixt us on the bare table of my office room, for each to serve himself as he would; but I now proposed that, having a lady in our company, we should pay more regard to the decencies by going upstairs to my parlour, and there laying a tablecloth and napkins for our repast.

"Aye, certainly!" cries Moll, who had grown mighty fastidious in these particulars since she had been mistress of Hurst Court; "this dirty table would spoil the best appetite in the world."

So I carried a faggot and some apple logs upstairs, and soon had a brave fire leaping up the chimney, by which time Moll and her father, with abundant mirth, had set forth our victuals on a clean white cloth, and to each of us a clean plate, knife, and fork, most proper. Then, all things being to our hand, we sat down and made a most hearty meal of Mrs. Butterby's good cheer, and all three of us as merry as grigs, with not a shadow of misgiving.

There had seemed something piteous to me in that appeal of Moll's, that she might be herself for this night; and indeed I marvelled now how she could have so trained her natural disposition to an artificial manner, and did no longer wonder at the look of fatigue and weariness in her face on her return to London. For the old reckless, careless, daredevil spirit was still alive in her, as I could plainly see now that she abandoned herself entirely to the free sway of impulse; the old twinkle of mirth and mischief was in her eyes; she was no longer a fine lady, but a merry vagabond again, and when she laughed 'twas with her hands clasping her sides, her head thrown back, and all her white teeth gleaming in the light.

"Now," says I, when at length our meal was finished, "I will clear the table."

"Hoop!" cries she, catching up the corners of the tablecloth, and flinging them over the fragments; "'tis done. Let us draw round the fire, and tell old tales. Here's a pipe, dear dad; I love the smell of tobacco; and you" (to me) "do fetch me a pipkin, that I may brew a good drink to keep our tongues going."

About the time this drink was brewed, Simon, leading Mr. Godwin by a circuitous way, came through the garden to the back of the house, where was a door, which I had never opened for lack of a key td fit the lock. This key was now in Simon's hand, and putting it with infinite care into the hole, he softly turned it in the wards. Then, with the like precaution, he lifts the latch and gently thrusts the door open, listening at every inch to catch the sounds within. At length 'tis opened wide; and so, turning his face to Mr. Godwin, who waits behind, sick with mingled shame and creeping dread, he beckons him to follow.

Above, Dawson was singing at the top of his voice, a sea-song he had learnt of a mariner at the inn he frequented at

Greenwich, with a troll at the end, taken up by Moll and me. And to hear his wife's voice bearing part in this rude song, made Mr. Godwin's heart to sink within him. Under cover of this noise, Simon mounted the stairs without hesitation, Mr. Godwin following at his heels, in a kind of sick bewilderment. 'Twas pitch dark up there, and Simon, stretching forth his hands to know if Mr. Godwin was by, touched his hand, which was deadly cold and quivering; for here at the door he was seized with a sweating faintness, which so sapped his vigour that he was forced to hold by the wall to save himself from falling.

"Art thee ready?" asks Simon; but he can get no answer, for Mr. Godwin's energies, quickened by a word from within like a jaded beast by the sting of a whip, is straining his ears to catch what is passing within. And what hears he?— The song is ended, and Dawson cries:

"You han't lost your old knack of catching a tune, Moll. Come hither, wench, and sit upon my knee, for I do love ye more than ever. Give me a buss, chuck; this fine husband of thine shall not have all thy sweetness to himself."

At this moment, Simon, having lifted the latch under his thumb, pushes wide open the door, and there through the thick cloud of tobacco smoke Mr. Godwin sees the table in disorder, the white cloth flung back over the remnants of our repast and stained with a patch of liquor from an overturned mug, a smutty pipkin set upon the board beside a dish of tobacco, and a broken pipe — me sitting o' one side the hearth heavy and drowsy with too much good cheer, and on t'other side his young wife, sitting on Dawson's knee, with one arm about his neck, and he in his uncouth seaman's garb, with a pipe in one hand, the other about Moll's waist, a-kissing her yielded cheek. With a cry of fury, like any wild beast, he springs forward and clutches at a knife that lies ready to his hand upon the board, and this cry is answered with a shriek from Moll as she starts to her feet.

"Who is this drunken villain?" he cries, stretching the knife in his hand towards Dawson.

And Moll, flinging herself betwixt the knife and Dawson, with fear for his life, and yet with some dignity in her voice and gesture, answers swiftly:

"This drunken villain is my father."

CHAPTER XXXI.

Moll's conscience is quickened by grief and humiliation beyond the ordinary.

"STAND aside, Moll," cries Dawson, stepping to the fore, and facing Mr. Godwin. "This is my crime, and I will answer for it with my blood. Here is my breast" (tearing open his jerkin). "Strike, for I alone have done you wrong, this child of mine being but an instrument to my purpose."

Mr. Godwin's hand fell by his side, and the knife slipped from his fingers.

"Speak," says he, thickly, after a moment of horrible silence broken only by the sound of the knife striking the floor. "If this is your daughter, — if she has lied to me, — what in God's name is the truth? Who are you, I ask?"

"John Dawson, a player," answers he, seeing the time is past for lying.

Mr. Godwin makes no response, but turns his eyes upon Moll, who stands before him with bowed head and clasped hands, wrung to her innermost fibre with shame, remorse, and awful dread, and for a terrible space I heard nothing but the deep, painful breathing of this poor, overwrought man.

"You are my wife," says he, at length. "Follow me," and with that he turns about and goes from the room. Then Moll, without a look at us, without a word, her face ghastly pale and drawn with agony, with faltering steps, obeys, catching at table and chair, as she passes, for support.

Dawson made a step forward, as if he would have overtaken her; but I withheld him, shaking my head, and himself seeing 'twas in vain, he dropped into a chair, and, spreading his arms upon the table, hides his face in them with a groan of despair.

Moll totters down the dark stairs, and finds her husband standing in the doorway, his figure revealed against the patch of grey light beyond, for the moon was risen, though veiled by a thick pall of cloud. He sees, as she comes to his side, that she has neither cloak nor hood to protect her from the winter wind, and in silence he takes off his own cloak and lays it on her shoulder. At this act of mercy a ray of hope animates Moll's numbed soul, and she catches at her husband's hand to press it to her lips, yet can find never a word to express her gratitude. But his hand is cold as ice, and he draws it away from her firmly, with obvious repugnance. There was no love in this little act of giving her his cloak; 'twas but the outcome of that chivalry in gentlemen which doth exact lenience even to an enemy.

So he goes on his way, she following like a whipped dog at his heels, till they reach the Court gates, and these being fast locked, on a little further, to the wicket gate. And there, as Mr. Godwin is about to enter, there confronts him Peter, that sturdy Puritan hireling of old Simon's.

"Thee canst not enter here, friend," says he, in his canting voice, as he sets his foot against the gate.

"Know you who I am?" asks Mr. Godwin.

"Yea, friend; and I know who thy woman is also. I am bidden by friend Simon, the true and faithful steward of Mistress Godwin in Barbary, to defend her house and lands against robbers and evil-doers of every kind, and without respect of their degree; and, with the Lord's help," adds he, showing a stout cudgel, " that will I do, friend."

" 'Tis true, fellow," returns Mr. Godwin. " I have no right to enter here."

And then, turning about, he stands irresolute, as not knowing whither he shall go to find shelter for his wife. For very shame, he does not take her to the village inn, to be questioned by gaping servants and landlord, who, ere long, must catch the flying news of her shameful condition and overthrow. A faint light in the lattice of Anne Fitch's cottage catches his eye, and he crosses to her door, still humbly followed by poor Moll. There he finds the thumb-piece gone from the latch, to him a well-known sign that Mother Fitch has gone out a-nursing; so, pulling the hidden string he wots of, he lifts the latch within, and the door opens to his hand. A rush is burning in a cup of oil upon the table, casting a feeble glimmer round the empty room. He closes the door when Moll has entered, sets a chair before the hearth, and rakes the embers together to give her warmth.

" Forgive me, oh, forgive me !" cries Moll, casting herself at his feet as he turns, and clasping his knees to her stricken heart.

" Forgive you !" says he, bitterly. " Forgive you for dragging me down to the level of rogues and thieves, for making me party to this vile conspiracy of plunder. A conspiracy that, if it bring me not beneath the lash of Justice, must blast my name and fame for ever. You know not what you ask. As well might you bid me take you back to finish the night in drunken riot with those others of our gang."

" Oh, no, not now ! not now !" cries Moll, in agony. " Do but say that some day long hence, you will forgive me. Give me that hope, for I cannot live without it."

"That hope's my fear!" says he. "I have known men who, by mere contact with depravity, have so dulled their sense of shame that they could make light of sins that once appalled them. Who knows but that one day I may forgive you, chat easily upon this villany, maybe, regret I went no further in it."

"Oh, God forbid that shall be of my doing!" cries Moll, springing to her feet. "Broken as I am, I'll not accept forgiveness on such terms. Think you I'm like those plague-stricken wretches who, of wanton wickedness, ran from their beds to infect the clean with their foul ill? Not I."

"I spoke in heat," says Mr. Godwin, quickly. "I repent even now what I said."

"Am I so steeped in infamy," continues she, "that I am past all cure? Think," adds she, piteously, "I am not eighteen yet. I was but a child a year ago, with no more judgment of right and wrong than a savage creature. Until I loved you, I think I scarcely knew the meaning of conscience. The knowledge came when I yearned to keep no secret from you. I do remember the first struggle to do right. 'Twas on the little bridge; and there I balanced awhile, 'twixt cheating you and robbing myself. And then, for fear you would not marry me, I dared not own the truth. Oh, had I thought you'd only keep me for your mistress, I'd have told you I was not your cousin. Little as this is, there's surely hope in't. Is it more impossible that you, a strong man, should lift me, than that I, a weak girl,— no more than that,— should drag you down?"

"I did not weigh my words."

"Yet, they were true," says she. "'Tis bred in my body — part of my nature, this spirit of evil, and 'twill exist as long as I. For, even now, I do feel that I would do this wickedness again, and worse, to win you once more."

"My poor wife," says he, touched with pity; and holding forth his arms, she goes to them and lays her cheek against his breast, and there stands crying very silently with mingled thoughts — now of the room she had prepared with such delight against his return, of her little table in the corner, with the chiney image atop, and other trifles with which she had dreamed to give him pleasure — all lost! No more would she sit by his side there watching, with wonder and pride, the growth of beauty 'neath his dexterous hand; and then she feels that 'tis compassion, not love, that hath opened his arms to her, that she hath killed his respect for her, and with it his love. And so, stifling the sobs that rise in her throat, she weeps on, till her tears trickling from her cheek fall upon his hand.

The icy barrier of resentment is melted by the first warm tear, — this silent testimony of her smothered grief, — and bursting from the bonds of reason, he yields to the passionate impulse of his heart, and clasping this poor sorrowing wife to his breast, he seeks to kiss away the tears from her cheek, and soothe her with gentle words. She responds to his passion, kiss for kiss, as she clasps her hands about his head; but still her tears flow on, for with her readier wit she perceives that this is but the transport of passion on his side, and not the untaxed outcome of enduring love, proving again the truth of his unmeditated prophecy; for how can he stand who yields so quickly to the first assault, and if he cannot stand, how can he raise her? Surely and more surely, little by little, they must sink together to some lower depth, and one day, thinks she, repeating his words, "We may chat easily upon this villany and regret we went no further in it."

Mr. Godwin leads her to the adjoining chamber, which had been his, and says:

"Lie down, love. To-morrow we shall see things clearer, and think more reasonably."

"Yes," says she, in return, "more reasonably," and with that she does his bidding; and he returns to sit before the embers and meditate. And here he stays, striving in vain to bring the tumult of his thoughts to some coherent shape, until from sheer exhaustion he falls into a kind of lethargy of sleep.

Meanwhile, Moll, lying in the dark, had been thinking also, but (as women will at such times) with clearer perception, so that her ideas forming in logical sequence, and growing more clear and decisive (as an argument becomes more lively and conclusive by successful reasoning) served to stimulate her intellect and excite her activity. And the end of it was that she rose quickly from her bed and looked into the next room, where she saw her husband sitting, with his chin upon his breast and his hands folded upon his knee before the dead fire. Then wrapping his cloak about her, she steals toward the outer door; but passing him she must needs pause at his back to staunch her tears a moment, and look down upon him for the last time. The light shines in his brown hair, and she bending down till her lips touch a stray curl, they part silently, and she breathes upon him from her very soul, a mute "Fare thee well, dear love."

But she will wait no longer, fearing her courage may give way, and the next minute she is out in the night, softly drawing the door to that separates these two for ever.

CHAPTER XXXII.

How we fought a most bloody battle with Simon, the constable, and others.

FOR some time we spoke never a word, Dawson and I,— he with his head lying on his arm, I seated in a chair with my hands hanging down by my side, quite stunned by the blow that had fallen upon us. At length, raising his head, his eyes puffed, and his face bedaubed with tears, he says:

"Han't you a word of comfort, Kit, for a broken-hearted man?"

I stammered a few words that had more sound than sense; but indeed I needed consolation myself, seeing my own responsibility for bringing this misfortune upon Moll, and being most heartily ashamed of my roguery now 'twas discovered.

"You don't think he'll be too hard on poor Moll, tell me that, Kit?"

"Aye, he'll forgive her," says I, "sooner than us, or we ourselves."

"And you don't think he'll be for ever a-casting it in her teeth that her father's a — a drunken vagabond, eh?"

"Nay; I believe he is too good a man for that."

"Then," says he, standing up, "I'll go and tell him the whole story, and you shall come with me to bear me out."

"To-morrow will be time enough," says I, flinching from this office; "'tis late now."

"No matter for that. Time enough to sleep when we've settled this business. We'll not leave poor Moll to bear all the punishment of our getting. Mr. Godwin shall know what an innocent, simple child she was when we pushed her into this knavery, and how we dared not tell her of our purpose lest she should draw back. He shall know how she was ever an obedient, docile, artless girl, yielding always to my guidance; and you can stretch a point, Kit, to say you have ever known me for a headstrong, masterful sort of a fellow, who would take denial from none, but must have my own way in all things. I'll take all the blame on my own shoulders, as I should have done at first, but I was so staggered by this fall."

"Well," says I, "if you will have it so—"

"I will," says he, stoutly. "And now give me a bucket of water that I may souse my head, and wear a brave look. I would have him think the worst of me that he may feel the kinder to poor Moll. And I'll make what atonement I can," adds he, as I led him into my bed-chamber. "If he desire it, I will promise never to see Moll again; nay, I will offer to take the king's bounty, and go a-sailoring; and so, betwixt sickness and the Dutch, there'll be an end of Jack Dawson in a very short space."

When he had ducked his head in a bowl of water, and got our cloaks from the room below, we went to the door, and there, to my dismay, I found the lock fast and the key which I had left in its socket gone.

"What's amiss, Kit?" asks Dawson, perceiving my consternation.

"The key, the key!" says I, holding the candle here and there to seek it on the floor, then, giving up my search as it struck me that Mr. Godwin and Moll could not have left the house had the door been locked on the inside; "I do believe we are locked in and made prisoners," says I.

"Why, sure, this is not Mr. Godwin's doing!" cries he.

"'Tis Simon," says I, with conviction, seeing him again in my mind, standing behind Mr. Godwin, with wicked triumph in his face.

"Is there no other door but this one?" asks Dawson.

"There is one at the back, but I have never yet opened that, for lack of a key." And now setting one thing against another, and recalling how I had before found the door open, when I felt sure I had locked it fast, the truth appeared to me; namely, that Simon had that key and did get in the back way, going out by the front on that former occasion in haste upon some sudden alarm.

"Is there never a window we can slip through?" asks Jack.

"Only those above stairs; the lower are all barred."

"A fig for his bars. Does he think we have neither hands nor wits to be hindered by this silly woman's trick?"

"'Tis no silly trick. He's not the man to do an idle thing. There's mischief in this."

"What mischief can he do us more than he has done?— for I see his hand in our misfortune. What mischief, I say? — out with it, man, for your looks betray a fear of something worse."

"Faith, Jack, I dread he has gone to fetch help and will lodge us in gaol for this business."

"Gaol!" cries he, in a passion of desperation. "Why, this will undo Moll for ever. Her husband can never forgive her putting such shame upon him. Rouse yourself, man, from your stupor. Get me something in the shape of a hammer, for God's sake, that we may burst our way from this accursed trap."

I bethought me of an axe for splitting wood, that lay in the kitchen, and fetching it quickly, I put it in his hand. Bidding me stand aside, he let fly at the door like a madman. The splinters flew, but the door held good; and when he stayed a moment to take a new grip on his axe, I heard a clamour of voices outside — Simon's, higher than the rest, crying, "My new door, that cost me seven and eightpence!"

"The lock, the lock!" says I. "Strike that off."

Down came the axe, striking a spark of fire from the lock, which fell with a clatter at the next blow; but ere we had time to open the door, Simon and his party, entering by the back door, forced us to turn for our defence. Perceiving Dawson armed with an axe, however, these fellows paused, and the leader, whom I recognised for the constable of our parish, carrying a staff in one hand and a lanthorn in t'other, cried to us in the king's name to surrender ourselves.

"Take us, if you can," cries Dawson; "and the Lord have mercy on the first who comes within my reach!"

Deftly enough, old Simon, snatching the fellow's cap who stood next him, flings it at the candle that stands flaring on the floor, and justles the constable's lanthorn from his hand, so that in a moment we were all in darkness. Taking us at this disadvantage (for Dawson dared not lay about him with his axe, for fear of hitting me by misadventure), the rascals closed at once; and a most bloody, desperate fight ensued. For, after the first onslaught, in which

Dawson (dropping his axe, as being useless at such close quarters) and I grappled each our man, the rest, knowing not friend from foe in the obscurity, and urged on by fear, fell upon each other,—this one striking out at the first he met, and that giving as good as he had taken,—and so all fell a-mauling and belabouring with such lust of vengeance that presently the whole place was of an uproar with the din of cursing, howling, and hard blows. For my own lot I had old Simon to deal with, as I knew at once by the cold, greasy feel of his leathern jerkin, he being enraged to make me his prisoner for the ill I had done him. Hooking his horny fingers about my throat, he clung to me like any wildcat; but stumbling, shortly, over two who were rolling on the floor, we went down both with a crack, and with such violence that he, being undermost, was stunned by the fall. Then, my blood boiling at this treatment, I got astride of him, and roasted his ribs royally, and with more force than ever I had conceived myself to be possessed of. And, growing beside myself with this passion of war, I do think I should have pounded him into a pulp, but that two other combatants, falling across me with their whole weight, knocked all the wind out of my body, oppressing me so grievously, that 'twas as much as I could do to draw myself out of the fray, and get a gasp of breath again.

About this time the uproar began to subside, for those who had got the worst of the battle thought it advisable to sneak out of the house for safety, and those who had fared better, fearing a reverse of fortune, counted they had done enough for this bout, and so also withdrew.

"Are you living, Kit?" asks Dawson, then.

"Aye," says I, as valiantly as you please, "and ready to fight another half-dozen such rascals," but pulling the broken door open, all the same, to get out the easier, in case they returned.

"Why, then, let's go," says he, "unless any is minded to have us stay."

No one responding to this challenge, we made ado to find a couple of hats and cloaks for our use and sallied out.

"Which way do we turn?" asks Dawson, as we come into the road.

"Whither would you go, Jack?"

"Why, to warn Moll of her danger, to be sure."

I apprehended no danger to her, and believed her husband would defend her in any case better than we could, but Dawson would have it we should warn them, and so we turned towards the Court. And now upon examination we found we had come very well out of this fight; for save that the wound in Dawson's hand had been opened afresh, we were neither much the worse.

"But let us set our best foot foremost, Jack," says I, "for I do think we have done more mischief to-night than any we have before, and I shall not be greatly surprised if we are called to account for the death of old Simon or some of his hirelings."

"I know not how that may be," says he, "but I must answer for knocking of somebody's teeth out."

CHAPTER XXXIII.

We take Moll to Greenwich; but no great happiness for her there.

IN the midst of our heroics I was greatly scared by perceiving a cloaked figure coming hurriedly towards us in the dim light.

"'Tis another, come to succour his friends," whispers I. "Let us step into this hedge."

"Too late," returns he. "Put on a bold face, 'tis only one."

With a swaggering gait and looking straight before us, we had passed the figure, when a voice calls "Father!" and there turning, we find that 'tis poor Moll in her husband's cloak.

"Where is thy husband, child?" asks Dawson, as he recovers from his astonishment, taking Moll by the hand.

"I have no husband, father," answers she, piteously.

"Why, sure he hath not turned you out of doors?"

"No, he'd not do that," says she, "were I ten times more wicked than I am."

"What folly then is this?" asks her father.

"'Tis no folly. I have left him of my own free will, and shall never go back to him. For he's no more my husband than that house is mine" (pointing to the Court). "Both were got by the same means, and both are lost."

Then briefly she told how they had been turned from the

gate by Peter, and how Mr. Godwin was now as poor and homeless as we. And this news throwing us into a silence with new bewilderment, she asks us simply whither we are going.

"My poor Moll!" is all the answer Dawson can make, and that in a broken, trembling voice.

"'Tis no good to cry," says she, dashing aside hér tears that had sprung at this word of loving sympathy, and forcing herself to a more cheerful tone. "Why, let us think that we are just awake from a long sleep to find ourselves no worse off than when we fell a-dreaming. Nay, not so ill," adds she, "for you have a home near London. Take me there, dear."

"With all my heart, chuck," answers her father, eagerly. "There, at least, I can give you a shelter till your husband can offer better."

She would not dispute this point (though I perceived clearly her mind was resolved fully never to claim her right to Mr. Godwin's roof), but only begged we should hasten on our way, saying she felt chilled; and in passing Mother Fitch's cottage she constrained us to silence and caution; then when we were safely past she would have us run, still feigning to be cold, but in truth (as I think) to avoid being overtaken by Mr. Godwin, fearing, maybe, that he would overrule her will. This way we sped till Moll was fain to stop with a little cry of pain, and clapping her hand to her heart, being fairly spent and out of breath. Then we took her betwixt us, lending her our arms for support, and falling into a more regular pace made good progress. We trudged on till we reached Croydon without any accident, save that at one point,

Moll's step faltering and she with a faint sob weighing heavily upon our arms, we stopped, as thinking her strength overtaxed, and then glancing about me I perceived we were upon that little bridge where we had overtaken Mr. Godwin and he had offered to make Moll his wife. Then I knew 'twas not fatigue that weighed her down, and gauging her feelings by my own remorse, I pitied this poor wife even more than I blamed myself; for had she revealed herself to him at that time, though he might have shrunk from marriage, he must have loved her still, and so she had been spared this shame and hopeless sorrow.

At Croydon we overtook a carrier on his way to London for the Saturday market, who for a couple of shillings gave us a place in his waggon with some good bundles of hay for a seat, and here was rest for our tired bodies (though little for our tormented minds) till we reached Marsh End, where we were set down; and so, the ground being hard with frost, across the Marsh to Greenwich about daybreak. Having the key of his workshop with him, Dawson took us into his lodgings without disturbing the other inmates of the house (who might well have marvelled to see us enter at this hour with a woman in a man's cloak, and no covering but a handkerchief to her head), and Moll taking his bed, we disposed ourselves on some shavings in his shop to get a little sleep.

Dawson was already risen when I awoke, and going into his little parlour, I found him mighty busy setting the place in order, which was in a sad bachelor's pickle, to be sure — all littered up with odds and ends of turning, unwashed plates, broken victuals, etc., just as he had left it.

T

"She's asleep," says he, in a whisper. "And I'd have this room like a little palace against she comes into it, so do you lend me a hand, Kit, and make no more noise than you can help. The kitchen's through that door; carry everything in there, and what's of no use fling out of the window into the road."

Setting to with a will, we got the parlour and kitchen neat and proper, plates washed, tiles wiped, pots and pans hung up, furniture furbished up, and everything in its place in no time; then leaving me to light a fire in the parlour, Dawson goes forth a-marketing, with a basket on his arm, in high glee. And truly to see the pleasure in his face later on, making a mess of bread and milk in one pipkin and cooking eggs in another (for now we heard Moll stirring in her chamber), one would have thought that this was an occasion for rejoicing rather than grief, and this was due not to want of kind feeling, but to the fond, simple nature of him, he being manly enough in some ways, but a very child in others. He did never see further than his nose (as one says), and because it gave him joy to have Moll beside him once more, he must needs think hopefully, that she will quickly recover from this reverse of fortune, and that all will come right again.

Our dear Moll did nothing to damp his hopes, but played her part bravely and well to spare him the anguish of remorse that secretly wrung her own heart. She met us with a cheerful countenance, admired the neatness of the parlour, the glowing fire, ate her share of porridge, and finding the eggs cooked hard, declared she could not abide them soft. Then she would see her father work his lathe (to his great delight), and begged he would make her some cups for eggs, as being more to our present fashion than eating them from one's hand.

"Why," says he, "there's an old bed-post in the corner that will serve me to a nicety. But first I must see our landlord and engage a room for Kit and me; for I take it, my dear," adds he, "you will be content to stay with us here."

"Yes," answers she, "'tis a most cheerful view of the river from the windows."

She tucked up her skirt and sleeves to busy herself in household matters, and when I would have relieved her of this office, she begged me to go and bear her father company, saying with a piteous look in her eyes that we must leave her some occupation or she should weary. She was pale, there were dark lines beneath her eyes, and she was silent; but I saw no outward sign of grief till the afternoon, when, coming from Jack's shop unexpected, I spied her sitting by the window, with her face in her hands, bowed over a piece of cloth we had bought in the morning, which she was about to fashion into a plain gown, as being more suitable to her condition than the rich dress in which she had left the Court.

"Poor soul!" thinks I; "here is a sad awaking from thy dream of riches and joy."

Upon a seasonable occasion I told Dawson we must soon begin to think of doing something for a livelihood — a matter which was as remote from his consideration as the day of wrath.

"Why, Kit," says he, "I've as good as fifty pounds yet in a hole at the chimney back."

"Aye, but when that's gone — " says I.

"That's a good way hence, Kit, but there never was

such a man as you for going forth to meet troubles half way. However, I warrant I shall find some jobs of carpentry to keep us from begging our bread when the pinch comes."

Not content to wait for this pinch, I resolved I would go into the city and enquire there if the booksellers could give me any employment — thinking I might very well write some good sermons on honesty, now I had learnt the folly of roguery. Hearing of my purpose the morning I was about to go, Moll takes me aside and asks me in a quavering voice if I knew where Mr. Godwin might be found. This question staggered me a moment, for her husband's name had not been spoken by any of us since the catastrophe, and it came into my mind now that she designed to return to him, and I stammered out some foolish hint at Hurst Court.

"No, he is not there," says she, "but I thought maybe that Sir Peter Lely — "

"Aye," says I; "he will most likely know where Mr. Godwin may be found."

"Can you tell me where Sir Peter lives?"

"No; but I can learn easily when I am in the city."

"If you can, write the address and send him this," says she, drawing a letter from her breast. She had writ her husband's name on it, and now she pressed her lips to it twice, and putting the warm letter in my hand, she turned away, her poor mouth twitching with smothered grief. I knew then that there was no thought in her mind of seeing her husband again.

I carried the letter with me to the city, wondering what was in it. I know not now, yet I think it contained but a few words of explanation and farewell, with some prayer, maybe, that she might be forgiven and forgotten.

Learning where Sir Peter Lely lived, I myself went to his house, and he not being at home, I asked his servant if Mr. Godwin did sometimes come there.

" Why, yes, sir, he was here but yesterday," answers he. " Indeed, never a day passes but he calls to ask if any one hath sought him."

" In that case," says I, slipping a piece in his ready hand, and fetching out Moll's letter, " you will give him this when he comes next."

" That I will, sir, and without fail. But if you would see him, sir, he bids me say he is ever at his lodging in Holborn, from five in the evening to eight in the morning."

" 'Twill answer all ends if you give him that letter. He is in good health, I hope."

" Well, sir, he is and he isn't, as you may say," answers he, dropping into a familiar, confidential tone after casting his eye over me to be sure I was no great person. " He ails nothing, to be sure, for I hear he is ever afoot from morn till even a-searching hither and thither ; but a more down-hearted, rueful looking gentleman for his age I never see. 'Twixt you and me, sir, I think he hath lost his sweetheart, seeing I am charged, with Sir Peter's permission, to follow and not lose sight of any lady who may chance to call here for him."

I walked back to Greenwich across the fields, debating in my mind whether I should tell Moll of her husband's distress or not, so perplexed with conflicting arguments that I had come to no decision when I reached home.

Moll spying me coming, from her window in the front of the house, met me at the door, in her cloak and hood, and begged I would take her a little turn over the heath.

"What have you to tell me?" asks she, pressing my arm as we walked on.

"I have given your letter to Sir Peter Lely's servant, who promises to deliver it faithfully to your husband."

"Well," says she, after a little pause of silence, "that is not all."

"You will be glad to know that he is well in health," says I, and then I stop again, all hanging in a hedge for not knowing whether it were wiser to speak or hold my tongue.

"There is something else. I see it in your face. Hide nothing from me for love's sake," says she, piteously. Whereupon, my heart getting the better of my head (which, to be sure, was no great achievement), I told all as I have set it down here.

"My dear, dear love! my darling Dick!" says she, in the end. And then she would have it told all over again, with a thousand questions, to draw forth more; and these being exhausted, she asks why I would have concealed so much from her, and if I did fear she would seek him.

"Nay, my dear," says I; "'tis t'other way about. For if your husband does forgive you, and yearns but to take you back into his arms, it would be an unnatural, cruel thing to keep you apart. Therefore, to confess the whole truth, I did meditate going to him and showing how we and not you are to blame in this matter, and then telling him where he might find you, if on reflection he felt that he could honestly hold you guiltless. But ere I do that (as I see now), I must know if you are willing to this accommodation; for if you are not, then are our wounds all opened afresh to no purpose, but to retard their healing."

She made no reply nor any comment for a long time, nor did I seek to bias her judgment by a single word (doubting my wisdom). But I perceived by the quivering of her arm within mine that a terrible conflict 'twixt passion and principle was convulsing every fibre of her being. At the top of the hill above Greenwich she stopped, and, throwing back her hood, let the keen wind blow upon her face, as she gazed over the grey flats beyond the river. And the air seeming to give her strength and a clearer perception, she says, presently:

"Accommodation!" (And she repeats this unlucky word of mine twice or thrice, as if she liked it less each time.) "That means we shall agree to let bygones be bygones, and do our best to get along together for the rest of our lives as easily as we may."

"That's it, my dear," says I, cheerfully.

"Hush up the past," continues she, in the same calculating tone; "conceal it from the world, if possible. Invent some new lie to deceive the curious, and hoodwink our decent friends. Chuckle at our success, and come in time" (here she paused a moment) "to 'chat so lightly of our past knavery, that we could wish we had gone farther in the business.'" Then turning about to me, she asks: "If you were writing the story of my life for a play, would you end it thus?"

"My dear," says I, "a play's one thing, real life's another; and believe me, as far as my experience goes of real life, the less heroics there are in it the better parts are those for the actors in't."

She shook her head fiercely in the wind, and, turning about with a brusque vigour, cries, "Come on. I'll have no accommodation. And yet," says she, stopping short after a couple of hasty steps, and with a fervent earnestness in her voice, "and yet, if I could wipe out this stain, if by any act I could redeem my fault, God knows, I'd do it, cost what it might, to be honoured once again by my dear Dick."

"This comes of living in a theatre all her life," thinks I. And indeed, in this, as in other matters yet to be told, the teaching of the stage was but too evident.

CHAPTER XXXIV.

All agree to go out to Spain again in search of our old jollity.

ANOTHER week passed by, and then Dawson, short-sighted as he was in his selfishness, began to perceive that things were not coming all right, as he had expected. Once or twice when I went into his shop, I caught him sitting idle before his lathe, with a most woe-begone look in his face.

"What's amiss, Jack?" asks I, one day when I found him thus.

He looked to see that the door was shut, and then says he, gloomily:

"She don't sing as she used to, Kit; she don't laugh hearty."

I hunched my shoulders.

"She doesn't play us any of her old pranks," continues he. "She don't say one thing and go and do t'other the next moment, as she used to do. She's too good."

What could I say to one who was fond enough to think that the summer would come back at his wish and last for ever?

"She's not the same, Kit," he goes on. "No, not by twenty years. One would say she is older than I am, yet she's scarce the age of woman. And I do see she gets more pale and thin each day. D'ye think she's fretting for *him?*"

"Like enough, Jack," says I. "What would you? He's her husband, and 'tis as if he was dead to her. She cannot be a maid again. 'Tis young to be a widow, and no hope of being wife ever more."

"God forgive me," says he, hanging his head.

"We did it for the best," says I. "We could not foresee this."

"'Twas so natural to think we should be happy again being all together. Howsoever," adds he, straightening himself with a more manful vigour, "we will do something to chase these black dogs hence."

On his lathe was the egg cup he had been turning for Moll; he snapped it off from the chuck and flung it in the litter of chips and shavings, as if 'twere the emblem of his past folly.

It so happened that night that Moll could eat no supper, pleading for her excuse that she felt sick.

"What is it, chuck?" says Jack, setting down his knife and drawing his chair beside Moll's.

"The vapours, I think," says she, with a faint smile.

"Nay," says he, slipping his arm about her waist and drawing her to him. "My Moll hath no such modish humours. 'Tis something else. I have watched ye, and do perceive you eat less and less. Tell us what ails you."

"Well, dear," says she, "I do believe 'tis idleness is the root of my disorder."

"Idleness was never wont to have this effect on you."

"But it does now that I am grown older. There's not enough to do. If I could find some occupation for my thoughts, I should not be so silly."

"Why, that's a good thought. What say you, dear, shall we go a-play-acting again?"

Moll shook her head.

"To be sure," says he, scratching his jaw, "we come out of that business with no great encouragement to go further in it. But times are mended since then, and I do hear the world is more mad for diversion now than ever they were before the Plague."

"No, dear," says Moll, "'tis of no use to think of that. I couldn't play now."

After this we sat silent a while, looking into the embers; then Jack, first to give expression to his thoughts, says:

"I think you were never so happy in your life, Moll, as that time we were in Spain, nor can I recollect ever feeling so free from care myself,— after we got out of the hands of that gentleman robber. There's a sort of infectious brightness in the sun, and the winds, blow which way they may, do chase away dull thoughts and dispose one to jollity; eh, sweetheart? Why, we met never a tattered vagabond on the road but he was halloing of ditties, and a kinder, more hospitable set of people never lived. With a couple of rials in your pocket, you feel as rich and independent as with an hundred pounds in your hand elsewhere."

At this point Moll, who had hitherto listened in apathy to these eulogies, suddenly pushing back her chair, looks at us with a strange look in her eyes, and says under her breath, "Elche!"

"Barcelony for my money," responds Dawson, whose memories of Elche were not so cheerful as of those parts where we had led a more vagabond life.

"Elche!" repeats Moll, twining her fingers, and with a smile gleaming in her eyes.

"Does it please you, chuck, to talk of these matters?"

"Yes, yes!" returns she, eagerly. "You know not the joy it gives me" (clapping her hand on her heart). "Talk on."

Mightily pleased with himself, her father goes over our past adventures,— the tricks Moll played us, as buying of her petticoat while we were hunting for her, our excellent entertainment in the mountain villages, our lying abed all one day, and waking at sundown to think it was daybreak, our lazy days and jovial nights, etc., at great length; and when his memory began to give out, giving me a kick of the shin, he says:

"Han't you got anything to say? For a dull companion there's nothing in the world to equal your man of wit and understanding"; which, as far as my observation goes, was a very true estimation on his part.

But, indeed (since I pretend to no great degree of wit or understanding), I must say, as an excuse for my silence, that during his discourse I had been greatly occupied in observing Moll, and trying to discover what was passing in her mind. 'Twas clear this talk of Spain animated her spirit beyond ordinary measure, so that at one moment I conceived she did share her father's fond fancy that our lost happiness might be regained by mere change of scene, and I confess I was persuaded somewhat to this opinion by reflecting how much we owe to circumstances for our varying moods, how dull, sunless days will cast a gloom upon our spirits, and how a bright, breezy day will lift them up, etc. But I presently perceived that the stream of her thoughts was divided; for though she nodded or shook her head, as occasion required, the strained, earnest expression in her tightened lips and knitted brows showed that the stronger current of her ideas flowed in another and deeper channel. Maybe she only desired her father to talk that she might be left the freer to think.

"'Twas near about this time of the year that we started on our travels," said I, in response to Dawson's reminder.

"Aye, I recollect 'twas mighty cold when we set sail, and the fruit trees were all bursting into bloom when we came into France. I would we were there now; eh, Moll?"

"What, dear?" asks she, rousing herself at this direct question.

"I say, would you be back there now, child?"

"Oh, will you take me there if I would go?"

"With all my heart, dear Moll. Is there anything in the world I'd not do to make you happy?"

She took his hand upon her knee, and caressing it, says:

"Let us go soon, father."

"What, will you be dancing of fandangos again?" asks he; and she nods for reply, though I believe her thoughts had wandered again to some other matter.

"I warrant I shall fall into the step again the moment I smell garlic; but I'll rehearse it an hour to-morrow morning, that we may lose no time. Will you have a short petticoat and a waist-cloth again, Moll?"

She, with her elbows on her knees now, and her chin in her hands, looking into the fire, nodded.

"And you, Kit," continues he, "you'll get a guitar and play tunes for us, as I take it you will keep us company still."

"Yes, you may count on me for that," says I.

"We shan't have Don Sanchez to play the tambour for us, but I wager I shall beat it as well as he; though, seeing he owes us more than we owe him, we might in reason call upon him, and—"

"No, no; only we three," says Moll.

"Aye, three's enough, in all conscience, and seeing we know a bit of the language, we shall get on well enough without him. I do long, Moll, to see you a-flinging over my shoulder, with your clappers going, your pretty eye and cheek all aglow with pleasure, and a court full of señors and caballeros crying 'Holé!' and casting their handkerchiefs at your feet."

Moll fetched a long, fluttering sigh, and, turning to her father, says in an absent way: "Yes, dear; yes. When shall we go?"

Then, falling to discussing particulars, Dawson, clasping his hands upon his stomach, asked with a long face if at this season we were likely to fall in with the equinoxes on our voyage, and also if we could not hit some point of Spain so as to avoid crossing the mountains of Pyranee and the possibility of falling again into the hands of brigands. To which I replied that, knowing nothing of the northern part of Spain and its people, we stood a chance of finding a rude climate, unsuitable to travelling at this time of year, and an inhospitable reception, and that, as our object was to reach the South as quickly as possible, it would be more to our advantage to find a ship going through the straits which would carry us as far as Alicante or Valencia. And Moll supporting my argument very vigorously, Dawson gave way with much less reluctance than I expected at the outset. But, indeed, the good fellow seemed now ready to make any sacrifice of himself so that he might see his Moll joyous again.

When I entered his shop the next morning, I found him with his coat off, cutting capers, a wooden platter in his hand for a tambourine, and the sweat pouring down his face.

"I am a couple of stone or so too heavy for the boleros," gasps he, coming to a stand, "but I doubt not, by the time we land at Alicante, there'll not be an ounce too much of me."

Learning that a convoy for the Levant was about to set sail with the next favourable wind from Chatham, we took horse and rode there that afternoon, and by great good luck we found the Faithful Friend, a good ship bound for Genoa in Italy, whereof Mr. Dixon, the master, having intent to enter and victual at Alicante, undertook to carry us there for ten pounds a head, so being we could get all aboard by the next evening at sundown.

Here was short grace, to be sure; but we did so despatch our affairs that we were embarked in due time, and by daybreak the following morning, were under weigh.

CHAPTER XXXV.

How we lost our poor Moll, and our long search for her.

WE reached Alicante the 15th March, after a long, tedious voyage. During this time I had ample opportunity for observing Moll, but with little relief to my gloomy apprehensions. She rarely quitted her father's side, being now as sympathetic and considerate of him in his sufferings, as before she had been thoughtless and indifferent. She had ever a gentle word of encouragement for him; she was ever kind and patient. Only once her spirit seemed to weary: that was when we had been beating about in the bay of Cadiz four days, for a favourable gale to take us through the straits. We were on deck, she and I, the sails flapping the masts idly above our heads.

"Oh," says she, laying her hand on my shoulder, and her wasted cheek against my arm, "oh, that it were all ended!"

She was sweeter with me than ever she had been before; it seemed as if the love bred in her heart by marriage must expend itself upon some one. But though this tenderness endeared her more to me, it saddened me, and I would have had her at her tricks once more, making merry at my expense. For I began to see that our happiness comes from within and not from without, and so fell despairing that ever this poor stricken heart of hers would be healed, which set me a-repenting more sincerely than ever the mischief I had helped to do her.

Dawson also, despite his stubborn disposition to see things as he would have them, had, nevertheless, some secret perception of the incurable sorrow which she, with all her art, could scarce dissimulate. Yet he clung to that fond belief in a return of past happiness, as if 'twere his last hope on earth. When at last our wind sprang up, and we were cutting through the waters with bending masts and not a crease in the bellied sails, he came upon deck, and spreading his hands out, cries in joy:

"Oh, this blessed sunlight! There is nought in the world like it — no, not the richest wine — to swell one's heart with content."

And then he fell again to recalling our old adventures and mirthful escapades. He gave the rascals who fetched us ashore a piece more than they demanded, hugely delighted to find they understood his Spanish and such quips as he could call to mind. Then being landed, he falls to extolling everything he sees and hears, calling upon Moll to justify his appreciation; nay, he went so far as to pause in a narrow street where was a most unsavoury smell, to sniff the air and declare he could scent the oranges in bloom. And Lord! to hear him praise the whiteness of the linen, the excellence of the meat and drink set before us at the posada, one would have said he had never before seen clean sheets or tasted decent victuals.

Seeing that neither Moll nor I could work ourselves up (try as we might) to his high pitch of enthusiasm, he was ready with an excuse for us.

"I perceive," says he, "you are still suffering from your voyage. Therefore, we will not quit this town before tomorrow" (otherwise I believe he would have started off on our expedition as soon as our meal was done). "However," adds he, "do you make enquiry, Kit, if you can get yourself understood, if there be ever a bull to be fought to-day or any diversion of dancing or play-acting to-night, that the time hang not too heavy on our hands."

As no such entertainments were to be had (this being the season of Lent, which is observed very strictly in these parts), Dawson contented himself with taking Moll out to visit the shops, and here he speedily purchased a pair of clappers for her, a tambour for himself, and a guitar for me, though we were difficult to please, for no clappers pleased Moll as those she had first bought; and it did seem to me that I could strike no notes out of any instrument but they had a sad, mournful tone.

Then nothing would satisfy him but to go from one draper's to another, seeking a short petticoat, a waist-cloth, and a round hat to Moll's taste, which ended to his disappointment, for she could find none like the old.

"Why, don't you like this?" he would say, holding up a gown; "to my eyes 'tis the very spit of t'other, only fresher."

And she demurring, whispers, "To-morrow, dear, to-morrow," with plaintive entreaty for delay in her wistful eyes.

Disheartened, but not yet at the end of his resources, her father at last proposed that she should take a turn through the town alone and choose for herself. "For," says he, "I believe we do rather hinder than help you with our advice in such matters."

After a moment's reflection, Moll agreed to this, and saying she would meet us at the posada for supper, left us, and walked briskly back the way we had come.

When she was gone, Dawson had never a word to say,

nor I either, for dejection, yet, had I been questioned, I could have found no better reason for my despondency than that I felt 'twas all a mistake coming here for happiness.

Strolling aimlessly through the narrow back ways, we came presently to the market that stands against the port. And here, almost at the first step, Dawson catches my arm and nods towards the opposite side of the market-place. Some Moors were seated there in their white clothes, with bundles of young palm leaves, plaited up in various forms of crowns, crosses, and the like, — which the people of this country do carry to church to be blessed on Palm Sunday; and these Moors I knew came from Elche, because palms grow nowhere else in such abundance.

"Yes," says I, thinking 'twas this queer merchandise he would point out, "I noticed these Moors and their ware when we passed here a little while back with Moll."

"Don't you see her there now — at the corner?" asks he.

Then, to my surprise, I perceived Moll in very earnest conversation with two Moors, who had at first screened her from my sight.

"Come away," continues he. "She left us to go back and speak to them, and would not have us know."

Why should she be secret about this trifling matter, I asked myself. 'Twas quite natural that, if she recognised in these Moors some old acquaintance of Elche, she should desire to speak them.

We stole away to the port, and seating ourselves upon some timber, there we looked upon the sea nigh upon half an hour without saying a word. Then turning to me, Dawson says: "Unless she speak to us upon this matter,

Kit, we will say nought to her. But, if she say nothing, I shall take it for a sign her heart is set upon going back to Elche, and she would have it a secret that we may not be disheartened in our other project."

"That is likely enough," says I, not a little surprised by his reasoning. But love sharpens a man's wit, be it never so dull.

"Nevertheless," continues he, "if she can be happier at Elche than elsewhere, then must we abandon our scheme and accept hers with a good show of content. We owe her that, Kit."

"Aye, and more," says I.

"Then when we meet to-morrow morning, I will offer to go there, as if 'twas a happy notion that had come to me in my sleep, and do you back me up with all the spirit you can muster."

So after some further discussion we rose, and returned to our posada, where we found Moll waiting for us. She told us she had found no clothes to her liking (which was significant), and said not a word of her speaking to the Moors in the market-place, so we held our peace on these matters.

We did not part till late that night, for Moll would sit up with us, confessing she felt too feverish for sleep; and indeed this was apparent enough by her strange humour, for she kept no constant mood for five minutes together. Now, she would sit pensive, paying no heed to us, with a dreamy look in her eyes, as if her thoughts were wandering far away — to her husband in England maybe; then she would hang her head as though she dared not look him in the face even at that distance; and anon she would recover herself with a noble exaltation, lifting her head with a fearless mien. And so presently her body drooping gradually to a reflective posture, she falls dreaming again, to rouse herself suddenly at some new prompting of her spirit, and give us all her thoughts, all eagerness for two moments, all melting sweetness the next, with her pretty manner of clinging to her father's arm, and laying her cheek against his shoulder. And when at last we came to say good-night, she hangs about his neck as if she would fain sleep there, quitting him with a deep sigh and a passionate kiss. Also she kissed me most affectionately, but could say never a word of farewell to either of us — hurrying to her chamber to weep, as I think.

We knew not what to conclude from these symptoms, save that she might be sickening of some disorder; so we to our beds, very down in the mouth and faint at heart.

About six the next morning I was awoke by the door bursting suddenly open, and starting up in my bed, I see Dawson at my side, shaking in every limb, and his eyes wide with terror.

"Moll's gone!" cries he, and falls a-blubbering.

"Gone!" says I, springing out of bed. "'Tis not possible."

"She has not lain in her bed; and one saw her go forth last night as the doors were closing, knowing her for a foreigner by her hood. Come with me," adds he, laying his hand on a chair for support. "I dare not go alone."

"Aye, I'll go with ye, Jack; but whither?"

"Down to the sea," says he, hoarsely.

I stopped in the midst of dressing, overcome by this fearful hint; for, knowing Moll's strong nature, the thought had never occurred to me that she might do away with herself.

Yet now reflecting on her strange manner of late, especially her parting with us overnight, it seemed not so impossible neither. For here, seeing the folly of our coming hither, desponding of any happiness in the future, was the speediest way of ending a life that was burdensome to herself and a constant sorrow to us. Nay, with her notions of poetic justice drawn from plays, she may have regarded this as the only atonement she could make her husband; the only means of giving him back freedom to make a happier choice in marriage. With these conclusions taking shape, I shuffled on my clothes, and then, with shaking fear, we two, hanging to each other's arms for strength, made our way through the crooked streets to the sea; and there, seeing a group of men and women gathered at the water's edge some little distance from us, we dared not go further, conceiving 'twas a dead body they were regarding. But 'twas only a company of fishers examining their haul of fishes, as we presently perceived. So, somewhat cheered, we cast our eyes to the right and left, and, seeing nothing to justify our fears, advanced along the mole to the very end, where it juts out into the sea, with great stones around to break the surf. Here, then, with deadly apprehensions, we peered amongst the rocks, holding our breath, clutching tight hold of one another by the hand, in terror of finding that we so eagerly searched, — a hood, a woman's skirt clinging to the stones, a stiffened hand thrust up from the lapping waters. Never may I forget the sickening horror of the moment when, creeping out amidst the rocks, Dawson twitches my hand, and points down through the clear water to something lying white at the bottom. It looked for all the world like a dead face, coloured a greenish white by the water; but presently we saw, by one end curling over in the swell of a wave, that 'twas only a rag of paper.

Then I persuaded Dawson to give up this horrid search, and return to our posada, when, if we found not Moll, we might more justly conclude she had gone to Elche, than put an end to her life; and though we could learn nothing of her at our inn, more than Dawson had already told me, yet our hopes were strengthened in the probability of finding her at Elche by recollecting her earnest, secret conversation with the Moors, who might certainly have returned to Elche in the night, they preferring that time for their journey, as we knew. So, having hastily snatched a repast, whilst our landlord was procuring mules for our use, we set off across the plain, doing our best to cheer each other on the way. But I confess one thing damped my spirits exceedingly, and that was, having no hint from Moll the night before of this project, which then must have been fully matured in her mind, nor any written word of explanation and encouragement. For, thinks I, she being no longer a giddy, heedless child, ready to play any prank without regard to the consequences, but a very considerate, remorseful woman, would not put us to this anxiety without cause. Had she resolved to go to her friends at Elche, she would, at least, have comforted us with the hope of meeting her again; whereas, this utter silence did point to a knowledge on her part that we were sundered for ever, and that she could give us no hope, but such as we might glean from uncertainty.

Arriving at Elche, we made straight for the house of the merchant, Sidi ben Ahmed, with whose family Moll had been so intimate previously. Here we were met by Sidi himself, who, after laying his fingers across his lips, and setting his hand upon his heart, in token of recognition and respect, asked us very civilly our business, though without any show of surprise at seeing us. But these Moors do pride themselves upon a stoic behaviour at all times, and make it a point to conceal any emotion they may feel, so that men never can truly judge of their feelings.

Upon explaining our circumstances as well as our small knowledge of the tongue allowed us, he makes us a gesture of his open hands, as if he would have us examine his house for ourselves, to see that she was not hid away there for any reason, and then calling his servants, he bids them seek through all the town, promising them a rich reward if they bring any tidings of Lala Mollah. And while this search was being made, he entertained us at his own table, where we recounted so much of our miserable history as we thought it advisable he should know.

One by one the servants came in to tell that they had heard nothing, save that some market-men had seen and spoken with Moll at Alicante, but had not clapt eyes on her since. Not content with doing us this service, the merchant furnished us with fresh mules, to carry us back to Alicante, whither we were now all eagerness to return, in the hope of finding Moll at the posada. So, travelling all night, we came to our starting-place the next morning, to learn no tidings of our poor Moll.

We drew some grain of comfort from this; for, it being now the third day since the dear girl had disappeared, her body would certainly have been washed ashore, had she cast herself, as we feared, in the sea. It occurred to us that if Moll were still living, she had either returned to England, or gone to Don Sanchez at Toledo, whose wise counsels she had ever held in high respect. The former supposition seemed to me the better grounded; for it was easy to understand how, yearning for him night and day, she should at length abandon every scruple, and throw herself at his feet, reckless of what might follow. 'Twas not inconsistent with her impulsive character, and that more reasonable view of life she had gained by experience, and the long reflections on her voyage hither. And that which supported my belief still more was that a fleet of four sail (as I learnt) had set forth for England the morning after our arrival. So now finding, on enquiry, that a carrier was to set out for Toledo that afternoon, I wrote a letter to Don Sanchez, telling him the circumstances of our loss, and begging him to let us know, as speedily as possible, if he had heard aught of Moll. And in this letter I enclosed a second, addressed to Mr. Godwin, having the same purport, which I prayed Don Sanchez to send on with all expedition, if Moll were not with him.

And now, having despatched these letters, we had nothing to do but to await a reply, which, at the earliest, we could not expect to get before the end of the week — Toledo being a good eighty English leagues distant.

We waited in Alicante four days more, making seven in all from the day we lost Moll; and then, the suspense and torment of inactivity becoming insupportable, we set out again for Elche, the conviction growing strong upon us, with reflection, that we had little to hope from Don Sanchez. And we resolved we would not go this time to Sidi ben Ahmed, but rather seek to take him unawares, and make enquiry by more subtle means, we having our doubts of his veracity. For these Moors are not honest liars like plain Englishmen, who do generally give you some hint of their business by shifting of their eyes this way and that, hawking, stammering, etc., but they will ever look you calmly and straight in the face, never at a loss for the right word, or over-anxious to convince you, so that 'twill plague a conjurer to tell if they speak truth or falsehood. And here I would remark, that in all my observations of men and manners, there is no nation in the world to equal the English, for a straightforward, pious, horse-racing sort of people.

Well, then, we went about our search in Elche with all the slyness possible, prying here and there like a couple of thieves a-robbing a hen-roost, and putting cross-questions to every simple fellow we met, — the best we could with our small knowledge of their tongue, — but all to no purpose, and so another day was wasted. We lay under the palms that night, and in the morning began our perquisition afresh; now hunting up and down the narrow lanes and alleys of the town, as we had scoured those of Alicante, in vain, until, persuaded of the uselessness of our quest, we agreed to return to Alicante, in the hope of finding there a letter from Don Sanchez. But (not to leave a single stone unturned), we settled we would call once again on Sidi ben Ahmed, and ask if he had any tidings to give us, but, openly, feeling we were no match for him at subterfuge. So, to his house we went, where we were received very graciously by the old merchant, who, chiding us gently for being in the neighbourhood a whole day without giving him a call, prayed us to enter his unworthy parlour, adding that we should find there a friend who would be very pleased to see us.

At this, my heart bounded to such an extent that I could

utter never a word (nor could Dawson either), for I expected nothing less than to find this friend was our dear Moll; and so, silent and shaking with feverish anticipation, we followed him down the tiled passage and round the inner garden of his house by the arcade, till we reached a doorway, and there, lifting aside the heavy hangings, he bade us enter. We pushed by him in rude haste, and then stopped of a sudden, in blank amazement; for, in place of Moll, whom we fully thought to find, we discovered only Don Sanchez, sitting on some pillows gravely smoking a Moorish chibouk.

"My daughter—my Moll!" cries Dawson, in despair. "Where is she?"

"By this time," replies Don Sanchez, rising, "your daughter should be in Barbary."

CHAPTER XXXVI.

We learn what hath become of Moll; and how she nobly atoned for our sins.

"BARBARY — Barbary!" gasps Dawson, thunderstruck by this discovery. "My Moll in Barbary?"

"She sailed three days ago," says the Don, laying down his pipe, and rising.

Dawson regards him for a moment or two in a kind of stupor, and then his ideas taking definite shape, he cries in a fury of passion and clenching his fists:

"Spanish dog! you shall answer this. And you" (turning in fury upon Sidi), "you — I know your cursed traffic — you've sold her to the Turk!"

Though Sidi may have failed to comprehend his words, he could not misunderstand his menacing attitude, yet he faced him with an unmoved countenance, not a muscle of his body betraying the slightest fear, his stoic calm doing more than any argument of words to overthrow Dawson's mad suspicion. But his passion unabated, Dawson turns again upon Don Sanchez, crying:

"Han't you won enough by your villany, but you must rob me of my daughter? Are you not satisfied with bringing us to shame and ruin, but this poor girl of mine must be cast to the Turk? Speak, rascal!" adds he, advancing a step, and seeking to provoke a conflict. "Speak, if you have any reason to show why I shouldn't strangle you."

"You'll not strangle me," answers the Don, calmly, "and here's my reason if you would see it." And with that he tilts his elbow, and with a turn of the wrist displays a long knife that lay concealed under his forearm. "I know no other defence against the attack of a madman."

"If I be mad," says Dawson, "and mad indeed I may be, and no wonder,—why, then, put your knife to merciful use and end my misery here."

"Nay, take it in your own hand," answers the Don, offering the knife. "And use it as you will — on yourself if you are a fool, or on me if, being not a fool, you can hold me guilty of such villany as you charged me with in your passion."

Dawson looks upon the offered knife an instant with distraction in his eyes, and the Don (not to carry this risky business too far), taking his hesitation for refusal, claps up the blade in his waist-cloth, where it lay mighty convenient to his hand.

"You are wise," says he, "for if that noble woman is to be served, 'tis not by spilling the blood of her best friends."

"You, her friend!" says Dawson.

"Aye, her best friend!" replies the other, with dignity, "for he is best who can best serve her."

"Then must I be her worst," says Jack, humbly, "having no power to undo the mischief I have wrought."

"'Tell me, Señor," says I, "who hath kidnapped poor Moll?"

"Nobody. She went of her free will, knowing full well the risk she ran — the possible end of her noble adventure — against the dissuasions and the prayers of all her friends here. She stood in the doorway there, and saw you cross the garden when you first came to seek her — saw you, her father, distracted with grief and fear, and she suffered you to go away. As you may know, nothing is more sacred to a Moor than the laws of hospitality, and by those laws Sidi was bound to respect the wishes of one who had claimed his protection. He could not betray her secret, but he and his family did their utmost to persuade her from her purpose. While you were yet in the town, they implored her to let them call you back, and she refused. Failing in their entreaties, they despatched a messenger to me; alas! when I arrived, she was gone. She went with a company of merchants bound for Alger, and all that her friends here could do was to provide her with a servant and letters, which will ensure her safe conduct to Thadviir."

"But why has she gone there, Señor?" says I, having heard him in a maze of wonderment to the end.

"Cannot you guess? Surely she must have given you some hint of her purposes, for 'twas in her mind, as I learn, when she agreed to leave England and come hither."

"Nothing — we know nothing," falters Dawson. "'Tis all mystery and darkness. Only we did suppose to find happiness a-wandering about the country, dancing and idling, as we did before."

"That dream was never hers," answers the Don. "She never thought to find happiness in idling pleasure. 'Tis the joy of martyrdom she's gone to find, seeking redemption in self-sacrifice."

"Be more explicit, sir, I pray," says I.

"In a word, then, she has gone to offer herself as a ransom for the real Judith Godwin."

We were too overwrought for great astonishment; indeed,

my chief surprise was that I had not foreseen this event in Moll's desire to return to Elche, or hit upon the truth in seeking an explanation of her disappearance. 'Twas of a piece with her natural romantic disposition and her newly awaked sense of poetic justice, — for here at one stroke she makes all human atonement for her fault and ours, — earning her husband's forgiveness by this proof of dearest love, and winning back for ever an honoured place in his remembrance. And I bethought me of our Lord's saying that greater love is there none than this: that one shall lay down his life for another.

For some time Dawson stood silent, his arms folded upon his breast, and his head bent in meditation, his lips pressed together, and every muscle in his face contracted with pain and labouring thought. Then, raising his head and fixing his eyes on the Don, he says:

"If I understand aright, my Moll hath gone to give herself up for a slave, in the place of her whose name she took."

The Don assents with a grave inclination of his head, and Dawson continues:

"I ask your pardon for that injustice I did you in my passion; but now that I am cool I cannot hold you blameless for what has befallen my poor child, and I call upon you as a man of honour to repair the wrong you've done me."

Again the Don bows very gravely, and then asks what we would have him do.

"I ask you," says Dawson, "as we have no means for such an expedition, to send me across the sea there to my Moll."

"I cannot ensure your return," says the Don, "and I warn you that once in Barbary you may never leave it."

"I do not want to return if she is there; nay," adds he,

"if I may move them to any mercy, they shall do what they will with this body of mine, so that they suffer my child to be free."

The Don turns to Sidi, and tells him what Dawson has offered to do; whereupon the Moor lays his finger across his lips, then his hand on Dawson's breast, and afterwards upon his own, with a reverence, to show his respect. And so he and the Don fall to discussing the feasibility of this project (as I discovered by picking up a word here and there); and, this ended, the Don turns to Dawson, and tells him there is no vessel to convey him at present, wherefore he must of force wait patiently till one comes in from Barbary.

"But," says he, "we may expect one in a few days, and rest you assured that your wish shall be gratified if it be possible."

We went down, Dawson and I, to the sea that afternoon; and, sitting on the shore at that point where we had formerly embarked aboard the Algerine galley, we scanned the waters for a sail that might be coming hither, and Dawson with the eagerness of one who looked to escape from slavery rather than one seeking it.

As we sat watching the sea, he fell a-regretting he had no especial gift of nature, by which he might more readily purchase Moll's freedom of her captors.

"However," says he, "if I can show 'em the use of chairs and benches, for lack of which they are now compelled, as we see, to squat on mats and benches, I may do pretty well with Turks of the better sort who can afford luxuries, and so in time gain my end."

"You shall teach me this business, Jack," says I, "for at present I'm more helpless than you."

"Kit," says he, laying hold of my hand, "let us have no misunderstanding on this matter. You go not to Barbary with me."

"What!" cries I, protesting. "You would have the heart to break from me after we have shared good and ill fortune together like two brothers all these years?"

"God knows we shall part with sore hearts o' both sides, and I shall miss you sadly enough, with no Christian to speak to out there. But 'tis not of ourselves we must think now. Some one must be here to be a father to my Moll when she returns, and I'll trust Don Sanchez no farther than I can see him, for all his wisdom. So, as you love the dear girl, you will stay here, Kit, to be her watch and ward, and as you love me you will spare me any further discussion on this head. For I am resolved."

I would say nothing then to contrary him, but my judgment and feeling both revolted against his decision. For, thinks I, if one Christian is worth but a groat to the Turk, two must be worth eightpence, therefore we together stand a better chance of buying Moll's freedom than either singly. And, for my own happiness, I would easier be a slave in Barbary with Jack than free elsewhere and friendless. Nowhere can a man be free from toil and pain of some sort or another, and there is no such solace in the world for one's discomforts as the company of a true man.

But I was not regardless of Moll's welfare when she returned, neither. For I argued with myself that Mr. Godwin had but to know of her condition to find means of coming hither for her succour. So the next time I met Don Sanchez, I took him aside and told him of my concern, asking him the speediest manner of sending a letter to England (that I had enclosed in mine to the Don having missed him through his leaving Toledo before it arrived).

"There is no occasion to write," says he. "For the moment I learnt your history from Sidi I sent a letter, apprising him of his wife's innocence in this business, and the noble reparation she had made for the fault of others. Also, I took the liberty to enclose a sum of money to meet his requirements, and I'll answer for it he is now on his way hither. For no man living could be dull to the charms of his wife, or bear resentment to her for an act that was prompted by love rather than avarice, and with no calculation on her part."

This cheered me considerably, and did somewhat return my faith in Don Sanchez, who certainly was the most extraordinary gentlemanly rascal that ever lived.

Day after day Dawson and I went down to the sea, and on the fifth day of our watching (after many false hopes and disappointments) we spied a ship, which we knew to be of the Algerine sort by the cross-set of its lateen sails, — making it to look like some great bird with spread wings on the water, — bearing down upon the shore.

We watched the approach of this ship in a fever of joy and expectation, for though we dared not breathe our hopes one to another, we both thought that maybe Moll was there. And this was not impossible. For, supposing Judith was married happily, she would refuse to leave her husband, and her mother, having lived so long in that country, might not care to leave it now and quit her daughter; so might they refuse their ransom and Moll be sent back to us. And, besides this reasoning, we had that clinging belief of the unfortunate that some unforeseen accident might turn to our advantage and overthrow our fears.

The Algerine came nearer and nearer, until at length we could make out certain figures moving upon the deck; then Dawson, laying a trembling hand on my sleeve, asked if I did not think 'twas a woman standing in the fore part; but I couldn't truly answer yes, which vexed him.

But, indeed, when the galley was close enough to drop anchor, being at some distance from the shore because of the shoals, I could not distinguish any women, and my heart sank, for I knew well that if Moll were there, she, seeing us, would have given us some signal of waving a handkerchief or the like. As soon as the anchor was cast, a boat was lowered, and being manned, drew in towards us; then, truly, we perceived a bent figure sitting idle in the stern, but even Dawson dared not venture to think it might be Moll.

The boat running on a shallow, a couple of Moors stepped into the water, and lifting the figure in their arms carried it ashore to where we stood. And now we perceived 'twas a woman muffled up in the Moorish fashion, a little, wizen old creature, who, casting back her head clothes, showed us a wrinkled face, very pale and worn with care and age. Regarding us, she says in plain English:

"You are my countrymen. Is one of you named Dawson?"

"My name is Dawson," says Jack.

She takes his hand in hers, and holding it in hers looks in his face with great pity, and then at last, as if loath to tell the news she sees he fears to hear, she says:

"I am Elizabeth Godwin."

What need of more to let us know that Moll had paid her ransom?

CHAPTER XXXVII.

Don Sanchez again proves himself the most mannerly rascal in the world.

IN silence we led Mrs. Godwin to the seat we had occupied, and seating ourselves we said not a word for some time. For my own part, the realisation of our loss threw my spirits into a strange apathy; 'twas as if some actual blow had stunned my senses. Yet I remember observing the Moors about their business, — despatching one to Elche for a train of mules, charging a second boat with merchandise while the first returned, etc.

"I can feel for you," says Mrs. Godwin at length, addressing Dawson, "for I also have lost an only child."

"Your daughter Judith, Madam?" says I.

"She died two years ago. Yours still lives," says she, again turning to Dawson, who sat with a haggard face, rocking himself like one nursing a great pain. "And while there is life, there's hope, as one says."

"Why, to be sure," says Jack, rousing himself. "This is no more, Kit, than we bargained for. Tell me, Madam, you who know that country, do you think a carpenter would be held in esteem there? I'm yet a strong man, as you see, with some good serviceable years of life before me. D'ye think they'd take me in exchange for my Moll, who is but a bit of a girl?"

"She is beautiful, and beauty counts for more than strength and abilities there, poor man," says she.

"I'll make 'em the offer," says he, "and though they do not agree to give her freedom, they may yet suffer me to see her time and again, if I work well."

"'Tis strange," says she. "Your child has told me all your history. Had I learnt it from other lips, I might have set you down for rogues, destitute of heart or conscience; yet, with this evidence before me, I must needs regard you and your dear daughter as more noble than many whose deeds are writ in gold. 'Tis a lesson to teach me faith in the goodness of God, who redeems his creatures' follies, with one touch of love. Be of good cheer, my friend," adds she, laying her thin hand on his arm. "There *is* hope. I would not have accepted this ransom — no, not for all your daughter's tears and entreaties — without good assurance that I, in my turn, might deliver her."

I asked the old gentlewoman how this might be accomplished.

"My niece," says she, dwelling on the word with a smile, as if happy in the alliance, "my niece, coming to Barbary of her free will, is not a slave like those captured in warfare and carried there by force. She remains there as a hostage for me, and will be free to return when I send the price of my ransom."

"Is that a great sum?"

"Three thousand gold ducats,— about one thousand pounds English."

"Why, Madam," says Dawson, "we have nothing, being now reduced to our last pieces. And if you have the goodness to raise this money, Heaven only knows how long it may be ere you succeed. 'Tis a fortnight's journey, at the least, to England, and then you have to deal with your steward, who will seek only to put obstacles in your way, so that six weeks may pass ere Moll is redeemed, and what may befall her in the meantime?"

"She is safe. Ali Oukadi is a good man. She has nought to fear while she is under his protection. Do not misjudge the Moors. They have many estimable qualities."

"Yet, Madam," says I, "by your saying there is hope, I gather there must be also danger."

"There is," answers she, at which Jack nods with conviction. "A beautiful young woman is never free from danger" (Jack assents again). "There are good and bad men amongst the Moors as amongst other people."

"Aye, to be sure," says Dawson.

"I say she is safe under the protection of Ali Oukadi, but when the ransom is paid and she leaves Thadviir, she may stand in peril."

"Why, that's natural enough," cries Dawson, "be she amongst Moors or no Moors; 'tis then she will most need a friend to serve her, and one that knows the ins and outs of the place and how to deal with these Turks must surely be better than any half-dozen fresh landed and raw to their business." Then he fell questioning Mrs. Godwin as to how Moll was lodged, the distance of Thadviir from Alger, the way to get there, and divers other particulars, which, together with his eager, cheerful vivacity, showed clearly enough that he was more firmly resolved than ever to go into Barbary and be near Moll without delay. And presently, leaving me with Mrs. Godwin, he goes down to the captain of the galley, who is directing the landing of goods from the play-boat, and, with such small store of words as he possessed, aided by plentiful gesture, he enters into a very lively debate with him, the upshot of which was that the captain tells him he shall start the next morning at daybreak if there be but a puff of air, and agrees to carry him to Alger for a couple of pieces (upon which they clap hands), as Dawson, in high glee, informs us on his return.

"And now, Kit," says he, "I must go back to Elche to borrow those same two pieces of Don Sanchez, so I pray you, Madam, excuse me."

But just then the train of mules from Elche appears, and with them Sidi ben Ahmed, who, having information of Mrs. Godwin coming, brings a litter for her carriage, at the same time begging her to accept his hospitality as the true friend of her niece Moll. So we all return to Elche together, and none so downcast as I at the thought of losing my friend, and speculating on the mischances that might befall him; for I did now begin to regard him as an ill-fated man, whose best intentions brought him nothing but evil and misfortune.

Being come to Elche, Don Sanchez presented himself to Mrs. Godwin with all the dignity and calm assurance in the world, and though she received him with a very cold, distant demeanour, as being the deepest rascal of us all and the one most to blame, yet it ruffled him never a bit, but he carried himself as if he had never benefited himself a penny by his roguery and at her expense.

On Dawson asking him for the loan of a couple of pieces and telling his project, the Don drew a very long serious face and tried his utmost to dissuade him from it, so that at first I suspected him of being loath to part with this petty sum; but herein I did him injustice, for, finding

Dawson was by no means to be turned from his purpose, he handed him his purse, advising him the first thing he did on arriving at Alger to present himself to the Dey and purchase a firman, giving him protection during his stay in Barbary (which he said might be done for a few silver ducats). Then, after discussing apart with Sidi, he comes to Mrs. Godwin, and says he:

"Madam, with your sanction my friend Sidi ben Ahmed will charge Mr. Dawson with a letter to Ali Oukadi, promising to pay him the sum of three thousand gold ducats upon your niece being safely conducted hither within the space of three weeks."

"Señor," answers she, "I thank Sidi ben Ahmed very deeply — and you also," adds she, overcoming her compunctions, "for this offer. But unhappily, I cannot hope to have this sum of money in so short a time."

"It is needless to say, Madam," returns he, with a scrape, "that in making this proposal I have considered of that difficulty; my friend has agreed to take my bond for the payment of this sum when it shall be convenient to you to discharge it."

Mrs. Godwin accepted this arrangement with a profound bow, which concealed the astonishment it occasioned her. But she drew a long breath, and I perceived she cast a curious glance at all three of us, as if she were marvelling at the change that must have taken place in civilised countries since her absence, which should account for a pack of thieves nowadays being so very unlike what a pack of thieves was in her young days.

CHAPTER XXXVIII.

How we hear Moll's sweet voice through the walls of her prison, and speak two words with her, though almost to our undoing.

HAVING written his letter, Sidi ben Ahmed proposed that Mrs. Godwin should await the return of Moll before setting out for England, very graciously offering her the hospitality of his house meanwhile, and this offer she willingly accepted. And now, there being no reason for my staying in Elche, Dawson gladly agreed I should accompany him, the more so as I knew more of the Moors' language than he. Going down with us to the water side, Don Sanchez gave us some very good hints for our behaviour in Barbary, bidding us, above everything, be very careful not to break any of the laws of that country. "For," says he, "I have seen three men hanged there for merely casting a Turk into the sea in a drunken frolic."

"Be assured, I'll touch nothing but water for my drink," says Dawson, taking this warning to his share.

"Be careful," continues the Don, "to pay for all you have, and take not so much as an orange from a tree by the wayside without first laying a fleece or two on the ground. I warn you that they, though upright enough amongst themselves, are crafty and treacherous towards strangers, whom they regard as their natural enemies; and they will tempt you to break the law either by provoking a quarrel, or putting you to some unlawful practice, that they may annul your firman and claim you as convicted outlaws for their slaves. For stealing a pullet I have seen the flesh beaten off the soles of an English sailor's feet, and he and his companions condemned to slavery for life."

"I'll lay a dozen fleeces on the ground for every sour orange I may take," says Dawson. "And as for quarrelling, a Turk shall pull my nose before ever a curse shall pass my lips."

With these and other exhortations and promises, we parted, and lying aboard that night, we set sail by daybreak the next morning, having a very fair gale off the land; and no ships in the world being better than these galleys for swiftness, we made an excellent good passage, so that ere we conceived ourselves half over the voyage, we sighted Alger looking like nothing but a great chalk quarry for the white houses built up the side of the hill.

We landed at the mole, which is a splendid construction some fifteen hundred feet or thereabouts in length (with the forts), forming a beautiful terrace walk supported by arches, beneath which large, splendid magazines, all the most handsome in the world, I think. Thence our captain led us to the Cassanabah, a huge, heavy, square, brick building, surrounded by high, massive walls and defended by a hundred pieces of ordnance, cannons, and mortars, all told. Here the Dey or Bashaw lives with his family, and below are many roomy offices for the discharge of business. Our captain takes us into a vast waiting-hall where over a hundred Moors were patiently attending an audience of the Dey's minister, and there we also might have lingered the whole day and gone away at night unsatisfied (as many of these Moors do, day after day, but that counts for nothing with these enduring people), but having a hint from our friend we found occasion to slip a ducat in the hand of a go-between officer, who straightway led us to his master. Our captain having presented us, with all the usual ceremonies, the grandee takes our letter from Sidi ben Ahmed, reads it, and without further ado signs and seals us a trader's pass for twenty-eight days, to end at sunset the day after the festival of Ranadal. With this paper we went off in high glee, thinking that twenty-eight hours of safe-conduct would have sufficed us. And so to an eating-house, where we treated our friendly captain to the best, and greasing his palm also for his good services, parted in mighty good humour on both sides.

By this time it was getting pretty late in the day; nevertheless, we burnt with such impatience to be near our dear Moll that we set forth for Thadviir, which lies upon the seacoast about seven English leagues east of Alger. But a cool, refreshing air from the sea and the great joy in our hearts made this journey seem to us the most delightful of our lives. And indeed, after passing through the suburbs richly planted with gardens, and crossing the river, on which are many mills, and so coming into the plain of Mettegia, there is such an abundance of sweet odours and lovely fertile views to enchant the senses, that a dull man would be inspirited to a happy, cheerful mood.

'Twas close upon nine o'clock when we reached the little town, and not a soul to be seen anywhere nor a light in any window, but that troubled us not at all (having provided ourselves with a good store of victuals before quitting Alger), for here 'tis as sweet to lie of nights in the open air as in the finest palace elsewhere. Late as it was, however, we could not dispose ourselves to sleep before we had gone all round the town to satisfy our curiosity. At the further extremity we spied a building looking very majestic in the moonlight, with a large garden about it enclosed with high walls, and deciding that this must be the residence of Ali Oukadi, who, we had learnt, was the most important merchant of these parts, we lay us down against the wall, and fell asleep, thinking of our dear Moll, who perchance, all unconscious, was lying within.

Rising at daybreak, for Dawson was mightily uneasy unless we might be breaking the law by sleeping out-of-doors (but there is no cruel law of this sort in Barbary), we washed ourselves very properly at a neighbouring stream, made a meal of dry bread and dates, then, laying our bundles in a secret place whence we might conveniently fetch them, if Ali Oukadi insisted on entertaining us a day or two, we went into the town, and finding, upon enquiry, that this was indeed his palace, as we had surmised, bethought us what to say and how to behave the most civil possible, and so presented ourselves at his gate, stating our business.

Presently, we were admitted to an outer office, and there received by a very bent, venerable old Moor, who, having greeted us with much ceremony, says, "I am Ali Oukadi. What would you have of me?"

"My daughter Moll," answers Jack, in an eager, choking voice, offering his letter. The Moor regarded him keenly, and, taking the letter, sits down to study it; and while he is at this business a young Moor enters, whose name, as we shortly learnt, was Mohand ou Mohand. He was, I take it, about twenty-five or thirty years of age, and as handsome a man of his kind as ever I saw, with wondrous soft dark eyes, but a cruel mouth and a most high, imperious bearing which, together with his rich clothes and jewels, betokened him a man of quality. Hearing who we were, he saluted us civilly enough; but there was a flash of enmity in his eyes and a tightening of his lips, which liked me not at all.

When the elder man had finished the letter, he hands it to the younger, and he having read it in his turn, they fall to discussing it in a low tone, and in a dialect of which not one word was intelligible to us. Finally, Ali Oukadi, rising from his cushions, says gravely, addressing Dawson:

"I will write without delay to Sidi ben Ahmed in answer to his letter."

"But my daughter," says Dawson, aghast, and as well as he could in the Moorish tongue. "Am I not to have her?"

"My friend says nothing here," answers the old man, regarding the letter, "nothing that would justify my giving her up to you. He says the money shall be paid upon her being brought safe to Elche."

"Why, your Excellency, I and my comrade here will undertake to carry her safely there. What better guard should a daughter have than her father?"

"Are you more powerful than the elements? Can you command the tempest? Have you sufficient armament to combat all the enemies that scour the seas? If any accident befall you, what is this promise of payment? — Nothing."

"At least, you will suffer me to make this voyage with my child."

"I do not purpose to send her to Elche," returned the old man, calmly. "'Tis a risk I will not undertake. I have said that when I am paid three thousand ducats, I will give Lala Mollah freedom, and I will keep my word. To send her to Elche is a charge that does not touch my compact. This I will write and tell my friend, Sidi ben Ahmed, and upon his payment and expressed agreement I will render you your daughter. Not before."

We could say nothing for a while, being so foundered by this reverse; but at length Dawson says in a piteous voice:

"At least you will suffer me to see my daughter. Think, if she were yours and you had lost her — believing her a while dead — "

Mohand ou Mohand muttered a few words that seemed to fix the old Moor's wavering resolution.

"I cannot agree to that," says he. "Your daughter is becoming reconciled to her position. To see you would open her wounds afresh to the danger of her life, maybe. Reflect," adds he, laying his hand on the letter, "if this business should come to nought, what could recompense your daughter for the disappointment of those false hopes your meeting would inspire? It cannot be."

With this he claps his hands, and a servant, entering at a nod from his master, lifts the hangings for us to go.

Dawson stammered a few broken words of passionate protest, and then breaking down as he perceived the folly of resisting, he dropped his head and suffered me to lead him out. As I saluted the Moors in going, I caught, as I fancied, a gleam of triumphant gladness in the dark eyes of Mohand ou Mohand.

Coming back to the place where we had hid our bundles, Dawson cast himself on the ground and gave vent to his passion, declaring he would see his Moll though he should tear the walls down to get at her, and other follies; but after a time he came to his senses again so that he could reason, and then I persuaded him to have patience, and forbear from any outburst of violence such as we had been warned against, showing him that certainly Don Sanchez, hearing of our condition, would send the money speedily, and so we should get Moll by fair means instead of losing her (and ourselves) by foul; that after all, 'twas but the delay of a week or so that we had to put up with, and so forth. Then, discussing what we should do next, I offered that we should return to Elche and make our case known rather than trust entirely to Ali Oukadi's promise of writing; for I did suspect some treacherous design on the part of Mohand ou Mohand, by which Mrs. Godwin failing of her agreement, he might possess himself of Moll; and this falling in with Dawson's wishes, we set out to return to Alger forthwith. But getting to Alger half-dead with the fatigue of trudging all that distance in the full heat of the day, we learnt to our chagrin that no ship would be sailing to Elche for a fortnight at the least, and all the money we had would not tempt any captain to carry us there; so here were we cast down again beyond everything for miserable, gloomy apprehensions.

After spending another day in fruitless endeavour to obtain a passage, nothing would satisfy Dawson's painful, restless spirit but we must return to Thadviir; so thither we went once more to linger about the palace of Ali Oukadi, in the poor hope that we might see Moll come out to take the air.

One day as we were standing in the shade of the garden wall, sick and weary with dejection and disappointment, Dawson, of a sudden, starts me from my lethargy by clutching my arm and raising his finger to bid me listen and be silent. Then straining my ear, I caught the distant sound of female voices, but I could distinguish not one from another, though by Dawson's joyous, eager look I perceived he recognised Moll's voice amongst them. They came nearer and nearer, seeking, as I think, the shade of those palm trees which sheltered us. And presently, quite close to us, as if but on the other side of the wall, one struck a lute and began to sing a Moorish song; when she had concluded her melancholy air a voice, as if saddened by the melody, sighed:

"Ah me! ah me!"

There was no misdoubting that sweet voice: 'twas Moll's.

Then very softly Dawson begins to whistle her old favourite ditty "Hearts will break." Scarce had he finished the refrain when Moll within took it up in a faint trembling voice, but only a bar, to let us know we were heard; then she fell a-laughing at her maids, who were whispering in alarm, to disguise her purpose; and so they left that part, as we knew by their voices dying away in the distance.

"She'll come again," whispers Dawson, feverishly.

And he was in the right; for, after we had stood there best part of an hour, we hear Moll again gently humming "Hearts will break," but so low, for fear of being heard by others, that only we who strained so hard to catch a sound could be aware of it.

"Moll, my love!" whispers Dawson, as she comes to an end.

"Dear father!" answers she, as low.

"We are here—Kit and I. Be comforted, sweet chuck,—you shall be free ere long."

"Shall I climb the wall?" asks she.

"No, no,—for God's sake, refrain!" says I, seeing that Jack was half minded to bid her come to him. "You will undo all—have patience."

At this moment other voices came to us from within, calling Lala Mollah; and presently the quick witch answers them from a distance, with a laugh, as if she had been playing at catch-who-can.

Then Dawson and I, turning about, discovered to our consternation Ali Oukadi standing quite close beside us, with folded arms and bent brows.

"You are unwise," says he, in a calm tone.

"Nay, master," says Jack, piteously. "I did but speak a word to my child."

"If you understand our tongue," adds I, "you will know that we did but bid her have patience, and wait."

"Possibly," says he. "Nevertheless, you compel me henceforth to keep her a close prisoner, when I would give her all the liberty possible."

"Master," says Jack, imploring, "I do pray you not to punish her for my fault. Let her still have the freedom of your garden, and I promise you we will go away this day and return no more until we can purchase her liberty for ever."

"Good," says the old man, "but mark you keep your promise. Know that 'tis an offence against the law to incite a slave to revolt. I tell you this, not as a threat, for I bear you no ill will, but as a warning to save you from consequences which I may be powerless to avert."

This did seem to me a hint at some sinister design of Mohand ou Mohand—a wild suspicion, maybe, on my part, and yet, as I think, justified by evils yet to come.

CHAPTER XXXIX.

Of our bargaining with a Moorish seaman; and of an English slave.

WE lost no time, be sure, in going back to Alger, blessing God on the way for our escape, and vowing most heartily that we would be led into no future folly, no matter how simple and innocent the temptation might seem.

And now began again a tedious season of watching on the mole of Alger; but not to make this business as wearisome to others, I will pass that over and come at once to that joyful, happy morning, when, with but scant hope, looking down upon the deck of a galley entering the port, to our infinite delight and amazement we perceived Richard Godwin waving his hand to us in sign of recognition. Then sure, mad with joy, we would have cast ourselves in the sea had we thereby been able to get to him more quickly. Nor was he much less moved with affection to meet us, and springing on the quai he took us both in his open arms and embraced us. But his first word was of Moll. "My beloved wife?" says he, and could question us no further.

We told him she was safe, whereat he thanks God most fervently, and how we had spoken with her; and then he tells us of his adventures — how on getting Don Sanchez's letter he had started forth at once with such help as Sir Peter Lely generously placed at his disposition, and how coming to Elche, he found Mrs. Godwin there in great anxiety because we had not returned, and how Don Sanchez, guessing at our case, had procured money from Toledo to pay Moll's ransom, and did further charter a neutral galley to bring him to Alger — which was truly as handsome a thing as any man could do, be he thief or no thief. All these matters we discussed on our way to the Cassanabah, where Mr. Godwin furnished himself as we had with a trader's permit for twenty-eight days.

This done, we set out with a team of good mules, and reaching Thadviir about an hour before sundown, we repaired at once to Ali Oukadi's, who received us with much civility, although 'twas clear to see he was yet loath to give up Moll; but the sight of the gold Mr. Godwin laid before him did smooth the creases from his brow (for these Moors love money before anything on earth), and having told it carefully he writes an acknowledgment and fills up a formal sheet of parchment bearing the Dey's seal, which attested that Moll was henceforth a free subject and entitled to safe-conduct within the confines of the Dey's administration. And having delivered these precious documents into Mr. Godwin's hands, he leaves us for a little space and then returns leading dear Moll by the hand. And she, not yet apprised of her circumstances, seeing her husband with us, gives a shrill cry, and like to faint with happiness totters forward and falls in his ready arms.

I will not attempt to tell further of this meeting and our passionate, fond embraces, for 'twas past all description; only in the midst of our joy I perceived that Mohand ou Mohand had entered the room and stood there, a silent spectator of Moll's tender yielding to her husband's caresses, his nostrils pinched, and his jaundiced face overcast with a wicked look of mortification and envy. And Moll seeing him, paled a little, drawing closer to her husband; for, as I learnt later on, and 'twas no more than I had guessed, he had paid her most assiduous attentions from the first moment he saw her, and had gone so far as to swear by Mahomet that death alone should end his burning passion to possess her. And I observed that when we parted, and Moll in common civility offered him her hand, he muttered some oath as he raised it to his lips.

Declining as civilly as we might Ali Oukadi's tender of hospitality, we rested that night at the large inn or caravansary, and I do think that the joy of Moll and her husband lying once more within each other's arms was scarcely less than we felt, Dawson and I, at this happy ending of our long tribulations; but one thing it is safe to say, we slept as sound as they.

And how gay were we when we set forth the next morning for Alger — Moll's eyes twinkling like stars for happiness, and her cheeks all pink with blushes like any new bride, her husband with not less pride than passion in his noble countenance, and Dawson and I as blithe and jolly as schoolboys on a holiday. For now had Moll by this act of heroism and devotion redeemed not only herself, but us also, and there was no further reason for concealment or deceit, but all might be themselves and fear no man.

Thus did joy beguile us into a false sense of security.

Coming to Alger about midday, we were greatly surprised to find that the sail chartered by Don Sanchez was no longer in the port, and the reason of this we presently learnt was that the Dey, having information of a descent being about to be made upon the town by the British fleet at Tangier, he had commanded, the night before, all alien ships to be gone from the port by daybreak. This put us to a quake, for in view of this descent not one single Algerine would venture to put to sea for all the money Mr. Godwin could offer or promise. So here we were forced to stay in trepidation and doubt as to how we, being English, might fare if the town should be bombarded as we expected, and never did we wish our own countrymen further. Only our Moll and her husband did seem careless in their happiness; for so they might die in each other's arms, I do think they would have faced death with a smile upon their faces.

However, a week passing, and no sign of any English flag upon the seas, the public apprehension subsided; and now we began very seriously to compass our return to Elche, our trader's passes (that is, Dawson's and mine) being run out within a week, and we knowing full well that we should not get them renewed after this late menace of an English attack upon the town. So, one after the other, we tried every captain in the port, but all to no purpose. And one of these did openly tell me the Dey had forbidden any stranger to be carried out of the town, on pain of having his vessel confiscated and being bastinadoed to his last endurance.

"And so," says he, lifting his voice, "if you offered me all the gold in the world, I would not carry you a furlong hence." But at the same time, turning his back on a janizary who stood hard by, he gave me a most significant wink and a little beck, as if I were to follow him presently.

And this I did as soon as the janizary was gone, following him at a distance through the town and out into the suburbs, at an idle, sauntering gait. When we had got out beyond the houses, to the side of the river I have mentioned, he sits him down on the bank, and I, coming up, sit down beside him as if for a passing chat. Then he, having glanced to the right and left, to make sure we were not observed, asks me what we would give to be taken to Elche; and I answered that we would give him his price so we could be conveyed shortly.

"When would you go?" asks he.

"Why," says I, "our passes expire at sundown after the day of Ramadah, so we must get hence, by hook or by crook, before that."

"That falls as pat as I would have it," returns he (but not in these words), "for all the world will be up at the Cassanabah on that day, to the feast the Dey gives to honour his son's coming of age. Moreover, the moon by then will not rise before two in the morning. So all being in our favour, I'm minded to venture on this business. But you must understand that I dare not take you aboard in the port, where I must make a pretence of going out a-fishing with my three sons, and give the janizaries good assurance that no one else is aboard, that I may not fall into trouble on my return."

"That's reasonable enough," says I, "but where will you take us aboard?"

"I'll show you," returns he, "if you will stroll down this bank with me, for my sons and I have discussed this matter ever since we heard you were seeking a ship for this project, and we have it all cut and dried properly."

So up we get and saunter along the bank leisurely, till we

reached a part where the river spreads out very broad and shallow.

"You see that rock," says he, nodding at a huge boulder lapped by the incoming sea. "There shall you be at midnight. We shall lie about a half a mile out to sea, and two of my sons will pull to the shore and take you up; so may all go well and nought be known, if you are commonly secret, for never a soul is seen here after sundown."

I told him I would consult with my friends and give him our decision the next day, meeting him at this spot.

"Good," says he, "and ere you decide, you may cast an eye at my ship, which you shall know by a white moon painted on her beam; 'tis as fast a ship as any that sails from Alger, though she carry but one mast, and so be we agree to this venture, you shall find the cabin fitted for your lady and everything for your comfort."

On this we separated presently, and I, joining my friends at our inn, laid the matter before them. There being still some light, we then went forth on the mole, and there we quickly spied the White Moon, which, though a small craft, looked very clean, and with a fair cabin house, built up in the Moorish fashion upon the stern. And here, sitting down, we all agreed to accept this offer, Mr. Godwin being not less eager for the venture than we, who had so much more to dread by letting it slip, though his pass had yet a fortnight to run.

So the next day I repaired to the rock, and meeting Haroun (as he was called), I closed with him, and put a couple of ducats in his hand for earnest money.

"'Tis well," says he, pocketing the money, after kissing it and looking up to heaven with a " Dill an," which means

"It is from God." "We will not meet again till the day of Ramadah at midnight, lest we fall under suspicion. Farewell."

We parted as we did before, he going his way, and I mine; but, looking back by accident before I had gone a couple of hundred yards, I perceived a fellow stealing forth from a thicket of canes that stood in the marshy ground near the spot where I had lately stood with Haroun, and turning again presently, I perceived this man following in my steps. Then, fairly alarmed, I gradually hastened my pace (but not so quick neither as to seem to fly), making for the town, where I hoped to escape pursuit in the labyrinth of little, crooked, winding alleys. As I rounded a corner, I perceived him out of the tail of my eye, still following, but now within fifty yards of me, he having run to thus overreach me; and ere I had turned up a couple of alleys he was on my heels and twitching me by the sleeve.

"Lord love you, Master," says he, in very good English, but gasping for breath. "Hold hard a moment, for I've a thing or two to say to you as is worth your hearing."

So I, mightily surprised by these words, stop; and he seeing the alley quite empty and deserted, sits down on a doorstep, and I do likewise, both of us being spent with our exertions.

"Was that man you were talking with a little while back named Haroun?" asks he, when he could fetch his breath. I nodded.

"Did he offer to take you and three others to Elche, aboard a craft called the White Moon?"

I nodded again, astonished at his information, for we had not discussed our design to-day, Haroun and I.

"Did he offer to carry you off in a boat to his craft from the rock on the mouth?"

Once more I nodded.

"Can you guess what will happen if you agree to this?"

Now I shook my head.

"The villain," says he, "will run you on a shoal, and there will he be overhauled by the janizaries, and you be carried prisoners back to Alger. Your freedom will be forfeited, and you will be sold for slaves. And that's not all," adds he; "the lass you have with you will be taken from you and given to Mohand ou Mohand, who has laid this trap for your destruction and the gratification of his lust."

I fell a-shaking only to think of this crowning calamity, and could only utter broken, unintelligible sounds to express my gratitude for this warning.

"Listen, Master, if you cannot speak," said he; "for I must quit you in a few minutes, or get my soles thrashed when I return home. What I have told you is true, as there is a God in heaven; 'twas overheard by my comrade, who is a slave in Mohand's household. If you escape this trap, you will fall in another, for there is no bounds to Mohand's devilish cunning. I say, if you stay here you are doomed to share our miserable lot, by one device or another. But I will show you how you may turn the tables on this villain, and get to a Christian country ere you are a week older, if you have but one spark of courage amongst you."

CHAPTER XL.

Of our escape from Barbary, of the pursuit and horrid, fearful slaughter that followed, together with other moving circumstances.

So Groves, as my man was named, told me how he and eight other poor Englishmen, sharing the same bagnio, had endured the hardships and misery of slavery, some for thirteen, and none less than seven, years; how for three years they had been working a secret tunnel by which they could escape from their bagnio (in which they were locked up every night at sundown) at any moment; how for six months, since the completion of their tunnel, they had been watching a favourable opportunity to seize a ship and make good their escape (seven of them being mariners); and how now they were, by tedious suspense, wrought to such a pitch of desperation that they were ripe for any means of winning their freedom. "And here," says he, in conclusion, "hath merciful Providence given us the power to save not only ourselves from this accursed bondage, but you, also, if you are minded to join us."

Asking him how he proposed to accomplish this end, he replies:

"'Tis as easy as kiss your hand. First, do you accept Haroun's offer?"

"I have," says I.

"Good!" says he, rubbing his hands, and speaking thick with joy. "You may be sure that Mohand will suffer no one to interfere with your getting aboard, to the achievement of his design. When is it to be?"

I hesitated a moment, lest I should fall into another trap, trying to escape from the first; but, seeing he was an Englishman, I would not believe him capable of playing into the Turks' hands for our undoing, and so I told him our business was for midnight on the feast of Ramadah.

"Sure, nought but Providence could have ordered matters so well," says he, doubling himself up, as if unable to control his joy. "We shall be there, we nine sturdy men. Some shall hide in the canes, and others behind the rock; and when Haroun rows to shore, four of us will get into his boat (muffled up as you would be to escape detection), and as soon as they lay themselves to their oars, their business shall be settled."

"As how?" asks I, shrinking (as ever) from deeds of violence.

"Leave that to us; but be assured they shall not raise a cry that shall fright your lady. Oh, we know the use of a bow-string as well as any Turk amongst them. We have that to thank 'em for. Well, these two being despatched, we return to shore, and two more of our men will get in; then we four to the felucca, and there boarding, we serve the others as we served the first two; so back comes one of us to fetch off our other comrades and you four. Then, all being aboard, we cut our cable, up with our sail, and by the time Mohand comes, in the morning, to seek his game on the sand-bank, we shall be half way to Elche, and farther, if Providence do keep pace with this happy beginning. What say you, friend?" adds he, noting my reflective mood.

Then I frankly confessed that I would have some assurance of his honesty.

"I can give you none, Master," says he, "but the word of a good Yorkshireman. Surely, you may trust me as I trust you; for 'tis in your power to reveal all to Haroun, and so bring us all to the galleys. Have you no faith in a poor broken Englishman?"

"Yes," says I; "I'll trust you."

Then we rose, clapping hands, and he left me, with tears of gratitude and joy in his eyes. Telling my friends I had something of a secret nature to impart, we went out to the end of the mole, where we were secure from eavesdroppers, and there I laid the whole story before them, whereupon we fell debating what we should do, looking at this matter from every side, with a view to our security; but, slavery lying before us, and no better means of escaping it coming to our minds, we did at last unanimously agree to trust Joe Groves rather than Haroun.

The next day there fell a great deluge of rain, and the morrow being the feast of Ramadah, we regarded this as highly favourable to our escape; for here when rain falls it ceases not for forty-eight hours, and thus might we count upon the aid of darkness. And that evening as we were regarding some merchandise in a bazaar, a fellow sidles up to me, and whispers (fingering a piece of cloth as if he were minded to buy it):

"Does all go well?"

Then perceiving this was Joe Groves, I answered in the same manner:

"All goes well."

"To-morrow at midnight?"

"To-morrow at midnight," I return. Upon which, casting down the cloth, he goes away without further sign.

And now comes in the feast of Ramadah with a heavy, steady downpour of rain all day, and no sign of ceasing at sundown, which greatly contented us. About ten, the house we lodged in being quite still, and our fear of accident pressing us to depart, we crept silently out into the street without let or hindrance (though I warrant some spy of Mohand's was watching to carry information of our flight to his master), and so through the narrow deserted alleys to the outskirts of the town, and thence by the river side to the great rock, with only just so much light as enabled us to hang together, and no more. And I do believe we should have floundered into the river o' one side of the marsh of canes or t'other, but that having gone over this road the last time with the thought that it might lead us to liberty, every object by the way impressed itself upon my mind most astonishingly.

Here under this rock stood we above an hour with no sound but the beating of the rain, and the lap of the water running in from the sea. Then, as it might be about half-past eleven, a voice close beside us (which I knew for Joe Groves, though I could see no one but us four, Jack by my side, and Moll bound close to her husband) says:

"All goes well?"

"Yes, all goes well," says I; whereupon he gives a cry like the croak of a frog, and his comrades steal up almost unseen and unheard, save that each as he came whispered his name, as Spinks, Davis, Lee, Best, etc., till their number was all told. Then Groves, who was clearly chosen their captain, calls Spinks, Lee, and Best to stand with him, and bids the others and us to stand back against the canes till we are called. So we do his bidding, and fall back to the growth of canes, whence we could but dimly make out the mass of the rock for the darkness, and there waited breathless, listening for the sound of oars. But these Moors, for a better pretence of secrecy, had muffled their oars, so that we knew not they were at hand until we heard Haroun's voice speaking low.

"Englishmen, are you there?" asks he.

"Aye, we four," whispers Groves, in reply.

Then we hear them wade into the water and get into the boat with whispering of Haroun where they are to dispose themselves, and so forth. After that silence for about ten minutes, and no sound but the ceaseless rain until we next hear Groves' voice.

"Davis, Negus," whispers he, on which two of our number leave us and go out to the boat to replace Haroun and that other Moor, who, in the manner of the Turks, had been strangled and cast overboard.

And now follows a much longer period of silence, but at length that comes to an end, and we hear Groves' voice again whispering us to come. At the first sound of his voice his three comrades rush forward; but Groves, recognising them, says hoarsely, "Back, every one of you but those I called, or I'll brain you! There's room but for six in the boat, and those who helped us shall go first, as I ordered. The rest must wait their time."

So these fellows, who would have ousted us, give way, grumbling, and Mr. Godwin carrying Moll to the boat, Dawson and I wade in after him, and so, with great gratitude, take our places as Groves directs. We being in, he and his mate lay to their oars, and pull out to the felucca, guided by the lanthorn on her bulwarks.

Having put us aboard safely, Groves and his mate fetch the three fellows that remained ashore, and now all being embarked, they abandon the small boat, slip the anchor, and get out their long sweeps, all in desperate haste; for that absence of wind, which I at first took to be a blessing, appeared now to be a curse, and our main hope of escape lay in pulling far out to sea before Mohand discovered the trick put upon him, and gave chase. All night long we toiled with most savage energy, dividing our number into two batches, so that one might go to the oars as the other tired, turn and turn about. Not one of us but did his utmost — nay, even Moll would stand by her husband, and strain like any man at this work. But for all our labour, Alger was yet in sight when the break of day gave us light to see it. Then was every eye searching the waters for sign of a sail, be it to save or to undo us. Sail saw we none, but about nine o'clock Groves, scanning the waters over against Alger, perceived something which he took to be a galley; nor were we kept long in uncertainty, for by ten it was obvious to us all, showing that it had gained considerably upon us in spite of our frantic exertions, which convinced us that this was Mohand, and that he had discovered us with the help of a spy-glass, maybe.

At the prospect of being overtaken and carried back to slavery, a sort of madness possessed those at the oars, the first oar pulling with such a fury of violence that it snapped at the rowlock, and was of no further use. Still we made good progress, but what could we with three oars do against the galley which maybe was mounted with a dozen? Some were for cutting down the mast and throwing spars, sails, and every useless thing overboard to lighten our ship, but Groves would not hear of this, seeing by a slant in the rain that a breeze was to be expected; and surely enough, the rain presently smote us on the cheek smartly, whereupon Groves ran up our sail, which, to our infinite delight, did presently swell out fairly, careening us so that the oar on t'other side was useless.

But that which favoured us favoured also our enemies, and shortly after we saw two sails go up to match our one. Then Groves called a council of us and his fellows, and his advice was this: that ere the galley drew nigh enough for our number to be sighted, he and his fellows should bestow themselves away in the stern cabin, and lie there with such arms of knives and spikes as they had brought with them ready to their hands, and that, on Mohand boarding us with his men, we four should retire towards the cabin, when he and his comrades would spring forth and fight every man to the death for freedom. And he held out good promise of a successful issue. "For," says he, "knowing you four" (meaning us) "are unarmed, 'tis not likely he will have furnished himself with any great force; and as his main purpose is to possess this lady, he will not suffer his men to use their firepieces to the risk of her destruction; therefore," adds he, "if you have the stomach for your part of this business, which is but to hold the helm as I direct, all must go well. But for the lady, if she hath any fear, we may find a place in the cabin for her."

This proposal was accepted by all with gladness, except Moll, who would on no account leave her husband's side;

but had he not been there, I believe she would have been the last aboard to feel fear, or play a cowardly part.

So without further parley, the fellows crept into the little cabin, each fingering his naked weapon, which made me feel very sick with apprehension of bloodshed.

The air of wind freshening, we kept on at a spanking rate for another hour, Groves lying on the deck with his eyes just over the bulwarks and giving orders to Dawson and me, who kept the helm; then the galley, being within a quarter of a mile of us, fired a shot as a signal to us to haul down our sail, and this having no effect, he soon after fires another, which, striking us in the stem, sent great splinters flying up from the bulwarks there.

"Hold her helm, stiff," whispers Groves, and then he backs cautiously into the cabin without rising from his belly, for the men aboard the galley were now clearly distinguishable.

Presently bang goes another gun, and the same moment, its shot taking our mast a yard or so above the deck, our lateen falls over upon the water with a great slap, and so are we brought to at once.

Dropping her sail, the galley sweeps up alongside us, and casting out divers hooks and tackle they held ready for their purpose, they grappled us securely. My heart sank within me as I perceived the number of our enemies, thirty or forty, as I reckon (but happily not above half a dozen armed men), and Mohand ou Mohand amongst them with a scimitar in his hand; for now I foresaw the carnage which must ensue when we were boarded.

Mohand ou Mohand was the first to spring upon our deck, and behind came his janizaries and half a score of seamen. We four, Mr. Godwin holding Moll's hand in his, stood in a group betwixt Mohand and his men and the cabin where Joe Groves lay with his fellows, biding his time. One of the janizaries was drawing his scimitar, but Mohand bade him put it up, and making an obeisance to Moll, he told us we should suffer no hurt if we surrendered peaceably.

"Never, you Turkish thief!" cries Dawson, shaking his fist at him.

Mohand makes a gesture of regret, and turning to his men tells them to take us, but to use no weapons, since we had none. Then, he himself leading, with his eyes fixed hungrily upon Moll, the rest came on, and we fell back towards the cabin.

The next instant, with a wild yell of fury, the hidden men burst out of the cabin, and then followed a scene of butchery which I pray Heaven it may nevermore be my fate to witness.

Groves was the first to spill blood. Leaping upon Mohand, he buried a long curved knife right up to the hilt in his neck striking downwards just over the collar bone, and he fell, the blood spurting from his mouth upon the deck. At the same time our men, falling upon the janizaries, did most horrid battle — nay, 'twas no battle, but sheer butchery; for these men, being taken so suddenly, had no time to draw their weapons, and could only fly to the fore end of the boat for escape, where, by reason of their number and the narrow confines of the deck, they were so packed and huddled together that none could raise his hand to ward a blow even, and so stood, a writhing, shrieking mass of humanity, to be hacked and stabbed and ripped and cut down to their death.

And their butchers had no mercy. They could think

only of their past wrongs, and of satiating the thirst for vengeance, which had grown to a madness by previous restraint.

"There's for thirteen years of misery," cries one, driving his spike into the heart of one. "Take that for hanging of my brother," screams a second, cleaving a Moor's skull with his hatchet. "Quits for turning an honest lad into a devil," calls a third, drawing his knife across the throat of a shrieking wretch, and so forth, till not one of all the crowd was left to murder.

Then still devoured by their lust for blood, they swarmed over the side of the galley to finish this massacre — Groves leading with a shout of "No quarter," and all echoing these words with a roar of joy. But here they were met with some sort of resistance, for the Moors aboard, seeing the fate of their comrades, forewarning them of theirs, had turned their swivel gun about and now fired — the ball carrying off the head of Joe Groves, the best man of all that crew, if one were better than another. But this only served to incense the rest the more, and so they went at their cruel work again, and ceased not till the last of their enemies was dead. Then, with a wild hurrah, they signal their triumph, and one fellow, holding up his bloody hands, smears them over his face with a devilish scream of laughter.

And now, caring no more for us or what might befall us, than for the Turks who lay all mangled on our deck, one cuts away the tackle that lashes their galley to us, while the rest haul up the sail, and so they go their way, leaving us to shift for ourselves.

CHAPTER XLI.

How Dawson counts himself an unlucky man who were best dead; and so he quits us, and I, the reader.

THE galley bent over to the wind and sped away, and I watched her go without regret, not thinking of our own hapless condition, but only of the brutal ferocity of that mad crew aboard her.

Their shouts of joy and diabolical laughter died away, and there was no sound but the lapping of the waves against the felucca's side. They had done their work thoroughly; not a moan arose from the heaps of butchered men, not a limb moved, but all were rigid, some lying in grotesque postures as the death agony had drawn them. And after the tumult that had prevailed this stillness of death was terrific. From looking over this ghastly picture I turned and clutched at Dawson's hand for some comforting sense of life and humanity.

We were startled at this moment by a light laugh from the cabin, whither Mr. Godwin had carried Moll, fainting with the horror of this bloody business, and going in there we found her now lying in a little crib, light-headed, — clean out of her wits indeed, for she fancied herself on the dusty road to Valencia, taking her first lesson in the fandango from Don Sanchez. Mr. Godwin knelt by the cot side, with his arm supporting her head, and soothing her the best he could. We found a little cask of water and a cup, that he might give her drink, and then, seeing we could be of no further service, Dawson and I went from the cabin, our thoughts awaking now to the peril of our position, without sail in mid-sea.

And first we cast our eyes all round about the sea, but we could descry no sail save the galley (and that at a great distance), nor any sign of land. Next, casting our eyes upon the deck, we perceived that the thick stream of blood that lay along that side bent over by the broken mast, was greatly spread, and not so black, but redder, which was only to be explained by the mingling of water; and this was our first notice that the felucca was filling and we going down.

Recovering presently from the stupor into which this suspicion threw us, we pulled up a hatch, and looking down into the hold perceived that this was indeed true, a puncheon floating on the water there within arms' reach. Thence, making our way quickly over the dead bodies, which failed now to terrify us, to the fore part of our felucca, we discovered that the shot which had hit us had started a plank, and that the water leaked in with every lap of a wave. So now, our wits quickened by our peril, we took a scimitar and a dirk from a dead janizary, to cut away the cordage that lashed us to the fallen mast, to free us of that burden and right the ship if we might. But ere we did this, Dawson, spying the great sail lying out on the water, bethought him to hack out a great sheet as far as we could reach, and this he took to lay over the started plank and staunch the leakage, while I severed the tackle and freed us from the great weight of the hanging mast and long spar. And certainly we thought ourselves safe when this was done, for the hull lifted at once and righted itself upon the water. Nevertheless, we were not easy, for we knew not what other planks below the water line were injured, nor how to sink our sheet or bind it over the faulty part. So, still further to lighten us, we mastered our qualms and set to work casting the dead bodies overboard. This horrid business, at another time, would have made me sick as any dog, but there was no time to yield to mawkish susceptibilities in the face of such danger as menaced us. Only when all was done, I did feel very weakened and shaky, and my gorge rising at the look of my jerkin, all filthy with clotted blood, I tore it off and cast it in the sea, as also did Dawson; and so, to turn our thoughts (after washing of our hands and cleaning our feet), we looked over the side, and agreed that we were no lower than we were, but rather higher for having lightened our burden. But no sail anywhere on the wide sea to add to our comfort.

Going into the cabin, we found that our dear Moll had fallen into a sleep, but was yet very feverish, as we could see by her frequent turning, her sudden starts, and the dreamy, vacant look in her eyes, when she opened them and begged for water. We would not add to Mr. Godwin's trouble by telling him of ours (our minds being still restless with apprehensions of the leak), but searching about, and discovering two small, dry loaves, we gave him one, and took the other to divide betwixt us, Dawson and I. And truly we needed this refreshment (as our feeble, shaking limbs testified), after all our exertions of the night and day (it being now high noon), having eaten nothing since supper the night before. But, famished as we were, we must needs steal to the side and look over to mark where the water rose; and neither of us dared say the hull was no lower, for we perceived full well it had sunk somewhat in the last hour.

Jack took a bite of his loaf, and offered me the rest, saying he had no stomach for food; but I could not eat my own, and so we thrust the bread in our breeches pockets and set to work, heaving everything overboard that might lighten us, and for ever a-straining our eyes to sight a ship. Then we set to devising means to make the sheet cling over the damaged planks, but to little purpose, and so Dawson essayed to get at it from the inside by going below, but the water was risen so high there was no room between it and the deck to breathe, and so again to wedging the canvas in from the outside till the sun sank. And by that time the water was beginning to lap up through the hatchway. Then no longer able to blink the truth, Jack turns to me and asks:

"How long shall we last?"

"Why," says I, "we have sunk no more than a foot these last six hours, and at this slow pace we may well last out eight or nine more ere the water comes over the bulwarks."

He shook his head ruefully, and, pointing to a sluice hole in the side, said he judged it must be all over with us when the water entered there.

"Why, in that case," says I, "let us find something to fill the sluice hole."

So having nothing left on deck, we went into the cabin on a pretence of seeing how Moll fared, and Jack sneaked away an old jacket and I a stone bottle, and with these we stopped the sluice hole the best we could.

By the time we had made a job of this 'twas quite dark, and having nothing more to do but to await the end, we stood side by side, too dejected to speak for some time, thinking of the cruelty of fate which rescued us from one evil only to plunge us in a worse. At length, Jack fell to talking in a low tone of his past life, showing how things had ever gone ill with him and those he loved.

"I think," says he in conclusion, "I am an unlucky man, Kit. One of those who are born to be a curse against their will to others rather than a blessing."

"Fie, Jack," says I, "'tis an idle superstition."

"Nay," says he, "I am convinced 'tis the truth. Not one of us here but would have been the happier had I died a dozen years ago. 'Tis all through me that we drown to-night."

"Nay, 'tis a blessing that we die all together, and none left to mourn."

"That may be for you and me who have lived the best years of our life, but for those in there but just tasting the sweets of life, with years of joy unspent, 'tis another matter."

Then we were silent for a while, till feeling the water laving my feet, I asked if we should not now tell Mr. Godwin of our condition.

"'Twas in my mind, Kit," answers he; "I will send him out to you."

He went into the cabin, and Mr. Godwin coming out, I showed him our state. But 'twas no surprise to him. Only, it being now about three in the morning, and the moon risen fair and full in the heavens, he casts his eyes along the silver path on the water in the hope of rescue, and finding none, he grasps my hand and says:

"God's will be done! 'Tis a mercy that my dear love is spared this last terror. Our pain will not be long."

A shaft of moonlight entered the cabin, and there we perceived Dawson kneeling by the crib, with his head laid upon the pillow beside his daughter.

He rose and came out without again turning to look on Moll, and Mr. Godwin took his place.

"I feel more happy, Kit," says Jack, laying his hand upon my shoulder. "I do think God will be merciful to us."

"Aye, surely," says I, wilfully mistaking his meaning. "I think the water hath risen no higher this last hour."

"I'll see how our sheet hangs; do you look if the water comes in yet at the sluice hole."

And so, giving my arm a squeeze as he slips his hand from my shoulder, he went to the fore part of the vessel, while I crossed to the sluice hole, where the water was spurting through a chink.

I rose after jamming the jacket to staunch the leak, and turning towards Jack I perceived him standing by the bulwark, with the moon beyond. And the next moment he was gone. And so ended the life of this poor, loving, unlucky man.

I know not whether it was this lightening of our burden, or whether at that time some accident of a fold in the sail sucking into the leaking planks, stayed the further ingress of waters, but certain it is that after this we sank no deeper to any perceptible degree; and so it came about that we were sighted by a fishing-boat from Carthagena, a little after daybreak, and were saved — we three who were left.

*   *   *   *   *   *

I have spent the last week at Hurst Court, where Moll and her husband have lived ever since Lady Godwin's death. They are making of hay in the meadows there; and 'twas sweet to see Moll and her husband, with their two boys, cocking the sweet grass. And all very merry at supper; only one sad memory cast me down as I thought of poor Jack, sorrowing to think he could not see the happiness which, as much as our past troubles, was due to him.

THE END.

www.ingramcontent.com/pod-product-compliance
Lightning Source LLC
Chambersburg PA
CBHW020245240426

43672CB00006B/642